THE NELSON PHILOSOPHICAL TEXTS

BERKELEY

*

PHILOSOPHICAL WRITINGS

Selected and edited by
T. E. JESSOP
Ferens Professor of Philosophy
University College, Hull

UNIVERSITY OF TEXAS PRESS
AUSTIN
1953

Library of Congress Catalog
Card Number 53-6392

Printed in Great Britain

CONTENTS

* Translated by the Editor.

In a large sense indeed, we may be said to have an idea of Spirit, that is, we understand the meaning of the word, otherwise we could not affirm or deny any thing of it. Moreover, as we conceive the ideas that are in the minds of other Spirits by means of our own, which we suppose to be resemblances of them; so we know other Spirits by means of our own soul, which in that sense is the image or idea of them, it having a like respect to other Spirits, that blueness or heat by me perceived hath to those ideas perceived by another.

MS IN BERKELEY'S HAND
Showing *Principles*, Sect. 140
From British Museum Additional MS 39304.
Reproduced by permission of the Director

INTRODUCTION

OF Berkeley's philosophical works the two major ones, *Principles* and *Three Dialogues*, are here printed with as little omission as possible, in order to leave the lines of his arguing virtually intact. More omissions had to be made in the *Essay of Vision* and *De Motu*, but the main stages of the arguments have been preserved. The latter tract, neglected because Fraser left it in its Latin, is given in translation. The liveliest of the seven dialogues of *Alciphron* has been included almost in its entirety, as an illustration of Berkeley's ethical criticism (he did not work out an ethical system). Just enough room was left for passages of *Siris* that show that in this last phase of his thought he retained the distinctive doctrines of the first. The six writings have been placed in chronological order. In every case the text of Berkeley's last edition has been followed, with the spelling, and occasionally the punctuation, modernised. Omissions, when not evident from the section-numbers, have been indicated by three points. A few of Berkeley's own back-references, to sections which I have had to omit, have been retained in case the reader should wish to consult the full text.

Berkeley's Life and Character

The provenance of genius and talent is usually hard to trace. Berkeley's kinship with the Earls of Berkeley, and with the General Wolfe who stormed Quebec, throws no light on his gifts of intellectual perspicacity, literary grace, moral purity and religious serenity. However these came to him, at least the first two were favoured by the places where he was educated ; for the school he went to at Kilkenny, very near to where he was born in 1685—an Irishman of English stock—had just reared Congreve and Swift ; and Trinity College, Dublin, which he entered in 1700, was a nursery of distinguished minds. Here he rose to a Fellowship in 1707, and within three years precociously published a psychological masterpiece (*Essay on Vision*) and a philosophical masterpiece (*Principles*). In 1709 he was ordained.

In 1713 he left Dublin for London, not returning (except for one brief visit) until 1721. During this period he began his acquisition of that large knowledge of the world which surprises those who approach his writings with the assumption that he was only a cloistered dreamer. In London he was welcomed at Court, and, more congenially, in the literary circles that included Addison, Steele, Pope, Prior, Gay and Swift. For Steele's *Guardian* he wrote a dozen essays, and with Swift formed a lasting friendship. Even in this galaxy he shone, not primarily as a thinker—his philosophical genius was inadequately measured in his lifetime—but as a man of unique charm of character, manner and conversation. His stay in the capital was broken by two visits to France and Italy, the one in 1713-14 as chaplain to a travelling ambassador, the other in 1716-20 as tutor to a young man doing the ' grand tour '. These journeys made him a connoisseur of the visual arts, chiefly of architecture, on which subject he was thereafter occasionally consulted. Of part of the second tour we have his diary, which reveals a quickness, competence and tirelessness of response to all points of natural history, to local customs, old or lovely buildings and their artistic furnishings. On his return from the second tour, besides re-asserting his philosophical interest by publishing *De Motu*, he wrote on a public issue, the sorry business of the South Sea Bubble, an *Essay towards preventing the Ruin of Great Britain.*

The Bubble, and the similar Mississippi debacle which he had learned of at first hand in France, mark a crucial stage in Berkeley's life. They brought to a head a conviction that the civilisation of Europe had become decrepit and perverse, and gave him the ambition to carry the lamp of godly learning and living from the Old World to the New. He decided to found, and spend the rest of his life in, a college in Bermuda for the Christian education of the colonists and natives of the American mainland. The noble dream, partly expressed in his poem ' America, or the Muses' Refuge ',[1] set him the most arduous task of his life, and its failure gave him his greatest agony. To raise the requisite funds he concentrated on two methods —to augment his personal income by preferment to high ecclesiastical office, and to extract a charter and grant from the Crown. He succeeded in the first by becoming Dean of Derry in 1724 (thus ending his Fellowship of Trinity College). As for the second, after years of lobbying he secured, by a miracle of persuasiveness, the approval by Parliament of a grant of £20,000. In 1728 he set sail, with his newly wed wife and a handful of partners in his scheme, landed at Newport, Rhode Island, and there awaited the promised grant. It never came : the Government of Great Britain had yielded to his famous personal charm, and when this was withdrawn, recovered its flinty realism. In 1731 he accepted the inevitable, and returned to England. Yet his stay of two and a half years had not been fruitless for America. In Newport he was long remembered as a superior visitant. He strongly influenced the father of American philosophy, Samuel Johnson, whose *Elementa Philosophica* (1752) is dedicated to him. He stimulated learning by making large gifts of books to Harvard and Yale, which latter still has three scholarships in Classics endowed by him. His advice was

[1] See A. A. Luce, *Life of George Berkeley*, p. 96.

sought in the early shaping of the colleges that were to become the universities of Columbia and Pennsylvania. It was ' in remembrance of one of the very best of the early friends of college education in America ' and of his westward look that America's westernmost university-town, facing the Golden Gate, was called Berkeley.

After two years in London, marked by the publication of *Alciphron* (written in Newport), his wandering days ended : in 1735 he was presented to the see of Cloyne, in the south-east corner of Ireland. Here, remote from Court, savants and men of letters, he gave himself for eighteen years to his pastoral cure, his family, and his books, refusing to be drawn from this busy tranquillity into any post of greater social repute. He had just issued *The Analyst* (1734), a critique of the Newtonian method of fluxions, which started a fruitful controversy among the mathematicians. This was followed by *The Querist* (1735-7), in which he showed himself to be both a lover of Ireland and an economist with insights ahead of his day. Some years later an epidemic treading on the heels of a famine diverted his philanthropy to medicine : in the sphere of practice he administered tar-water (which he had learned of while in America) to his family and people, and made the drinking of it a vogue ; and in the sphere of theory he composed his strange and beautiful *Siris* (1744), in which, by meditative transitions, from the pharmacology of tar he passes through cosmological speculations about Aether to a Trinitarian theism.

In the autumn of 1752, permitted by the Crown to leave his see, though forbidden to resign it, he moved to Oxford, to enjoy as a tired man its learned peace. There he died in the following year, and there was buried in the Cathedral.

Berkeley's Philosophy

It is a mistake to approach Berkeley as though he were simply a Lockian trying to improve on his master.

We have to keep in mind, besides Locke, at least Descartes, the Occasionalists, Spinoza, Hobbes, the new physicists and mathematicians, and the 'free-thinking' dilettanti who found in the new science reasons or excuses for breaking the old restraints on thought and conduct. The seventeenth-century thinkers, founding the scientific way of studying Nature, had jettisoned everyday notions, disparaged sense, invented subtleties of method and statement, and proclaimed or implied the doctrine of determinism. Berkeley entered the lists in order to rescue science from its complexities and to deprive it of its materialistic suggestions.

Following a fashion set by Descartes, he undertakes an examination of the cognitive value of the senses. The distinctively contemporary view, among philosophers and scientists alike, was that the objects of sense are wholly within the minds that apprehend them, are the effects of material entities that exist independently of all apprehension, and are—strictly, some of them only—copies of the material entities that produce them. Berkeley rejects all these propositions.

(1) Berkeley cannot bring himself to depart so far from the commonsense attitude as to believe that Nature is destitute of colour and sound. These, he notes, are just as integrally parts of the data of sense as solidity, shape and motion are ; are unimaginable apart from the latter, as, indeed, the latter are from them (*e.g.*, colour is extended, and extension coloured) ; and therefore belong where the rest belong. As for the common contention that they are *peculiarly* relative to the position or state of the perceiver, that is an error of fact. There is no tenable ground for distinguishing the data of sense into an objective group, 'primary qualities', and a merely subjective group, 'secondary qualities' (the current talk of colour and sound as 'really' motion, Berkeley stigmatises as nonsense).

The conclusion is that all sensa are cognitively on the same level. Are they all alike, then, copies of a material reality beyond them ? Berkeley's answer is that not one of them is : he rejects the representative theory of perception outright. He points out that the supposition of two parallel orders, one of sensed qualities in the sensing mind and one of similar qualities beyond the mind, issues in scepticism ; for if, *ex hypothesi*, we are face to face only with the former, we can never verify it by comparing it with the latter, since comparison involves the compresence to the mind of the things compared. He has a further objection, typically expressed as an axiom, namely, that a sensum cannot be like anything else than another sensum. The seen, *e.g.* cannot be like the invisible, or the heard like the inaudible ; yet that they can be is assumed when we suppose sensa to be copies of entities that are held to be always beyond the intuition of sense. If the supposed material entities are like the visible, etc., they must themselves be visible, etc., in which event they would be directly presentable to sense, needing no surrogates, no mental representatives or copies. Conversely, if, as the current theory declared, they are not visible, etc., what we do see, etc., cannot represent their nature. The realm of sense, therefore, can have no relation of similitude to anything outside itself. From which the conclusion follows that the realm of sense is itself the corporeal realm, since all corporeal qualities are sensory. To speak of a corporeal world beyond sense is to use words, not to think. The copy-theory is here inapplicable. Sensa present simply themselves ; they represent nothing ; therefore it is meaningless to ask whether they are veracious or fallacious representatives. This is Berkeley's vindication of sense.

But has not Berkeley mentalised the corporeal by bringing it wholly within the mind ? Is he not a subjective idealist, and therefore logically a solipsist ? Indeed, is not ' in the mind ' his own recurrent phrase ? It is ; but since the philosophical vocabulary of his day was less developed than ours, we must catch his meaning instead of simply repeating his phrase. In fact, he does not subjectivise sensa. (*a*) These are just what they appear to be ; what is seen as colour *is* colour, and what is seen as extended *is* extended. Now colour, extension and suchlike sensa are plainly not mental. They are the very constitutive properties of the corporeal. To assign them to the mind as parts of its being, as qualifications of its nature or phases of its process, is unthinkable. The mental and the corporeal are radically opposite, incapable of being assimilated to each other. This opposition of mind and body is an explicit, emphatic and basic part of Berkeley's doctrine, repeated in all his philosophical works. (*b*) Sensa, he says, are related to mind not as modes or attributes to substance, but as objects to subjects. They are over against the mind, not parts of it. (*c*) They are given to us. This also is the plain testimony of experience. Descartes' suggestion, at his sceptical stage, that they might be produced by us, is dismissed by Berkeley as requiring the irresponsible postulation of an occult cause. (*d*) Reflection on experience forces us to believe that sensa, or at least some of them, persist when we are not sensing them. My desk does not vanish when I leave my room ; nor does my fire during the night—it passes through the sequence of changes which we call ' dying out '.

That is Berkeley's realism. There is nothing *per quod percipitur* but simply *id quod percipitur*. The sensed is itself the real corporeal world, perception interposing no screen, whether opaque or diaphanous, of mental entities between us and it.

Yet is not this realism excluded by Berkeley's axiom ' *esse* is *percipi* ' ? Not at all. It does not, indeed, wholly follow from the axiom (but from the givenness, continuity, and intrinsic difference from mind, of the corporeal), but it is permitted by this. The axiom certainly means that the existence of the corporeal *consists* in being perceived, that the sensory is the sensible, that a colour that cannot be seen, a shape that cannot be seen or touched, is a contradiction in terms : in other words, that the corporeal is by nature a *menti objectum*, essentially tied to mind. It is in order to indicate this bond that Berkeley calls everything sensory or corporeal an ' idea ' (*Princ.*, Sect. 39). But it should be noted that the doctrine, because axiomatic, is entirely general. It is not the empirical allegation that each of us in fact enters into relation with the corporeal only by sensations that are his own. This was a commonplace of the day (the situation recently called the ' egocentric predicament '), and one of the several commonplaces against which Berkeley was arguing. The axiom rests on the objective content of the sensory. It says that the sensory as such is relative to mind as such, not that it is bound to this or that mind. It is intended to express not a psychological fact but an epistemological necessity. This is why he laid it down as an axiom. It has nothing to do with subjectivism.

Consequently it is compatible with his realism. Shape, motion, colour, etc.—the qualities that *define* the corporeal—*entail* a reference to mind. Yet experience shows that when I perceive them they are not relative to me only, not existent for me only. The axiom can be satisfied, then, only by postulating a cosmic perceiver. The corporeal world is a system of objects—truly corporeal, not mental—relative essentially to God's mind, and accidentally to our minds. It exists in virtue of God's awareness of it. Berkeley's epistemology thus culminates in a grand ontological conclusion. Sensa force thought to God as their immediate condition ; and as we are always meeting sensa, the evidence for God is very ample and very near. This is a new proof of God. The only earlier epistemological proof was that of St. Augustine, who argued, as a Platonist would, not from sensa but from the eternal verities.

(2) So much for one strand of Berkeley's philosophy, separated out for clearness' sake. Another strand, plaited with it, turns on the application of the principle of causality. The principle itself is not questioned, but only the range of its application. What is maintained is that only mind has causal power. In noting that in the corporeal realm nothing more is observed than regular connexion, Berkeley was only reaffirming what the Occasionalists and Locke had said and what Hume was to say again. The only causal power shown in experience is, as Locke had admitted, that of will (we can summon and dismiss images and thoughts, and move our limbs). Therefore, by the sole analogy we have, all corporeal things and changes must be produced—both brought into existence and presented to our minds—by a cosmic mind. This is Berkeley's form of the cosmological proof of God. The passivity of the corporeal, besides being evident in fact, is evident rationally, being implied by the axiom ' *esse* is *percipi* ', for ' being perceived ' is a passive relation. The connexions among corporeal things are, then, from our finite point of view, merely empirical. No necessity can be discerned in them. They are related not as cause and effect but as sign and thing signified. They can be understood neither causally nor logically, but only teleologically : dependent on the will of God, they are the signs, the language, by which He instructs our expectations, and thereby express His beneficence towards us. ' As if Nature were anything but the ordinance of the free will of God ! ' is one of the comments which Berkeley made in his note-books. Cf. *Princ.*, Sect. 107 *ad fin.*

(3) A third strand is Berkeley's denial of the very possibility of abstract ' ideas '. We have mentioned that by

' idea ' he means anything sensory (and therefore corporeal).
Now the sensory, when not being sensed, can only be
imagined, not thought. In imagination we can, indeed,
abstract within the limits of the sensorily possible ; but
when we go beyond these to pure intellection we leave
the sensory entirely behind, and therefore cannot present
it at all to the mind. Alleged abstract ' ideas ' involve
one or other of two claims, either that we can think apart
what are necessarily bound together in sense, *e.g.* colour
and extension ; or that we can form general concepts
(universals) of classes of sensory things, *e.g.* triangles.
Neither is psychologically possible. Colour and extension
cannot be sensed apart and cannot be imagined apart,
and outside sense and imagination cannot be apprehended
at all. As for the supposed universal triangle, one that is
not equilateral, scalene, etc., and has no determinate
magnitude, it is just nothing, and is not made something by
being called triangle-as-such or triangularity. When
particularity is taken from the sensory, all is taken. We
have, it is true, general *names*, but these can bring before
the mind nothing but one or other, indifferently, of the
particular ' ideas ' which they denote. The concrete
cannot be presented abstractly ; it is necessarily the object
of sensuous intuition.

Berkeley brings this denial of abstract ' ideas ' to bear on
the recent theories of an absolute time, an absolute space,
infinitesimals, and an absolute motion. These, he declares,
are not only not real ; they are simply words. No object
corresponding to them can come before the mind : for
space is essentially sensory (as Kant also held), and therefore cannot appear when we abstract from its sensory
determinations and limits ; and time is but the order of
our experiences ; and, space and time being thus relative,
motion also is bound to be relative. A wider alleged
abstraction, and according to Berkeley the worst of all,

is that which claims to conceive the corporeal in separation from any apprehending mind whatever.

(4) Having considered separately three aspects of Berkeley's total argument, we may now pull them together in order to summarise what he said about matter and mind respectively.

In its negative aspect Berkeley's philosophy is notoriously a denial of 'matter'. He calls those against whom he was arguing 'materialists', and he would approve our calling him an 'immaterialist'. If his terms have proved to be misleading, the fault is not his, for he explained their meaning clearly. Not only he but also his contemporaries meant by 'matter' either corporeal things regarded as existing by themselves, in their own right, beyond sense, independently of all apprehension; or else something that was believed to underlie corporeal phenomena as their substance, point of attachment, or unifying ground and source. Berkeley dismisses both meanings. (a) That 'matter' in the first sense is not a datum was on all hands agreed; all known corporeal properties are sensa, and therefore, according to the current view, sensa private to each mind. 'Matter', then, is something inferred, epistemologically as the 'reality', and ontologically as the cause, of such allegedly private sensa. In neither way, Berkeley argues, can the inference be justified—not in the first way, because sensa, being experienced as objective, are real enough in themselves (as he slyly observes, it is sensed, not insensible, bread that feeds us), and because it is self-contradictory to suppose beyond sensa, and therefore as essentially insensible, anything that has to be described in sensory terms; and not in the second way, because there is no warrant in experience or in reason for adducing any cause except mind for anything at all (a contention for which there was much contemporary support). (b) In the expression 'material substance'

Berkeley can find no coherent meaning. By definition it is not identical with any or all of the corporeal phenomena (space, colour, etc.) which sense presents to us. It is what 'stands under' these. But this cannot be taken literally, for that which is posited as different from space cannot have a spatial relation to space. It must therefore be taken metaphorically ; but then it evaporates into a vague expression like 'some sort of support', or into Locke's frank phrase, 'a something we know not what'. Since this can explain nothing, it can be dropped without loss. It explains nothing because it is nothing, being neither an 'idea', *i.e.* something sensory, nor a 'notion', *i.e.* something mental.

The demand for 'matter' in either sense is due, Berkeley maintains, to our looking in the wrong direction for the explanation of the given world of sense. When we see that the corporeal *means* the perceptible, we connect it essentially with mind, and thereby instantly preclude the first sense ; and at the same time we expose the nature of the connexion—that the corporeal requires not a substance to inhere in but only a subject to appear to—and thereby preclude the second sense. Further, 'matter' being denied, the realm of sense cannot be stigmatised as the distorted shadow of it. The world we seem to live in is the world we do live in, being all that it is experienced to be—given to us, independent of us, and composed of everything it appears to contain. We thus get rid, not only of sub-jectivism, but also of the intermediate nonsense of having to say, for example, that sound is 'really' motion, that 'real' sound cannot possibly be heard, that what is essentially audible is 'really' inaudible.

'Matter', then, does not exist at all. The corporeal certainly does ; but in the last analysis as object. In this remarkably original way Berkeley retains the radical distinction of the mental and the corporeal without falling into dualism; for, while preserving the full corporeality of the latter, he makes it ultimately dependent on the former. He alone among the prominent thinkers of the early period of modern philosophy exposed the absurdity of placing sensa of space and colour in the mind, an absurdity because it involves the double howler of mentalising the corporeal and corporealising the mental.

(5) That ' *esse* is *percipi* ' is said only of the sensory, the corporeal. The *esse* of mind is *percipere* and *velle*. The corporeal, existing only as object, and manifestly inert, cannot be conceived as ultimate. It is not substantial. The only substance, the only thing that is known as a unity expressing itself variously, as a fount of activity, and as capable of existing in its own right, itself apprehending and therefore not dependent on being apprehended, is mind. The concept of mental substance is both coherent and empirically grounded, so that it is free from the objections that dispose of the pretended concept of material substance. We are bound to posit a mental substance, for ' ideas ' do not apprehend themselves or one another, and anyhow we know it directly, each of us in himself, ' by a sort of internal awareness ' (*De Motu*, Sect. 21). Other minds each of us knows by analogy—finite minds from their bodily evidence, God by the evidence of that entire corporeal realm which can only exist in relation to a cosmic perceiver. All minds alike, when we think about them, turning them into objects, are, and have to be, thought of as subjects : they are objects accidentally, subjects essentially. As objects they are utterly different from the corporeal—not sensory but sensing, not passive but active, and not extended but spaceless. To mark this distinction Berkeley calls them, when treating them both as objects, ' ideas ' and ' notions ' respectively. When we bear in mind that ' notion ' means any object the content of which is mental, we shall see the sheer oddity of two common

criticisms of Berkeley's introduction of that term—first, that he ought to say that the *esse* of a notion must be *concipi*, *i.e.* that even the existence of minds consists in being thought of, and secondly, that the abstract ' ideas ' which he had denied can, after all, be smuggled back into his system as ' notions '.

(6) Berkeley's last philosophical work, *Siris*, appeared thirty-four years after his first. It is a leisurely musing on old science and older metaphysics. Its theoretical purpose is to show that in the most venerated systems of antiquity the corporeal universe is placed under the control of a divine mind. On the way he repeats one after another of his earlier doctrines, so far as I can see neither adding nor changing anything. With those who have found here a *volte face* I am unable to agree. The doctrines which he here affirms (there are many which he is merely reporting) seem to me to be those he had affirmed before ; his interest in the sensible world is undiminished, for more than half of the book is concerned with it ; and though in the end he soars away from it, and from a metaphysical height gives a comparative disparagement of it and of our know-ledge of it, that height is the realm of mind, which he had always regarded as alone substantial and causative. Sense, he now says, knows nothing ; but all that he means is, as he had said earlier, that it apprehends merely the corporeal, not the mental, only the dependent, not the ultimate, only that which is to be explained and not that which explains. Sense, he still holds, apprehends the corporeal as it is, and natural science, he still holds, ascertains the given non-causal connexions of the corporeal ; but only metaphysics, leaving ' ideas ' for ' notions ', investigates mind and detects in this the epistemological and causal ground of the corporeal—which again is what he had asserted in his early days. There is but one Berkeleian system. What he willed to us in the first flush

of his career is not altered by any late codicil, for *Siris* is not a codicil, but the same will rewritten with an ornament of antique learning, a mood of deepened humility, and a speculative vision tinged with an unwonted mysticism.

T. E. J.

University College,
  Hull, 1952.

CHRONOLOGICAL TABLE
OF BERKELEY'S LIFE AND WRITINGS

1685.   (12 March). Born near Kilkenny.

1696.   Entered Kilkenny College.

1700-12.   In Dublin.

> 1700, entered Trinity College, Dublin. 1704, B.A. 1707, Fellow ; M.A. ; *Arithmetica* and *Miscellanea Mathematica*. 1709, ordained ; *Essay towards a new Theory of Vision*. 1710, *Treatise concerning the Principles of Human Knowledge*. 1712, Junior Lecturer in Greek; *Passive Obedience*.

1713-21.   Chiefly abroad.

> 1713 (Jan.-Oct.), in England; *Three Dialogues* ; essays in *The Guardian*. 1713-14, in Italy, as chaplain to the Earl of Peterborough. 1714-16, in England. 1715, *Advice to the Tories who have taken the Oaths*. 1716-20, in France, Italy and Sicily, as travelling tutor.

1721-4.   Chiefly in Dublin.

> 1721, D.D.; Lecturer in Divinity; *De Motu* ; *Essay towards preventing the Ruin of Great Britain*. 1722, Dean of Dromore (in title, not in office). 1723, executor and legatee of Swift's Vanessa. 1724, Dean of Derry; resigned offices in Trinity College; *Proposal for the better supplying of Churches in our foreign Plantations*.

1724-8.   In England, preparing plans for a college in Bermuda.

> 1728, married Anne Forster; sailed for America.

1729-31.   In Newport, Rhode Island.

1731-4.   In England.

     1732, *Alciphron.*   1733, *Theory of Vision . . . vindicated and explained.*

1734-52.   In Ireland, as Bishop of Cloyne.

     1734, Bishop of Cloyne; *Analyst.* 1735, *Defence of Free-thinking in Mathematics.* 1735-7, *Querist.* 1738, *Discourse addressed to Magistrates.* 1744, *Philosophical Reflexions and Inquiries concerning the Virtues of Tar water* (*Siris*). 1749, *A Word to the Wise.*

1753   (14 January).   Died in Oxford.

BIBLIOGRAPHICAL NOTE

THE FOLLOWING editions of Berkeley's works will be generally accessible to students :

> Ed. A. C. Fraser, *The Works of George Berkeley*, 4 vols., Oxford 1871 : second edn. 1901.
>
> Ed. G. Sampson, *The Works of George Berkeley*, 3 vols., London 1897-8.
>
> Edd. A. A. Luce and T. E. Jessop, *The Works of George Berkeley, Bishop of Cloyne*, 9 vols., Edinburgh 1948— . . . (Referred to below as L. and J.).

Besides the works represented in this volume, the following deserve particular mention :

> *Philosophical Commentaries*. Notes written by Berkeley *circa* 1707-08 in preparation of his *Essay on Vision* and the *Principles*. They were first transcribed and published (1871) by Fraser, who called them Berkeley's *Commonplace Book*. The new title is due to Dr Luce, who has given us a much more accurate transcription, a better arrangement, and a more perceptive interpretation, in his edn., Edinburgh 1944. Also in L. and J., vol. I.
>
> *Passive Obedience*, Dublin and London 1712. L. and J., vol. VI.
>
> *The Theory of Vision, or Visual Language showing the immediate Presence and Providence of a Deity, vindicated and explained* (short title, *Theory of Vision vindicated*), London 1712. L. and J., vol. I.
>
> *The Analyst*, Dublin and London 1734. L. and J., vol. IV.
>
> *The Querist*, Dublin and London 1735-7. L. and J., vol. VI.

On Berkeley's life, the following may be consulted :

> A. C. Fraser, *Life and Letters of George Berkeley*, *D.D.*, Oxford 1871.
>
> J. M. Hone and M. Rossi, *Bishop Berkeley*, London and New York 1931.
>
> A. A. Luce, *The Life of George Berkeley, Bishop of Cloyne*, Edinburgh 1949, which in accuracy supersedes its predecessors.

The following is a select list of works in English on Berkeley's philosophy :

A. C. Fraser, *Berkeley*, Edinburgh 1881, repr. 1901.

G. Dawes Hicks, *Berkeley*, London 1932.

G. A. Johnston, *The Development of Berkeley's Philosophy*, London 1923.

A. A. Luce, *Berkeley and Malebranche*, Oxford 1934; *Berkeley's Immaterialism*, Edinburgh 1945.

In French, German and Italian, the best general studies are respectively as follows :

A. Joussain, *Exposé critique de la philosophie de Berkeley*, Paris 1920.

R. Metz, *Berkeleys Leben und Lehre*, Stuttgart 1925.

A. Levi, *La filosofia di Giorgio Berkeley*, Turin 1922.

AN ESSAY
TOWARDS A NEW THEORY
OF VISION

First published 1709   Final edition 1732

EDITOR'S NOTE

The *Essay* exposes the inadequacy of the geometrical way of explaining vision, adducing instead the *experienced* basis of our spontaneous judgments of distance, magnitude and situation, and finding it chiefly in tactile (including what we now call kinaesthetic) data. It makes the novel point that visual extension and tactile extension have nothing in common.

Although the *Essay* is thus psychological in content, Berkeley wrote it to clear up a difficulty that arose when, already an immaterialist, he was composing his *Principles* (see *Princ.*, Sect. 43). Not having yet published his *esse-percipi* philosophy, he refrains from questioning the usual assumption that the objects of touch are the 'real' things. He does announce, however, two of his distinctive philosophical doctrines—that there are no abstract 'ideas' (Sects. 43, 122 ff., 130, 137), and that sensory objects are signs only, never causes, are connected not necessarily but arbitrarily, like words and what they denote, so that in this regard they form a natural language. Berkeley looked back upon the *Essay* from his philosophical point of view in his *Theory of Vision Vindicated* (1733).

The passages selected cover all the topics. (1) *Perception of distance*—from Sects. 1-51; (2) *Of magnitude*—from Sects. 54-65; (3) *Of situation*—from Sects. 88-119 ; (4) *The heterogeneity of the space (and motion) of sight and of touch, and remarks on the space of geometry*—from Sects. 121-58.

2

AN ESSAY TOWARDS A NEW
THEORY OF VISION

1 My design is to show the manner wherein we perceive by sight the distance, magnitude, and situation of objects. Also to consider the difference there is betwixt the ideas of sight and touch, and whether there be any idea common to both senses.

2 It is, I think, agreed by all that distance, of itself and immediately, cannot be seen. For distance being a line directed end-wise to the eye, it projects only one point in the fund of the eye, which point remains invariably the same, whether the distance be longer or shorter.

3 I find it also acknowledged that the estimate we make of the distance of objects considerably remote is rather an act of judgment grounded on experience than of sense. For example, when I perceive a great number of inter-mediate objects, such as houses, fields, rivers, and the like, which I have experienced to take up a considerable space, I thence form a judgment or conclusion that the object I see beyond them is at a great distance. Again, when an object appears faint and small, which at a near distance I have experienced to make a vigorous and large appearance, I instantly conclude it to be far off: and this, 'tis evident, is the result of experience; without which, from the faint-ness and littleness I should not have inferred anything concerning the distance of objects.

16 Now, it being already shown that distance is suggested to the mind by the mediation of some other idea which is itself perceived in the act of seeing, it remains that we inquire what ideas or sensations there be that attend vision, unto which we may suppose the ideas of distance are

connected, and by which they are introduced into the mind. And *first*, it is certain by experience that when we look at a near object with both eyes, according as it approaches or recedes from us, we alter the disposition of our eyes, by lessening or widening the interval between the pupils. This disposition or turn of the eyes is attended with a sensation, which seems to me to be that which in this case brings the idea of greater or lesser distance into the mind.

17 Not that there is any natural or necessary connexion between the sensation we perceive by the turn of the eyes and greater or lesser distance, but because the mind has by constant experience found the different sensations corresponding to the different dispositions of the eyes to be attended each with a different degree of distance in the object, there has grown an habitual or customary connexion between those two sorts of ideas, so that the mind no sooner perceives the sensation arising from the different turn it gives the eyes, in order to bring the pupils nearer or farther asunder, but it withal perceives the different idea of distance which was wont to be connected with that sensation; just as upon hearing a certain sound, the idea is immediately suggested to the understanding which custom had united with it.

21 *Secondly*, an object placed at a certain distance from the eye, to which the breadth of the pupil bears a considerable proportion, being made to approach, is seen more confusedly : and the nearer it is brought the more confused appearance it makes. And this being found constantly to be so, there ariseth in the mind an habitual connexion between the several degrees of confusion and distance ; the greater confusion still implying the lesser distance, and the lesser confusion the greater distance of the object.

22 This confused appearance of the object doth therefore seem to be the medium whereby the mind judgeth of

distance in those cases wherein the most approved writers of optics will have it judged by the different divergency with which the rays flowing from the radiating point fall on the pupil. . . .

27 *Thirdly*, an object being placed at the distance above specified, and brought nearer to the eye, we may nevertheless prevent, at least for some time, the appearances growing more confused by straining the eye. In which case that sensation supplies the place of confused vision in aiding the mind to judge of the distance of the object; it being esteemed so much the nearer by how much the effort or straining of the eye in order to distinct vision is greater.

28 I have here set down those sensations or ideas that seem to be the constant and general occasions of introducing into the mind the different ideas of near distance. It is true in most cases that divers other circumstances contribute to frame our idea of distance, to wit, the particular number, size, kind, etc., of the things seen. Concerning which, as well as all other the forementioned occasions which suggest distance, I shall only observe they have none of them, in their own nature, any relation or connexion with it : nor is it possible they should ever signify the various degrees thereof, otherwise than as by experience they have been found to be connected with them.

41 From what hath been premised it is a manifest consequence that a man born blind, being made to see, would at first have no idea of distance by sight ; the sun and stars, the remotest objects as well as the nearer, would all seem to be in his eye, or rather in his mind. The objects intromitted by sight would seem to him (as in truth they are) no other than a new set of thoughts or sensations, each whereof is as near to him as the perceptions of pain or pleasure, or the most inward passions of his soul. For

our judging objects perceived by sight to be at any distance, or without the mind, is (*vid.* Sect. 28) entirely the effect of experience, which one in those circumstances could not yet have attained to.

43 And perhaps upon a strict inquiry we shall not find that even those who from their birth have grown up in a continued habit of seeing are irrecoverably prejudiced on the other side, to wit, in thinking what they see to be at a distance from them. For at this time it seems agreed on all hands by those who have had any thoughts of that matter, that colours, which are the proper and immediate object of sight, are not without the mind. But then it will be said, by sight we have also the ideas of extension, and figure, and motion; all which may well be thought without, and at some distance from the mind, though colour should not. In answer to this I appeal to any man's experience, whether the visible extension of any object doth not appear as near to him as the colour of that object; nay, whether they do not both seem to be in the very same place. Is not the extension we see coloured, and is it possible for us, so much as in thought, to separate and abstract colour from extension? Now, where the extension is, there surely is the figure, and there the motion too.[1] I speak of those which are perceived by sight.

44 But for a fuller explication of this point, and to show that the immediate objects of sight are not so much as the ideas or resemblances of things placed at a distance, it is requisite that we look nearer into the matter and carefully observe what is meant in common discourse, when one says that which he sees is at a distance from him. Suppose, for example, that looking at the moon I should say it were fifty or sixty semidiameters of the earth distant from me. Let us see what moon this is spoken of: it is plain it cannot be the visible moon, or anything like the visible

---

[1] [See *Princ.*, Sects. 10 and 99.—ED.]

moon, or that which I see, which is only a round, luminous plane of about thirty visible points in diameter. For in case I am carried from the place where I stand directly towards the moon, it is manifest the object varies, still as I go on; and by the time that I am advanced fifty or sixty semidiameters of the earth, I shall be so far from being near a small, round, luminous flat that I shall perceive nothing like it; this object having long since disappeared, and if I would recover it, it must be by going back to the earth from whence I set out. Again, suppose I perceive by sight the faint and obscure idea of something which I doubt whether it be a man, or a tree, or a tower, but judge it to be at the distance of about a mile. It is plain I cannot mean that what I see is a mile off, or that it is the image or likeness of anything which is a mile off, since that every step I take towards it the appearance alters, and from being obscure, small, and faint, grows clear, large, and vigorous. And when I come to the mile's end, that which I saw first is quite lost, neither do I find anything in the likeness of it.

45 In these and the like instances the truth of the matter stands thus: Having of a long time experienced certain ideas, perceivable by touch as distance, tangible figure, and solidity, to have been connected with certain ideas of sight, I do upon perceiving these ideas of sight forthwith conclude what tangible ideas are by the wonted ordinary course of Nature like to follow. Looking at an object, I perceive a certain visible figure and colour, with some degree of faintness and other circumstances, which from what I have formerly observed, determine me to think that if I advance forward so many paces or miles, I shall be affected with such and such ideas of touch: so that in truth and strictness of speech I neither see distance itself, nor anything that I take to be at a distance. I say, neither distance nor things placed at a distance are themselves, or

their ideas, truly perceived by sight. This I am persuaded of, as to what concerns myself : and I believe whoever will look narrowly into his own thoughts and examine what he means by saying he sees this or that thing at a distance, will agree with me that what he sees only suggests to his understanding that after having passed a certain distance, to be measured by the motion of his body, which is perceivable by touch, he shall come to perceive such and such tangible ideas which have been usually connected with such and such visible ideas. But that one might be deceived by these suggestions of sense, and that there is no necessary connexion between visible and tangible ideas suggested by them, we need go no further than the next looking-glass or picture to be convinced. Note that when I speak of tangible ideas, I take the word ' idea ' for any the immediate object of sense or understanding, in which large signification it is commonly used by the moderns.

46 From what we have shown it is a manifest consequence that the ideas of space, outness, and things placed at a distance are not, strictly speaking, the object of sight ; they are not otherwise perceived by the eye than by the ear. Sitting in my study I hear a coach drive along the street ; I look through the casement and see it ; I walk out and enter into it ; thus, common speech would incline one to think I heard, saw, and touched the same thing, to wit, the coach. It is nevertheless certain, the ideas intromitted by each sense are widely different and distinct from each other ; but having been observed constantly to go together, they are spoken of as one and the same thing. By the variation of the noise I perceive the different distances of the coach, and know that it approaches before I look out. Thus by the ear I perceive distance, just after the same manner as I do by the eye.

48 . . . It is thought a great absurdity to imagine that one and the same thing should have any more than one

extension and one figure. But the extension and figure
of a body, being let into the mind two ways, and that
indifferently either by sight or touch, it seems to follow
that we see the same extension and the same figure which
we feel.

49 But if we take a close and accurate view of things, it
must be acknowledged that we never see and feel one and
the same object. / That which is seen is one thing, and
that which is felt is another. / If the visible figure and
extension be not the same with the tangible figure and
extension, we are not to infer that one and the same thing
has divers extensions. (The true consequence is that the
objects of sight and touch are two distinct things. / It
may perhaps require some thought rightly to conceive
this distinction. And the difficulty seems not a little
increased, because the combination of visible ideas hath
constantly the same name as the combination of tangible
ideas wherewith it is connected : which doth of necessity
arise from the use and end of language.

50 In order therefore to treat accurately and uncon-
fusedly of vision, we must bear in mind that there are two
sorts of objects apprehended by the eye, the one primarily
and immediately, the other secondarily and by intervention of the former. Those of the first sort neither are,
nor appear to be, without the mind, or at any distance off ;
they may indeed grow greater or smaller, more confused,
or more clear, or more faint, but they do not, cannot,
approach or recede from us. Whenever we say an object is
at a distance, whenever we say it draws near, or goes farther
off, we must always mean it of the latter sort, which properly
belong to the touch, and are not so truly perceived as
suggested by the eye in like manner as thoughts by the ear.

51 No sooner do we hear the words of a familiar language
pronounced in our ears, but the ideas corresponding thereto present themselves to our minds : in the very same

9

instant the sound and the meaning enter the understanding : so closely are they united that it is not in our
power to keep out the one, except we exclude the other
also. We even act in all respects as if we heard the
very thoughts themselves. So likewise the secondary
objects, or those which are only suggested by sight, do
often more strongly affect us, and are more regarded than the
proper objects of that sense ; along with which they enter
into the mind, and with which they have a far more strict
connexion, than ideas have with words. Hence it is we
find it so difficult to discriminate between the immediate
and mediate objects of sight, and are so prone to attribute
to the former what belongs only to the latter. They are, as
it were, most closely twisted, blended, and incorporated
together. And the prejudice is confirmed and riveted in
our thoughts by a long tract of time, by the use of language,
and want of reflexion. However, I believe any one that
shall attentively consider what we have already said, and
shall say, upon this subject before we have done (especially
if he pursue it in his own thoughts) may be able to deliver
himself from that prejudice. Sure I am it is worth some
attention, to whoever would understand the true nature
of vision.

54 It hath been shown there are two sorts of objects
apprehended by sight ; each whereof hath its distinct
magnitude, or extension. The one, properly tangible, *i.e.* to
be perceived and measured by touch, and not immediately
falling under the sense of seeing : the other, properly and
immediately visible, by mediation of which the former is
brought in view. Each of these magnitudes are greater
or lesser, according as they contain in them more or fewer
points, they being made up of points or minimums. For,
whatever may be said of extension in abstract, it is certain
sensible extension is not infinitely divisible. There is a

minimum tangibile and a *minimum visibile,* beyond which sense cannot perceive. This every one's experience will inform him.

55 The magnitude of the object which exists without the mind, and is at a distance, continues always invariably the same : but the visible object still changing as you approach to, or recede from, the tangible object, it hath no fixed and determinate greatness. Whenever, therefore, we speak of the magnitude of anything, for instance a tree or a house, we must mean the tangible magnitude, otherwise there can be nothing steady and free from ambiguity spoken of it. But though the tangible and visible magnitude in truth belong to two distinct objects : I shall nevertheless (especially since those objects are called by the same name, and are observed to coexist), to avoid tediousness and singularity of speech, sometimes speak of them as belonging to one and the same thing.

56 Now in order to discover by what means the magnitude of tangible objects is perceived by sight, I need only reflect on what passes in my own mind, and observe what those things be which introduce the ideas of greater or lesser into my thoughts, when I look on any object. And these I find to be, *first*, the magnitude or extension of the visible object, which being immediately perceived by sight, is connected with that other which is tangible and placed at a distance. *Secondly*, the confusion or distinctness. And *thirdly*, the vigorousness or faintness of the aforesaid visible appearance.[1] *Ceteris paribus*, by how much the greater or lesser the visible object is, by so much the greater or lesser do I conclude the tangible object to be. But, be the idea immediately perceived by sight never so large, yet if it be withal confused, I judge the magnitude of the thing to be

---

[1] [See Sect. 35 (not here included).—ED.]

but small. If it be distinct and clear, I judge it greater. And if it be faint, I apprehend it to be yet greater. . . .

57 Moreover the judgments we make of greatness do, in like manner as those of distance, depend on the disposition of the eye, also on the figure, number, and situation of objects and other circumstances that have been observed to attend great or small tangible magnitudes. Thus, for instance, the very same quantity of visible extension, which in the figure of a tower doth suggest the idea of great magnitude, shall in the figure of a man suggest the idea of much smaller magnitude. That this is owing to the experience we have had of the usual bigness of a tower and a man no one, I suppose, need be told.

58 It is also evident that confusion or faintness have no more a necessary connexion with little or great magnitude than they have with little or great distance. As they suggest the latter, so they suggest the former to our minds. And by consequence, if it were not for experience, we should no more judge a faint or confused appearance to be connected with great or little magnitude, than we should that it was connected with great or little distance.

59 Nor will it be found that great or small visible magnitude hath any necessary relation to great or small tangible magnitude, so that the one may certainly be inferred from the other. But before we come to the proof of this, it is fit we consider the difference there is betwixt the extension and figure which is the proper object of touch, and that other which is termed visible ; and how the former is principally though not immediately taken notice of, when we look at any object. This has been before mentioned, but we shall here inquire into the cause thereof. We regard the objects that environ us in proportion as they are adapted to benefit or injure our own bodies, and thereby produce in our minds the sensations of pleasure or pain. Now bodies operating on our organs by an immediate application, and the hurt

or advantage arising therefrom, depending altogether on the tangible, and not at all on the visible, qualities of any object: this is a plain reason why those should be regarded by us much more than these: and for this end the visive sense seems to have been bestowed on animals, to wit, that by the perception of visible ideas (which in themselves are not capable of affecting or any wise altering the frame of their bodies) they may be able to foresee (from the experience they have had what tangible ideas are connected with such and such visible ideas) the damage or benefit which is like to ensue, upon the application of their own bodies to this or that body which is at a distance. Which foresight, how necessary it is to the preservation of an animal, every one's experience can inform him. Hence it is that when we look at an object, the tangible figure and extension thereof are principally attended to; whilst there is small heed taken of the visible figure and magnitude, which, though more immediately perceived, do less concern us, and are not fitted to produce any alteration in our bodies.

60 That the matter of fact is true will be evident to anyone who considers that a man placed at ten foot distance is thought as great as if he were placed at a distance only of five foot: which is true not with relation to the visible, but tangible greatness of the object; the visible magnitude being far greater at one station than it is at the other.

61 Inches, feet, etc., are settled stated lengths whereby we measure objects and estimate their magnitude: we say, for example, an object appears to be six inches or six foot long. Now, that this cannot be meant of visible inches, etc., is evident, because a visible inch is itself no constant, determinate magnitude, and cannot therefore serve to mark out and determine the magnitude of any other thing. Take an inch marked upon a ruler: view it, successively, at the distance of half a foot, a foot, a foot and a half, etc., from the eye: at each of which, and at all the intermediate

distances, the inch shall have a different visible extension, *i.e.* there shall be more or fewer points discerned in it. Now I ask which of all these various extensions is that stated, determinate one that is agreed on for a common measure of other magnitudes? No reason can be assigned why we should pitch on one more than another : and except there be some invariable, determinate extension fixed on to be marked by the word ' inch ', it is plain it can be used to little purpose; and to say a thing contains this or that number of inches shall imply no more than that it is extended, without bringing any particular idea of that extension into the mind. Farther, an inch and a foot, from different distances, shall both exhibit the same visible magnitude, and yet at the same time you shall say that one seems several times greater than the other. From all which it is manifest that the judgments we make of the magnitude of objects by sight are altogether in reference to their tangible extension. Whenever we say an object is great, or small, of this or that determinate measure, I say it must be meant of the tangible, and not the visible extension, which, though immediately perceived, is nevertheless little taken notice of.

65 As we see distance, so we see magnitude. And we see both in the same way that we see shame or anger in the looks of a man. Those passions are themselves invisible, they are nevertheless let in by the eye along with colours and alterations of countenance, which are the immediate object of vision : and which signify them for no other reason than barely because they have been observed to accompany them. Without which experience we should no more have taken blushing for a sign of shame than of gladness.

88 Having finished what I intended to say concerning the distance and magnitude of objects, I come now to treat

of the manner wherein the mind perceives by sight their situation. Among the discoveries of the last age, it is reputed none of the least that the manner of vision hath been more clearly explained than ever it had been before. There is at this day no one ignorant that the pictures of external objects are painted on the retina, or fund of the eye: that we can see nothing which is not so painted: and that, according as the picture is more distinct or confused, so also is the perception we have of the object: but then in this explication of vision there occurs one mighty difficulty. The objects are painted in an inverted order on the bottom of the eye: the upper part of any object being painted on the lower part of the eye, and the lower part of the object on the upper part of the eye: and so also as to right and left. Since therefore the pictures are thus inverted, it is demanded how it comes to pass that we see the objects erect and in their natural posture?

93 It is certain that a man actually blind, and who had continued so from his birth, would by the sense of feeling attain to have ideas of upper and lower. By the motion of his hand he might discern the situation of any tangible object placed within his reach. That part on which he felt himself supported, or towards which he perceived his body to gravitate, he would term lower and the contrary to this upper; and accordingly denominate whatsoever objects he touched.

96 To set this matter in a clearer light I shall make use of an example. Suppose the above-mentioned blind person by his touch perceived a man to stand erect. Let us inquire into the manner of this. By the application of his hand to the several parts of a human body he had perceived different tangible ideas, which being collected into sundry complex ones, have distinct names annexed to them. Thus one combination of a certain tangible figure, bulk, and consistency of parts is called the head, another the hand, a third the foot, and so of the rest: all

15

which complex ideas could, in his understanding, be made up only of ideas perceivable by touch. He had also by his touch obtained an idea of earth or ground, towards which he perceives the parts of his body to have a natural tendency. Now, by erect nothing more being meant than that perpendicular position of a man wherein his feet are nearest to the earth, if the blind person by moving his hand over the parts of the man who stands before him perceives the tangible ideas that compose the head to be farthest from, and those that compose the feet to be nearest to, that other combination of tangible ideas which he calls earth, he will denominate that man erect. But if we suppose him on a sudden to receive his sight, and that he behold a man standing before him, it is evident in that case he would neither judge the man he sees to be erect nor inverted; for he never having known those terms applied to any other save tangible things, or which existed in the space without him, and what he sees neither being tangible nor perceived as existing without, he could not know that in propriety of language they were applicable to it.

97 Afterwards, when upon turning his head or eyes up and down to the right and left he shall observe the visible objects to change, and shall also attain to know that they are called by the same names, and connected with the objects perceived by touch; then indeed he will come to speak of them and their situation in the same terms that he has been used to apply to tangible things; and those that he perceives by turning up his eyes he will call upper, and those that by turning down his eyes he will call lower.

98 And this seems to me the true reason why he should think those objects uppermost that are painted on the lower part of his eye: for by turning the eye up they shall be distinctly seen: as likewise those that are painted on the highest part of the eye shall be distinctly seen by turning the eye down, and are for that reason esteemed lowest; for

we have shown that to the immediate objects of sight considered in themselves, he would not attribute the terms high and low. It must therefore be on account of some circumstances which are observed to attend them : and these, it is plain, are the actions of turning the eye up and down, which suggest a very obvious reason why the mind should denominate the objects of sight accordingly high or low. And without this motion of the eye, this turning it up and down in order to discern different objects, doubtless erect, inverse, and other the like terms relating to the position of tangible objects, would never have been transferred, or in any degree apprehended to belong, to the ideas of sight : the mere act of seeing including nothing in it to that purpose ; whereas the different situations of the eye naturally direct the mind to make a suitable judgment of the situation of objects intromitted by it.

99 Farther, when he has by experience learned the connexion there is between the several ideas of sight and touch, he will be able, by the perception he has of the situation of visible things in respect of one another, to make a sudden and true estimate of the situation of outward, tangible things corresponding to them. And thus it is he shall perceive by sight the situation of external objects which do not properly fall under that sense.

100 I know we are very prone to think that, if just made to see, we should judge of the situation of visible things as we do now : but we are also as prone to think that, at first sight, we should in the same way apprehend the distance and magnitude of objects as we do now : which hath been shown to be a false and groundless persuasion. And for the like reasons the same censure may be passed on the positive assurance that most men, before they have thought sufficiently of the matter, might have of their being able to determine by the eye at first view, whether objects were erect or inverse.

17

104 Farther, we have at large shown (*vid.* Sects. 63 and 64) there is no discoverable necessary connexion between any given visible magnitude and any one particular tangible magnitude; but that it is entirely the result of custom and experience, and depends on foreign and accidental circumstances, that we can by the perception of visible extension inform ourselves what may be the extension of any tangible object connected with it. Hence it is certain that neither the visible magnitude of head or foot would bring along with them into the mind, at first opening of the eyes, the respective tangible magnitudes of those parts.

105 By the foregoing section it is plain the visible figure of any part of the body hath no necessary connexion with the tangible figure thereof, so as at first sight to suggest it to the mind, for figure is the termination of magnitude: whence it follows that no visible magnitude having in its own nature an aptness to suggest any one particular tangible magnitude, so neither can any visible figure be inseparably connected with its corresponding tangible figure, so as of itself, and in a way prior to experience, it might suggest it to the understanding. This will be farther evident if we consider that what seems smooth and round to the touch may to sight, if viewed through a microscope, seem quite otherwise.

106 From all which laid together and duly considered, we may clearly deduce this inference. In the first act of vision no idea entering by the eye would have a perceivable connexion with the ideas to which the names earth, man, head, foot, etc., were annexed in the understanding of a person blind from his birth, so as in any sort to introduce them into his mind, or make themselves be called by the same names, and reputed the same things with them, as afterwards they come to be.

115 But, say you, the picture of the man is inverted,

and yet the appearance is erect : I ask, what mean you by the picture of the man, or, which is the same thing, the visible man's being inverted ? You tell me it is inverted, because the heels are uppermost and the head undermost ? Explain me this. You say that by the head's being undermost you mean that it is nearest to the earth ; and by the heels being uppermost that they are farthest from the earth. I ask again what earth you mean ? You cannot mean the earth that is painted on the eye, or the visible earth : for the picture of the head is farthest from the picture of the earth, and the picture of the feet nearest to the picture of the earth ; and accordingly the visible head is farthest from the visible earth, and the visible feet nearest to it. It remains, therefore, that you mean the tangible earth, and so determine the situation of visible things with respect to tangible things ; contrary to what hath been demonstrated in Sects. 111 and 112. The two distinct provinces of sight and touch should be considered apart, and as if their objects had no intercourse, no manner of relation one to another, in point of distance or position.

116 Farther, what greatly contributes to make us mistake in this matter is that when we think of the pictures in the fund of the eye, we imagine ourselves looking on the fund of another's eye, or another looking on the fund of our own eye, and beholding the pictures painted thereon. Suppose two eyes A and B : A from some distance looking on the pictures in B sees them inverted, and for that reason concludes they are inverted in B : but this is wrong. There are projected in little on the bottom of A the images of the pictures of, suppose, man, earth, etc., which are painted on B. And besides these the eye B itself, and the objects which environ it, together with another earth, are projected in a large size on A. Now, by the eye A these larger images are deemed the true objects, and the lesser only pictures in miniature. And it is with respect to those

greater images that it determines the situation of the smaller images : so that comparing the little man with the great earth, A judges him inverted, or that the feet are farthest from and the head nearest to the great earth. Whereas, if A compare the little man with the little earth, then he will appear erect, *i.e.*, his head shall seem farthest from, and his feet nearest to, the little earth. But we must consider that B does not see two earths as A does : it sees only what is represented by the little pictures in A, and consequently shall judge the man erect : for, in truth, the man in B is not inverted, for there the feet are next the earth ; but it is the representation of it in A which is inverted, for there the head of the representation of the picture of the man in B is next the earth, and the feet farthest from the earth, meaning the earth which is without the representation of the pictures in B. For if you take the little images of the pictures in B, and consider them by themselves, and with respect only to one another, they are all erect and in their natural posture.

117 Farther, there lies a mistake in our imagining that the pictures of external objects are painted on the bottom of the eye. It hath been shown there is no resemblance between the ideas of sight and things tangible. It hath likewise been demonstrated that the proper objects of sight do not exist without the mind. Whence it clearly follows that the pictures painted on the bottom of the eye are not the pictures of external objects. Let anyone consult his own thoughts, and then say what affinity, what likeness there is between that certain variety and disposition of colours which constitute the visible man, or picture of a man, and that other combination of far different ideas, sensible by touch, which compose the tangible man. But if this be the case, how come they to be accounted pictures or images, since that supposes them to copy or represent some originals or other ?

118 To which I answer : In the forementioned instance the eye A takes the little images, included within the representation of the other eye B, to be pictures or copies, whereof the archetypes are not things existing without, but the larger pictures projected on its own fund : and which by A are not thought pictures, but the originals, or true things themselves. Though if we suppose a third eye C from a due distance to behold the fund of A, then indeed the things projected thereon shall, to C, seem pictures or images in the same sense that those projected on B do to A.

119 Rightly to conceive this point we must carefully distinguish between the ideas of sight and touch, between the visible and tangible eye ; for certainly on the tangible eye nothing either is or seems to be painted. Again, the visible eye, as well as all other visible objects, hath been shown to exist only in the mind, which perceiving its own ideas, and comparing them together, calls some *pictures* in respect of others. What hath been said, being rightly comprehended and laid together, doth, I think, afford a full and genuine explication of the erect appearance of objects ; which phenomenon, I must confess, I do not see how it can be explained by any theories of vision hitherto made public.

121 We have shown the way wherein the mind by mediation of visible ideas doth perceive or apprehend the distance, magnitude, and situation of tangible objects. We come now to inquire more particularly concerning the difference between the ideas of sight and touch, which are called by the same names, and see whether there be any idea common to both senses. From what we have at large set forth and demonstrated in the foregoing parts of this treatise, it is plain there is no one self-same numerical extension perceived both by sight and touch ; but that the particular figures and extensions perceived by sight,

however they may be called by the same names and reputed the same things with those perceived by touch, are nevertheless different, and have an existence distinct and separate from them : so that the question is not now concerning the same numerical ideas, but whether there be any one and the same sort or species of ideas equally perceivable to both senses ; or, in other words, whether extension, figure, and motion perceived by sight are not specifically distinct from extension, figure, and motion perceived by touch.

122 But before I come more particularly to discuss this matter, I find it proper to consider extension in abstract[1] : for of this there is much talk, and I am apt to think that when men speak of extension as being an idea common to two senses, it is with a secret supposition that we can single out extension from all other tangible and visible qualities, and form thereof an abstract idea, which idea they will have common both to sight and touch. We are therefore to understand by extension in abstract an idea of extension, for instance, a line or surface entirely stripped of all other sensible qualities and circumstances that might determine it to any particular existence ; it is neither black nor white, nor red, nor hath it any colour at all, or any tangible quality whatsoever, and consequently it is of no finite determinate magnitude : for that which bounds or distinguishes one extension from another is some quality or circumstance wherein they disagree.

123 Now I do not find that I can perceive, imagine, or any wise frame in my mind such an abstract idea as is here spoken of. A line or surface which is neither black nor white, nor blue, nor yellow, etc., nor long, nor short, nor rough, nor smooth, nor square, nor round, etc., is perfectly incomprehensible. This I am sure of as to myself : how far the faculties of other men may reach they best can tell.

[1] [*Cf. Princ.*, Sect. 116 and *De Motu*, Sect. 53.—ED.]

22

124 It is commonly said that the object of geometry is abstract extension : but geometry contemplates figures : now, figure is the termination of magnitude : but we have shown that extension in abstract hath no finite determinate magnitude. Whence it clearly follows that it can have no figure, and consequently is not the object of geometry. It is indeed a tenet as well of the modern as of the ancient philosophers that all general truths are concerning universal abstract ideas ; without which, we are told, there could be no science, no demonstration of any general proposition in geometry. But it were no hard matter, did I think it necessary to my present purpose, to show that propositions and demonstrations in geometry might be universal, though they who make them never think of abstract general ideas of triangles or circles.

125 After reiterated endeavours to apprehend the general idea of a triangle, I have found it altogether incomprehensible. And surely if any one were able to introduce that idea into my mind, it must be the author of the *Essay concerning Human Understanding* ; he who has so far distinguished himself from the generality of writers by the clearness and significancy of what he says. Let us therefore see how this celebrated author describes the general or abstract idea of a triangle. ' It must be (says he) neither oblique nor rectangular, neither equilateral, equicrural, nor scalenum ; but all and none of these at once. In effect, it is somewhat imperfect that cannot exist ; an idea, wherein some parts of several different and inconsistent ideas are put together ' (*Essay*, Bk. IV, C. 7, Sect. 9). This is the idea which he thinks needful for the enlargement of knowledge, which is the subject of mathematical demonstration, and without which we could never come to know any general proposition concerning triangles. That author acknowledges it doth ' require some pains and skill to form this general idea of a triangle,'

ibid. But had he called to mind what he says in another place, to wit, ' That ideas of mixed modes wherein any inconsistent ideas are put together cannot so much as exist in the mind, *i.e.* be conceived,' *vid.* Bk. III, C. 10, Sect. 33, *ibid.* I say, had this occurred to his thoughts, it is not improbable he would have owned it above all the pains and skill he was master of to form the above-mentioned idea of a triangle, which is made up of manifest, staring contradictions. That a man who laid so great a stress on clear and determinate ideas should nevertheless talk at this rate seems very surprising. But the wonder will lessen if it be considered that the source whence this opinion flows is the prolific womb which has brought forth innumerable errors and difficulties in all parts of philosophy and in all the sciences : but this matter, taken in its full extent, were a subject too comprehensive to be insisted on in this place. And so much for extension in abstract.

127 It having been shown that there are no abstract ideas of figure, and that it is impossible for us by any precision of thought to frame an idea of extension separate from all other visible and tangible qualities which shall be common both to sight and touch : the question now remaining is, whether the particular extensions, figures, and motions perceived by sight be of the same kind with the particular extensions, figures, and motions perceived by touch ? In answer to which I shall venture to lay down the following proposition : *The extension, figures, and motions perceived by sight are specifically distinct from the ideas of touch called by the same names, nor is there any such thing as one idea or kind of idea common to both senses.* This proposition may without much difficulty be collected from what hath been said in several places of this essay. But because it seems so remote from, and contrary to, the received notions and settled opinion of mankind, I shall attempt to demonstrate it more particularly and at large by the following arguments.

128 When upon perception of an idea I range it under this or that sort, it is because it is perceived after the same manner, or because it has a likeness or conformity with, or affects me in the same way as, the ideas of the sort I rank it under. In short, it must not be entirely new, but have something in it old and already perceived by me. It must, I say, have so much at least in common with the ideas I have before known and named as to make me give it the same name with them. But it has been, if I mistake not, clearly made out that a man born blind would not at first reception of his sight think the things he saw were of the same nature with the objects of touch, or had anything in common with them ; but that they were a new set of ideas, perceived in a new manner, and entirely different from all he had ever perceived before : so that he would not call them by the same name, nor repute them to be of the same sort with anything he had hitherto known.

129 *Secondly*, light and colours are allowed by all to constitute a sort of species entirely different from the ideas of touch : nor will any man, I presume, say they can make themselves perceived by that sense : but there is no other immediate object of sight besides light and colours. It is therefore a direct consequence that there is no idea common to both senses.

130 It is a prevailing opinion, even amongst those who have thought and writ most accurately concerning our ideas and the ways whereby they enter into the understanding, that something more is perceived by sight than barely light and colours with their variations. Mr. Locke termeth sight, 'The most comprehensive of all our senses, conveying to our minds the ideas of light and colours, which are peculiar only to that sense ; and also the far different ideas of space, figure, and motion.' *Essay*, Bk. II, C. 9, Sect. 9. Space or distance, we have shown, is not otherwise the object of sight than of hearing ; *vid.* Sect. 46.

And as for figure and extension, I leave it to anyone that shall calmly attend to his own clear and distinct ideas to decide whether he has any idea intromitted immediately and properly by sight save only light and colours: or whether it be possible for him to frame in his mind a distinct abstract idea of visible extension or figure exclusive of all colour: and on the other hand, whether he can conceive colour without visible extension? For my own part, I must confess I am not able to attain so great a nicety of abstraction: in a strict sense, I see nothing but light and colours, with their several shades and variations. He who beside these doth also perceive by sight ideas far different and distinct from them hath that faculty in a degree more perfect and comprehensive than I can pretend to. It must be owned that by the mediation of light and colours other far different ideas are suggested to my mind: but so they are by hearing, which beside sounds which are peculiar to that sense, doth by their mediation suggest not only space, figure, and motion, but also all other ideas whatsoever that can be signified by words.

131 *Thirdly*, it is, I think, an axiom universally received that quantities of the same kind may be added together and make one entire sum. Mathematicians add lines together: but they do not add a line to a solid, or conceive it as making one sum with a surface: these three kinds of quantity being thought incapable of any such mutual addition, and consequently of being compared together in the several ways of proportion, are by them esteemed entirely disparate and heterogeneous. Now let any one try in his thoughts to add a visible line or surface to a tangible line or surface, so as to conceive them making one continued sum or whole. He that can do this may think them homogeneous: but he that cannot, must by the foregoing axiom think them heterogeneous. A blue and a red line I can conceive added together into one sum and

making one continued line: but to make in my thoughts one continued line of a visible and tangible line added together is, I find, a task far more difficult, and even insurmountable: and I leave it to the reflexion and experience of every particular person to determine for himself.

132 A farther confirmation of our tenet may be drawn from the solution of Mr. Molyneux's problem, published by Mr. Locke in his *Essay*: which I shall set down as it there lies, together with Mr. Locke's opinion of it. ' " Suppose a man born blind, and now adult, and taught by his touch to distinguish between a cube and a sphere of the same metal, and nighly of the same bigness, so as to tell, when he felt one and t'other, which is the cube and which the sphere. Suppose then the cube and sphere placed on a table, and the blind man to be made to see: *Quaere*, Whether by his sight, before he touched them, he could now distinguish and tell which is the globe, which the cube?" To which the acute and judicious proposer answers: " Not. For though he has obtained the experience of how a globe, how a cube, affects his touch, yet he has not yet attained the experience that what affects his touch so or so must affect his sight so or so: or that a protuberant angle in the cube that pressed his hand unequally shall appear to his eye as it doth in the cube." I agree with this thinking gentleman, whom I am proud to call my friend, in his answer to this his problem; and am of opinion that the blind man at first sight would not be able with certainty to say which was the globe, which the cube, whilst he only saw them ' (*Essay*, Bk. II, C. 9, Sect. 8).

133 Now, if a square surface perceived by touch be of the same sort with a square surface perceived by sight, it is certain the blind man here mentioned might know a square surface as soon as he saw it: it is no more but introducing into his mind by a new inlet an idea he has been already well acquainted with. Since, therefore, he is

supposed to have known by his touch that a cube is a body terminated by square surfaces, and that a sphere is not terminated by square surfaces : upon the supposition that a visible and tangible square differ only *in numero* it follows that he might know, by the unerring mark of the square surfaces, which was the cube, and which not, while he only saw them. We must therefore allow either that visible extension and figures are specifically distinct from tangible extension and figures, or else that the solution of this problem given by those two thoughtful and ingenious men is wrong.

137 Visible figure and extension having been demonstrated to be of a nature entirely different and heterogeneous from tangible figure and extension, it remains that we inquire concerning motion. Now, that visible motion is not of the same sort with tangible motion seems to need no farther proof, it being an evident corollary from what we have shown concerning the difference there is between visible and tangible extension : but for a more full and express proof hereof we need only observe that one who had not yet experienced vision would not at first sight know motion. Whence it clearly follows that motion perceivable by sight is of a sort distinct from motion perceivable by touch. The antecedent I prove thus : by touch he could not perceive any motion but what was up or down, to the right or left, nearer or farther from him ; besides these and their several varieties or complications, it is impossible he should have any idea of motion. He would not therefore think anything to be motion, or give the name motion to any idea which he could not range under some or other of those particular kinds thereof. But from Sect. 95 it is plain that by the mere act of vision he could not know motion upwards or downwards, to the right or left, or in any other possible direction. From which I conclude he would not know motion at all at first sight. As for the idea of motion in abstract, I shall not waste paper about it, but leave it to

my reader to make the best he can of it.[1]   To me it is perfectly unintelligible.

144 It must be confessed that we are not so apt to confound other signs with the things signified, or to think them of the same species, as we are visible and tangible ideas.   But a little consideration will show us how this may be without our supposing them of a like nature. These signs are constant and universal, their connexion with tangible ideas has been learnt at our first entrance into the world: and ever since, almost every moment of our lives, it has been occurring to our thoughts, and fastening and striking deeper on our minds.   When we observe that signs are variable, and of human institution; when we remember there was a time they were not connected in our minds with those things they now so readily suggest; but that their signification was learned by the slow steps of experience: this preserves us from confounding them.   But when we find the same signs suggest the same things all over the world; when we know they are not of human institution, and cannot remember that we ever learned their signification, but think that at first sight they would have suggested to us the same things they do now: all this persuades us they are of the same species as the things respectively represented by them, and that it is by a natural resemblance they suggest them to our minds.

145 Add to this that whenever we make a nice survey of any object, successively directing the optic axis to each point thereof, there are certain lines and figures described by the motion of the head or eye, which being in truth perceived by feeling, do nevertheless so mix themselves, as it were, with the ideas of sight, that we can scarce think but they appertain to that sense.   Again, the ideas of sight enter into the mind several at once, more distinct and unmingled than is usual in the other senses beside the

[1] [*Cf. Princ.*, Intro., Sect. 10, and *De Motu*, Sects. 43 ff.—ED.]

touch. Sounds, for example, perceived at the same instant, are apt to coalesce, if I may so say, into one sound: but we can perceive at the same time great variety of visible objects, very separate and distinct from each other. Now tangible extension being made up of several distinct coexistent parts, we may hence gather another reason that may dispose us to imagine a likeness or analogy between the immediate objects of sight and touch. But nothing, certainly, doth more contribute to blend and confound them together than the strict and close connexion they have with each other. We cannot open our eyes but the ideas of distance, bodies, and tangible figures are suggested by them. So swift and sudden and unperceived is the transition from visible to tangible ideas that we can scarce forbear thinking them equally the immediate object of vision.

147 Upon the whole, I think we may fairly conclude that the proper objects of vision constitute an universal language of the Author of Nature,[1] whereby we are instructed how to regulate our actions in order to attain those things that are necessary to the preservation and well-being of our bodies, as also to avoid whatever may be hurtful and destructive of them. It is by their information that we are principally guided in all the transactions and concerns of life. And the manner wherein they signify and mark unto us the objects which are at a distance is the same with that of languages and signs of human appointment, which do not suggest the things signified by any likeness or identity of nature, but only by an habitual connexion that experience has made us to observe between them.

153 Though what has been said may suffice to show what ought to be determined with relation to the object of geometry, I shall nevertheless, for the fuller illustration thereof, consider the case of an intelligence or unbodied

[1] [*Cf. Princ.*, Sect. 44, and *Siris*, Sect. 254.—ED.]

spirit which is supposed to see perfectly well, *i.e.*, to have a clear perception of the proper and immediate objects of sight, but to have no sense of touch. Whether there be any such being in nature or no is beside my purpose to inquire. It sufficeth that the supposition contains no contradiction in it. Let us now examine what proficiency such a one may be able to make in geometry. Which speculation will lead us more clearly to see whether the ideas of sight can possibly be the object of that science.

154 *First*, then, it is certain the aforesaid intelligence could have no idea of a solid, or quantity of three dimensions, which followeth from its not having any idea of distance. We indeed are prone to think that we have by sight the ideas of space and solids, which ariseth from our imagining that we do, strictly speaking, see distance and some parts of an object at a greater distance than others; which hath been demonstrated to be the effect of the experience we have had, what ideas of touch are connected with such and such ideas attending vision: but the intelligence here spoken of is supposed to have no experience of touch. He would not, therefore, judge as we do, nor have any idea of distance, outness, or profundity, nor consequently of space or body, either immediately or by suggestion. Whence it is plain he can have no notion of those parts of geometry which relate to the mensuration of solids and their convex or concave surfaces, and contemplate the properties of lines generated by the section of a solid. The conceiving of any part whereof is beyond the reach of his faculties.

155 Farther, he cannot comprehend the manner wherein geometers describe a right line or circle; the rule and compass with their use being things of which it is impossible he should have any notion: nor is it an easier matter for him to conceive the placing of one plane or angle on another, in order to prove their equality: since that supposeth some idea of distance or external space. All

which makes it evident our pure intelligence could never attain to know so much as the first elements of plane geometry. And perhaps upon a nice inquiry it will be found he cannot even have an idea of plane figures any more than he can of solids; since some idea of distance is necessary to form the idea of a geometrical plane, as will appear to whoever shall reflect a little on it.

157 I must confess men are tempted to think that flat or plane figures are immediate objects of sight, though they acknowledge solids are not. And this opinion is grounded on what is observed in painting, wherein (it seems) the ideas immediately imprinted on the mind are only of planes variously coloured, which by a sudden act of the judgment are changed into solids; but with a little attention we shall find the planes here mentioned as the immediate objects of sight are not visible but tangible planes. For when we say that pictures are planes, we mean thereby that they appear to the touch smooth and uniform. But then this smoothness and uniformity, or, in other words, this planeness of the picture, is not perceived immediately by vision: for it appeareth to the eye various and multiform.

158 From all which we may conclude that planes are no more the immediate object of sight than solids. What we strictly see are not solids, nor yet planes variously coloured: they are only diversity of colours. And some of these suggest to the mind solids, and others plane figures, just as they have been experienced to be connected with the one or the other: so that we see planes in the same way that we see solids, both being equally suggested by the immediate objects of sight, which accordingly are themselves denominated planes and solids. But though they are called by the same names with the things marked by them, they are nevertheless of a nature entirely different, as hath been demonstrated.

A TREATISE
CONCERNING THE PRINCIPLES
OF HUMAN KNOWLEDGE

Wherein the chief causes
of error and difficulty in the sciences,
with the grounds of scepticism, atheism, and irreligion,
are inquired into.

First published 1710   Second Edition 1734

EDITOR'S NOTE

What follows the Introduction is called Part I because other parts, to deal with the philosophy of mind (including ethics), of physics, and of mathematics, were projected, though not completed. Part I contains the groundwork, and is Berkeley's most careful statement of it.

The passages selected fall into the following divisions : (1) *The impossibility of abstract ideas of the sensory*—from the Introduction. (2) *Exposition of immaterialistic theism, on the basis of* 'esse *is* percipi '—Sects. 1-33. (3) *Some objections to immaterialism answered* : that it leaves no room for a really corporeal world— from Sects. 34-41 ; ignores the given externality of the seen world —Sects. 42-4; implies the fleetingness of corporeal things—from Sects. 45-8; makes mind extended—Sect. 49; nullifies mechanics —Sect. 50; denial of material causality is absurd—Sect. 53; inconsistent with the Copernican theory—Sect. 58; assigns no function to sensible things—from Sects. 60-6; matter may exist as an ' occasion ' of sensory experience—Sects. 67-72. (4) *The advantages of immaterialism,* (*a*) in the study of the corporeal-- from Sects. 85-128; (*b*) in the study of mind—from Sects. 135-56.

INTRODUCTION

4 My purpose is to try if I can discover what those principles are which have introduced all that doubtfulness and uncertainty, those absurdities and contradictions into the several sects of philosophy; insomuch that the wisest men have thought our ignorance incurable, conceiving it to arise from the natural dullness and limitation of our faculties. And surely it is a work well deserving our pains, to make a strict inquiry concerning the first principles of *human knowledge*, to sift and examine them on all sides: especially since there may be some grounds to suspect that those lets and difficulties, which stay and embarrass the mind in its search after truth, do not spring from any darkness and intricacy in the objects, or natural defect in the understanding, so much as from false principles which have been insisted on, and might have been avoided.

6 In order to prepare the mind of the reader for the easier conceiving what follows, it is proper to premise somewhat, by way of introduction, concerning the nature and abuse of language. But the unravelling this matter leads me in some measure to anticipate my design, by taking notice of what seems to have had a chief part in rendering speculation intricate and perplexed, and to have occasioned innumerable errors and difficulties in almost all parts of knowledge. And that is the opinion that the mind hath a power of framing *abstract ideas* or notions of things. He who is not a perfect stranger to the writings and disputes of philosophers must needs acknowledge that no small part of them are spent about abstract ideas. These are in a more especial manner thought to be the object of

35

those sciences which go by the name of logic and metaphysics, and of all that which passes under the notion of
the most abstracted and sublime learning, in all which one
shall scarce find any question handled in such a manner,
as does not suppose their existence in the mind, and that
it is well acquainted with them.

7 It is agreed on all hands, that the qualities or modes of
things do never really exist each of them apart by itself, and
separated from all others, but are mixed, as it were, and
blended together, several in the same object. But we are
told, the mind being able to consider each quality singly,
or abstracted from those other qualities with which it is
united, does by that means frame to itself abstract ideas.
For example, there is perceived by sight an object extended,
coloured, and moved : this mixed or compound idea the
mind resolving into its simple, constituent parts, and viewing
each by itself, exclusive of the rest, does frame the abstract
ideas of extension, colour, and motion. Not that it is
possible for colour or motion to exist without extension :
but only that the mind can frame to itself by *abstraction*
the idea of colour exclusive of extension, and of motion
exclusive of both colour and extension.

8 Again, the mind having observed that in the particular
extensions perceived by sense, there is something common
and alike in all, and some other things peculiar, as this or
that figure or magnitude, which distinguish them one from
another ; it considers apart or singles out by itself that
which is common, making thereof a most abstract idea
of extension, which is neither line, surface, nor solid, nor
has any figure or magnitude but is an idea entirely prescinded from all these. So likewise the mind by leaving out
of the particular colours perceived by sense, that which
distinguishes them one from another, and retaining that
only which is common to all, makes an idea of colour in
abstract which is neither red, nor blue, nor white, nor any

36

other determinate colour. And in like manner by considering motion abstractedly not only from the body moved, but likewise from the figure it describes, and all particular directions and velocities, the abstract idea of motion is framed; which equally corresponds to all particular motions whatsoever that may be perceived by sense.

9 And as the mind frames to itself abstract ideas of qualities or modes, so does it, by the same precision or mental separation, attain abstract ideas of the more compounded beings, which include several coexistent qualities. For example, the mind having observed that Peter, James, and John, resemble each other, in certain common agreements of shape and other qualities, leaves out of the complex or compounded idea it has of Peter, James, and any other particular man, that which is peculiar to each, retaining only what is common to all; and so makes an abstract idea wherein all the particulars equally partake, abstracting entirely from and cutting off all those circumstances and differences which might determine it to any particular existence. And after this manner it is said we come by the abstract idea of *man* or, if you please, humanity or human nature; wherein it is true, there is included colour, because there is no man but has some colour, but then it can be neither white, nor black, nor any particular colour; because there is no one particular colour wherein all men partake. So likewise there is included stature, but then it is neither tall stature nor low stature, nor yet middle stature, but something abstracted from all these. And so of the rest. Moreover, there being a great variety of other creatures that partake in some parts, but not all, of the complex idea of *man*, the mind leaving out those parts which are peculiar to men, and retaining those only which are common to all the living creatures, frameth the idea of *animal*, which abstracts not only from all particular men, but also all birds, beasts, fishes, and insects. The constituent parts of the

abstract idea of animal are body, life, sense and spontaneous motion. By *body* is meant, body without any particular shape or figure, there being no one shape or figure common to all animals, without covering, either of hair or feathers, or scales etc. nor yet naked: hair, feathers, scales, and nakedness being the distinguishing properties of particular animals, and for that reason left out of the *abstract idea*. Upon the same account the spontaneous motion must be neither walking, nor flying, nor creeping, it is nevertheless a motion; but what that motion is, it is not easy to conceive.

10 Whether others have this wonderful faculty of *abstracting their ideas*, they best can tell: for myself I find indeed I have a faculty of imagining, or representing to myself the ideas of those particular things I have perceived and of variously compounding and dividing them. I can imagine a man with two heads or the upper parts of a man joined to the body of a horse. I can consider the hand, the eye, the nose, each by itself abstracted or separated from the rest of the body. But then whatever hand or eye I imagine, it must have some particular shape and colour. Likewise the idea of man that I frame to myself, must be either of a white, or a black, or a tawny, a straight, or a crooked, a tall, or a low, or a middle-sized man. I cannot by any effort of thought conceive the abstract idea above described. And it is equally impossible for me to form the abstract idea of motion distinct from the body moving, and which is neither swift nor slow, curvilinear nor rectilinear; and the like may be said of all other abstract general ideas whatsoever. To be plain, I own myself able to abstract in one sense, as when I consider some particular parts or qualities separated from others, with which though they are united in some object, yet it is possible they may really exist without them. But I deny that I can abstract one from another, or conceive separately, those qualities which it is impossible should exist so separated;

or that I can frame a general notion by abstracting from particulars in the manner aforesaid. Which two last are the proper acceptations of *abstraction*. And there are grounds to think most men will acknowledge themselves to be in my case. The generality of men which are simple and illiterate never pretend to *abstract notions*. It's said they are difficult and not to be attained without pains and study. We may therefore reasonably conclude that, if such there be, they are confined only to the learned.

11 I proceed to examine what can be alleged in defence of the doctrine of abstraction, and try if I can discover what it is that inclines the men of speculation to embrace an opinion so remote from common sense as that seems to be. There has been a late deservedly esteemed philosopher [Locke], who, no doubt, has given it very much countenance by seeming to think the having abstract general ideas is what puts the widest difference in point of understanding betwixt man and beast. ' The having of general ideas ', saith he, ' is that which puts a perfect distinction betwixt man and brutes, and is an excellency which the faculties of brutes do by no means attain unto. For it is evident we observe no footsteps in them of making use of general signs for universal ideas; from which we have reason to imagine that they have not the faculty of *abstracting* or making general ideas, since they have no use of words or any other general signs.' And a little after: ' Therefore, I think we may suppose that it is in this that the species of brutes are discriminated from men, and 'tis that proper difference wherein they are wholly separated, and which at last widens to so wide a distance. For if they have any ideas at all, and are not bare machines (as some would have them) we cannot deny them to have some reason. It seems as evident to me that they do some of them in certain instances reason as that they have sense, but it is only in particular ideas, just as they receive them from their senses.

They are the best of them tied up within those narrow bounds, and have not (as I think) the faculty to enlarge them by any kind of *abstraction*.' (*Essay*, Bk. II, C. 11, Sects. 10 and 11). I readily agree with this learned author, that the faculties of brutes can by no means attain to *abstraction*. But then if this be made the distinguishing property of that sort of animals, I fear a great many of those that pass for men must be reckoned into their number. The reason that is here assigned why we have no grounds to think brutes have abstract general ideas is that we observe in them no use of words or any other general signs ; which is built on this supposition, to wit, that the making use of words implies the having general ideas. From which it follows, that men who use language are able to abstract or generalise their ideas. That this is the sense and arguing of the author will further appear by his answering the question he in another place puts. ' Since all things that exist are only particulars, how come we by general terms ? ' His answer is, ' Words become general by being made the signs of general ideas ' (*Essay*, Bk. III, C. 3, Sect. 6). But it seems that a word becomes general by being made the sign, not of an abstract general idea, but of several particular ideas, any one of which it indifferently suggests to the mind. For example, when it is said *the change of motion is proportional to the impressed force*, or that *whatever has extension is divisible* ; these propositions are to be understood of motion and extension in general, and nevertheless it will not follow that they suggest to my thoughts an idea of motion without a body moved, or any determinate direction and velocity, or that I must conceive an abstract general idea of extension, which is neither line, surface nor solid, neither great nor small, black, white, nor red, nor of any other determinate colour. It is only implied that whatever motion I consider, whether it be swift or slow, perpendicular, horizontal or oblique, or in whatever object, the axiom concerning it holds equally true. As does the other of every particular extension, it matters not whether line, surface or solid, whether of this or that magnitude or figure.

12 By observing how ideas become general, we may the better judge how words are made so. And here it is to be noted that I do not deny absolutely there are general ideas, but only that there are any *abstract general ideas*: for in the passages above quoted, wherein there is mention of general ideas, it is always supposed that they are formed *by abstraction*, after the manner set forth in Sects. 8 and 9. Now if we annex a meaning to our words, and speak only of what we can conceive, I believe we shall acknowledge that an idea, which considered in itself is particular, becomes general by being made to represent or stand for all other particular ideas of the same sort. To make this plain by an example, suppose a geometrician is demonstrating the method of cutting a line in two equal parts. He draws, for instance, a black line of an inch in length, this which in itself is a particular line is nevertheless with regard to its signification general, since as it is there used, it represents all particular lines whatsoever; for that what is demonstrated of it, is demonstrated of all lines, or, in other words, of a line in general. And as that particular line becomes general, by being made a sign, so the name *line* which taken absolutely is particular, by being a sign is made general. And as the former owes its generality, not to its being the sign of an abstract or general line, but of all particular right lines that may possibly exist, so the latter must be thought to derive its generality from the same cause, namely, the various particular lines which it indifferently denotes.

15 . . . It is, I know, a point much insisted on, that all knowledge and demonstration are about universal notions, to which I fully agree: but then it doth not appear to me

PRINCIPLES OF HUMAN KNOWLEDGE

that those notions are formed by *abstraction* in the manner premised; *universality*, so far as I can comprehend, not consisting in the absolute, positive nature or conception of anything, but in the relation it bears to the particulars signified or represented by it: by virtue whereof it is that things, names, or notions, being in their own nature *particular*, are rendered *universal*. Thus when I demonstrate any proposition concerning triangles, it is to be supposed that I have in view the universal idea of a triangle; which ought not to be understood as if I could frame an idea of a triangle which was neither equilateral nor scalenon nor equicrural. But only that the particular triangle I consider, whether of this or that sort it matters not, doth equally stand for and represent all rectilinear triangles whatsoever, and is in that sense *universal*. All which seems very plain and not to include any difficulty in it.

16 But here it will be demanded how we can know any proposition to be true of all particular triangles, except we have first seen it demonstrated of the abstract idea of a triangle which equally agrees to all. For because a property may be demonstrated to agree to some one particular triangle, it will not thence follow that it equally belongs to any other triangle, which in all respects is not the same with it. For example, having demonstrated that the three angles of an isosceles rectangular triangle are equal to two right ones, I cannot therefore conclude this affection agrees to all other triangles, which have neither a right angle, nor two equal sides. It seems therefore that, to be certain this proposition is universally true, we must either make a particular demonstration for every particular triangle, which is impossible, or once for all demonstrate it of the *abstract idea of a triangle*, in which all the particulars do indifferently partake, and by which they are all equally represented. To which I answer, that though the idea I have in view whilst I make the demonstration

be, for instance, that of an isosceles rectangular triangle, whose sides are of a determinate length, I may nevertheless be certain it extends to all other rectilinear triangles, of what sort or bigness soever; and that because neither the right angle, nor the equality, nor determinate length of the sides, are at all concerned in the demonstration. It is true the diagram I have in view includes all these particulars, but then there is not the least mention made of them in the proof of the proposition. It is not said, the three angles are equal to two right ones, because one of them is a right angle, or because the sides comprehending it are of the same length; which sufficiently shows that the right angle might have been oblique, and the sides unequal, and for all that the demonstration have held good. And for this reason it is, that I conclude that to be true of any obliqu-angular or scalenon, which I had demonstrated of a par-ticular right-angled, equicrural triangle; and not because I demonstrated the proposition of the abstract idea of a triangle. And here it must be acknowledged that a man may consider a figure merely as triangular, without attending to the particular qualities of the angles, or relations of the sides. So far he may abstract : but this will never prove that he can frame an abstract, general, inconsistent idea of a triangle. In like manner we may consider Peter so far forth as man, or so far forth as animal, without framing the forementioned abstract idea, either of man or of animal, inasmuch as all that is perceived is not considered.

18 I come now to consider the source of this prevailing notion, and that seems to me to be language. And surely nothing of less extent than reason itself could have been the source of an opinion so universally received. The truth of this appears, as from other reasons, so also from the plain confession of the ablest patrons of abstract ideas, who acknowledge that they are made in order to naming;

from which it is a clear consequence, that if there had been no such thing as speech or universal signs, there never had been any thought of abstraction. See Bk. III, C. 6, Sect. 39 and elsewhere of the *Essay on Human Understanding*. Let us therefore examine the manner wherein words have contributed to the origin of that mistake. First then, 'tis thought that every name hath, or ought to have, one only precise and settled signification, which inclines men to think there are certain *abstract, determinate ideas*, which constitute the true and only immediate signification of each general name. And that it is by the mediation of these abstract ideas that a general name comes to signify any particular thing. Whereas in truth, there is no such thing as one precise and definite signification annexed to any general name, they all signifying indifferently a great number of particular ideas. All which doth evidently follow from what has been already said, and will clearly appear to any one by a little reflexion. To this it will be objected, that every name that has a definition is thereby restrained to one certain signification. For example, a *triangle* is defined to be a *plane surface comprehended by three right lines ;* by which that name is limited to denote one certain idea and no other. To which I answer, that in the definition it is not said whether the surface be great or small, black or white, nor whether the sides are long or short, equal or unequal, nor with what angles they are inclined to each other ; in all which there may be great variety, and consequently there is no one settled idea which limits the signification of the word *triangle.* 'Tis one thing for to keep a name constantly to the same definition, and another to make it stand every where for the same idea : the one is necessary, the other useless and impracticable.

19 But to give a farther account how words came to produce the doctrine of abstract ideas, it must be observed that it is a received opinion, that language has no other

end but the communicating our ideas, and that every significant name stands for an idea. This being so, and it being withal certain that names, which yet are not thought altogether insignificant, do not always mark out particular conceivable ideas, it is straightway concluded that they stand for abstract notions. That there are many names in use amongst speculative men which do not always suggest to others determinate particular ideas, is what nobody will deny. And a little attention will discover that it is not necessary (even in the strictest reasonings) significant names which stand for ideas should, every time they are used, excite in the understanding the ideas they are made to stand for : in reading and discoursing, names being for the most part used as letters are in algebra, in which though a particular quantity be marked by each letter, yet to proceed right it is not requisite that in every step each letter suggest to your thoughts that particular quantity it was appointed to stand for.

20 Besides, the communicating of ideas marked by words is not the chief and only end of language, as is commonly supposed. There are other ends, as the raising of some passion, the exciting to, or deterring from an action, the putting the mind in some particular disposition ; to which the former is in many cases barely subservient, and sometimes entirely omitted, when these can be obtained without it, as I think doth not infrequently happen in the familiar use of language. I entreat the reader to reflect with himself, and see if it doth not often happen either in hearing or reading a discourse, that the passions of fear, love, hatred, admiration, disdain, and the like, arise immediately in his mind upon the perception of certain words, without any ideas coming between. At first, indeed, the words might have occasioned ideas that were fit to produce those emotions ; but, if I mistake not, it will be found that when language is once grown familiar, the hearing of the sounds

or sight of the characters is oft immediately attended with those passions which at first were wont to be produced by the intervention of ideas, that are now quite omitted. May we not, for example, be affected with the promise of a *good thing*, though we have not an idea of what it is? Or is not the being threatened with danger sufficient to excite a dread, though we think not of any particular evil likely to befall us, nor yet frame to ourselves an idea of danger in abstract? If anyone shall join ever so little reflection of his own to what has been said, I believe it will evidently appear to him, that general names are often used in the propriety of language without the speaker's designing them for marks of ideas in his own which he would have them raise in the mind of the hearer. Even proper names themselves do not seem always spoken with a design to bring into our view the ideas of those individuals that are supposed to be marked by them. For example, when a Schoolman tells me *Aristotle hath said it*, all I conceive he means by it, is to dispose me to embrace his opinion with the deference and submission which custom has annexed to that name. And this effect may be so instantly produced in the minds of those who are accustomed to resign their judgment to the authority of that philosopher, as it is impossible any idea either of his person, writings, or reputation should go before. Innumerable examples of this kind may be given, but why should I insist on those things which everyone's experience will, I doubt not, plentifully suggest unto him?

24 . . . He that knows he has no other than particular ideas will not puzzle himself in vain to find out and conceive the abstract idea annexed to any name. And he that knows names do not always stand for ideas will spare himself the labour of looking for ideas where there are none to be had. It were therefore to be wished that everyone would use his utmost endeavours to obtain a clear view of

the ideas he would consider, separating from them all that dress and encumbrance of words which so much contribute to blind the judgment and divide the attention. In vain do we extend our view into the heavens, and pry into the entrails of the earth, in vain do we consult the writings of learned men, and trace the dark footsteps of antiquity; we need only draw the curtain of words, to behold the fairest tree of knowledge, whose fruit is excellent, and within the reach of our hand.

25 Unless we take care to clear the first principles of knowledge from the embarras and delusion of words, we may make infinite reasonings upon them to no purpose; we may draw consequences from consequences, and be never the wiser. The farther we go we shall only lose ourselves the more irrecoverably, and be the deeper entangled in difficulties and mistakes. Whoever therefore designs to read the following sheets, I entreat him to make my words the occasion of his own thinking, and endeavour to attain the same train of thoughts in reading that I had in writing them. By this means it will be easy for him to discover the truth or falsity of what I say. He will be out of all danger of being deceived by my words, and I do not see how he can be led into an error by considering his own naked, undisguised ideas.

PART ONE

1 It is evident to anyone who takes a survey of the objects of human knowledge, that they are either ideas actually imprinted on the senses, or else such as are perceived by attending to the passions and operations of the mind,[1] or lastly ideas formed by help of memory and imagination, either compounding, dividing, or barely representing those originally perceived in the aforesaid ways. By sight I have the ideas of light and colours with their several degrees and variations. By touch I perceive, for example, hard and soft, heat and cold, motion and resistance, and of all these more and less either as to quantity or degree. Smelling furnishes me with odours, the palate with tastes, and hearing conveys sounds to the mind in all their variety of tone and composition. And as several of these are observed to accompany each other, they come to be marked by one name, and so to be reputed as one thing. Thus, for example, a certain colour, taste, smell, figure and consistence having been observed to go together, are accounted one distinct thing, signified by the name *apple*. Other collections of ideas constitute a stone, a tree, a book, and the like sensible things; which, as they are pleasing or disagreeable, excite the passions of love, hatred, joy, grief, and so forth.

2 But besides all that endless variety of ideas or objects of knowledge, there is likewise something which knows or perceives them, and exercises divers operations, as willing, imagining, remembering about them. This perceiving, active being is what I call *mind, spirit, soul* or *my self*. By

[1] [The distinction of sensory and mental objects is for Berkeley fundamental. *Cf.* Sects. 86, 89, 139, 142, and *De Motu*, 21, 30.—ED.]

which words I do not denote any one of my ideas, but a thing entirely distinct from them, wherein they exist, or, which is the same thing, whereby they are perceived; for the existence of an idea consists in being perceived.

3 That neither our thoughts, nor passions, nor ideas formed by the imagination, exist without the mind, is what everybody will allow. And it seems no less evident that the various sensations or ideas imprinted on the sense, however blended or combined together (that is, whatever objects they compose) cannot exist otherwise than in a mind perceiving them. I think an intuitive knowledge may be obtained of this by anyone that shall attend to what is meant by the term *exist* when applied to sensible things. The table I write on, I say, exists, that is, I see and feel it; and if I were out of my study I should say it existed, meaning thereby that if I was in my study I might perceive it, or that some other spirit actually does perceive it. There was an odour, that is, it was smelled; there was a sound, that is to say, it was heard; a colour or figure, and it was perceived by sight or touch. This is all that I can understand by these and the like expressions. For as to what is said of the absolute existence of unthinking things without any relation to their being perceived, that seems perfectly unintelligible. Their *esse* is *percipi*, nor is it possible they should have any existence out of the minds or thinking things which perceive them.

4 It is indeed an opinion strangely prevailing amongst men, that houses, mountains, rivers, and in a word all sensible objects, have an existence natural or real, distinct from their being perceived by the understanding. But with how great an assurance and acquiescence soever this principle may be entertained in the world; yet whoever shall find in his heart to call it in question may, if I mistake not, perceive it to involve a manifest contradiction. For what are the forementioned objects but the things we

perceive by sense, and what do we perceive besides our own ideas or sensations;[1] and is it not plainly repugnant that any one of these or any combination of them should exist unperceived?

5 If we thoroughly examine this tenet, it will, perhaps, be found at bottom to depend on the doctrine of *abstract ideas*. For can there be a nicer strain of abstraction than to distinguish the existence of sensible objects from their being perceived, so as to conceive them existing unperceived? Light and colours, heat and cold, extension and figures, in a word the things we see and feel, what are they but so many sensations, notions, ideas or impressions on the sense; and is it possible to separate, even in thought, any of these from perception? For my part I might as easily divide a thing from itself. I may indeed divide in my thoughts or conceive apart from each other those things which, perhaps, I never perceived by sense so divided. Thus I imagine the trunk of a human body without the limbs, or conceive the smell of a rose without thinking on the rose itself. So far I will not deny I can abstract, if that may properly be called *abstraction*, which extends only to the conceiving separately such objects as it is possible may really exist or be actually perceived asunder. But my conceiving or imagining power does not extend beyond the possibility of real existence or perception. Hence as it is impossible for me to see or feel anything without an actual sensation of that thing, so is it impossible for me to conceive in my thoughts any sensible thing or object distinct from the sensation or perception of it.

6 Some truths there are so near and obvious to the mind that a man need only open his eyes to see them. Such I take this important one to be, to wit, that all the choir of heaven and furniture of the earth, in a word all those

[1] [*I.e.*, the corporeal is analysable without remainder into sensa. See Sect. 49.—Ed.]

bodies which compose the mighty frame of the world, have not any subsistence without a mind, that their being is to be perceived or known; that consequently so long as they are not actually perceived by me, or do not exist in my mind or that of any other created spirit, they must either have no existence at all, or else subsist in the mind of some eternal spirit: it being perfectly unintelligible and involving all the absurdity of abstraction, to attribute to any single part of them an existence independent of a spirit. To be convinced of which, the reader need only reflect and try to separate in his own thoughts the being of a sensible thing from its being perceived.

7 From what has been said, it follows, there is not any other substance than *spirit*, or that which perceives. But for the fuller proof of this point, let it be considered, the sensible qualities are colour, figure, motion, smell, taste, and such like, that is, the ideas perceived by sense. Now for an idea to exist in an unperceiving thing is a manifest contradiction; for to have an idea is all one as to perceive: that therefore wherein colour, figure, and the like qualities exist, must perceive them; hence it is clear there can be no unthinking substance or *substratum* of those ideas.

8 But, say you, though the ideas themselves do not exist without the mind, yet there may be things like them whereof they are copies or resemblances, which things exist without the mind, in an unthinking substance. I answer, an idea can be like nothing but an idea; a colour or figure can be like nothing but another colour or figure. If we look but ever so little into our thoughts, we shall find it impossible for us to conceive a likeness except only between our ideas. Again, I ask whether those supposed originals or external things, of which our ideas are the pictures or representations, be themselves perceivable or no? If they are, then they are ideas, and we have gained our point; but if you say they are not, I appeal to anyone whether it be

sense to assert a colour is like something which is invisible; hard or soft, like something which is intangible; and so of the rest.

9 Some there are who make a distinction betwixt *primary* and *secondary* qualities: [1] by the former, they mean extension, figure, motion, rest, solidity or impenetrability, and number: by the latter they denote all other sensible qualities, as colours, sounds, tastes, and so forth. The ideas we have of these they acknowledge not to be the resemblances of any thing existing without the mind or unperceived; but they will have our ideas of the primary qualities to be patterns or images of things which exist without the mind, in an unthinking substance which they call *matter*. By matter therefore we are to understand an inert, senseless substance, in which extension, figure, and motion do actually subsist. But it is evident from what we have already shown, that extension, figure and motion are only ideas existing in the mind, and that an idea can be like nothing but another idea, and that consequently neither they nor their archetypes can exist in an unperceiving substance. Hence it is plain that the very notion of what is called *matter* or *corporeal substance* involves a contradiction in it.

10 They who assert that figure, motion, and the rest of the primary or original qualities do exist without the mind, in unthinking substances, do at the same time acknowledge that colours, sounds, heat, cold, and suchlike secondary qualities, do not, which they tell us are sensations existing in the mind alone, that depend on and are occasioned by the different size, texture and motion of the minute particles of matter. This they take for an undoubted truth, which they can demonstrate beyond all exception. Now if it be certain, that those original qualities are

---

[1] [The distinction of primary and secondary qualities is discussed more fully in the first of the *Three Dialogues*.—ED.]

inseparably united with the other sensible qualities, and not even in thought capable of being abstracted from them, it plainly follows that they exist only in the mind. But I desire any one to reflect and try, whether he can by any abstraction of thought conceive the extension and motion of a body without all other sensible qualities. For my own part, I see evidently that it is not in my power to frame an idea of a body extended and moved, but I must withal give it some colour or other sensible quality which is acknowledged to exist only in the mind. In short, extension, figure, and motion, abstracted from all other qualities, are inconceivable. Where therefore the other sensible qualities are, there must these be also, to wit, in the mind and nowhere else.

11 Again, *great* and *small*, *swift* and *slow*, are allowed to exist nowhere without the mind, being entirely relative, and changing as the frame or position of the organs of sense varies. The extension therefore which exists without the mind is neither great nor small, the motion neither swift nor slow, that is they are nothing at all. But, say you, they are extension in general, and motion in general: thus we see how much the tenet of extended, movable substances existing without the mind, depends on that strange doctrine of *abstract ideas*. And here I cannot but remark, how nearly the vague and indeterminate description of matter or corporeal substance, which the modern philosophers are run into by their own principles, resembles that antiquated and so much ridiculed notion of *materia prima*, to be met with in Aristotle and his followers. Without extension solidity cannot be conceived; since therefore it has been shown that extension exists not in an unthinking substance, the same must also be true of solidity.

12 That number is entirely the creature of the mind, even though the other qualities be allowed to exist without, will be evident to whoever considers that the same thing

bears a different denomination of number, as the mind views it with different respects. Thus, the same extension is one of three or thirty-six, according as the mind considers it with reference to a yard, a foot, or an inch. Number is so visibly relative, and dependent on men's understanding, that it is strange to think how anyone should give it an absolute existence without the mind. We say one book, one page, one line; all these are equally units, though some contain several of the others. And in each instance it is plain, the unit relates to some particular combination of ideas arbitrarily put together by the mind.

13 Unity I know some will have to be a simple or uncompounded idea, accompanying all other ideas into the mind.[1] That I have any such idea answering the word *unity*, I do not find; and if I had, methinks I could not miss finding it; on the contrary it should be the most familiar to my understanding, since it is said to accompany all other ideas, and to be perceived by all the ways of sensation and reflexion. To say no more, it is an *abstract idea*.

14 I shall farther add, that after the same manner as modern philosophers prove certain sensible qualities to have no existence in matter, or without the mind, the same thing may be likewise proved of all other sensible qualities whatsoever. Thus, for instance, it is said that heat and cold are affections only of the mind, and not at all patterns of real beings existing in the corporeal substances which excite them, for that the same body which appears cold to one hand seems warm to another. Now why may we not as well argue that figure and extension are not patterns or resemblances of qualities existing in matter, because

[1] [So Locke, *Essay* II, xvi, 1 : ' Amongst all the ideas we have . . . there is none more simple than that of unity. . . . Every object our senses are employed about, every idea in our understandings, every thought of our minds. brings this idea along with it.' *Cf.* below, Sect. 120.—Ed.]

to the same eye at different stations, or eyes of a different texture at the same station, they appear various, and cannot therefore be the images of anything settled and determinate without the mind ? Again, it is proved that sweetness is not really in the sapid thing, because the thing remaining unaltered the sweetness is changed into bitter, as in case of a fever or otherwise vitiated palate. Is it not as reasonable to say, that motion is not without the mind, since if the succession of ideas in the mind become swifter, the motion, it is acknowledged, shall appear slower without any alteration in any external object.

15 In short, let anyone consider those arguments, which are thought manifestly to prove that colours and tastes exist only in the mind, and he shall find they may with equal force be brought to prove the same thing of extension, figure, and motion. Though it must be confessed this method of arguing doth not so much prove that there is no extension or colour in an outward object, as that we do not know by sense which is the true extension or colour of the object.[1] But the arguments foregoing plainly show it to be impossible that any colour or extension at all, or other sensible quality whatsoever, should exist in an unthinking subject without the mind, or in truth that there should be any such thing as an outward object.

16 But let us examine a little the received opinion. It is said extension is a mode or accident of matter, and that matter is the *substratum* that supports it. Now I desire that you would explain what is meant by matter's *supporting* extension : say you, I have no idea of matter, and therefore cannot explain it. I answer, though you have no positive, yet if you have any meaning at all, you must at least have a relative idea of matter ; though you know not what it is, yet you must be supposed to know what relation it bears

[1] [Because the argument assumes physical things independent of mind. *Cf*. Sect. 87.—ED.]

to accidents, and what is meant by its supporting them. It is evident *support* cannot here be taken in its usual or literal sense, as when we say that pillars support a building: in what sense therefore must it be taken?

17 If we inquire into what the most accurate philosophers declare themselves to mean by *material substance*, we shall find them acknowledge, they have no other meaning annexed to those sounds, but the idea of being in general, together with the relative notion of its supporting accidents.[1] The general idea of being appeareth to me the most abstract and incomprehensible of all other; and as for its supporting accidents, this, as we have just now observed, cannot be understood in the common sense of those words; it must therefore be taken in some other sense, but what that is they do not explain. So that when I consider the two parts or branches which make the signification of the words *material substance* I am convinced there is no distinct meaning annexed to them. But why should we trouble ourselves any farther, in discussing this material *substratum* or support of figure and motion, and other sensible qualities? Does it not suppose they have an existence without the mind? And is not this a direct repugnancy, and altogether inconceivable?

18 But though it were possible that solid, figured, movable substances may exist without the mind, corresponding to the ideas we have of bodies, yet how is it possible for us to know this? Either we must know it by sense, or by reason. As for our senses, by them we have the knowledge only of our sensations, ideas, or those things that are immediately perceived by sense, call them what you will:

[5] [As Locke noted (*Essay* II, xxiii, 2): 'If anyone will examine himself concerning his notion of pure substance in general, he will find he has no other idea of it at all but only a supposition of he knows not what support of such qualities which are capable of producing simple ideas in us.'—ED.]

but they do not inform us that things exist without the mind, or unperceived, like to those which are perceived. This the materialists themselves acknowledge. It remains therefore that if we have any knowledge at all of external things, it must be by reason, inferring their existence from what is immediately perceived by sense. But what reason can induce us to believe the existence of bodies without the mind, from what we perceive, since the very patrons of matter themselves do not pretend there is any necessary connexion betwixt them and our ideas ? I say it is granted on all hands (and what happens in dreams, frenzies, and the like, puts it beyond dispute) that it is possible we might be affected with all the ideas we have now, though no bodies existed without, resembling them. Hence it is evident the supposition of external bodies is not necessary for the producing our ideas, since it is granted they are produced sometimes, and might possibly be produced always in the same order we see them in at present, without their concurrence.

19 But though we might possibly have all our sensations without them, yet perhaps it may be thought easier to conceive and explain the manner of their production, by supposing external bodies in their likeness rather than otherwise ; and so it might be at least probable there are such things as bodies that excite their ideas in our minds. But neither can this be said ; for though we give the materialists their external bodies, they by their own confession are never the nearer knowing how our ideas are produced : since they own themselves unable to comprehend in what manner body can act upon spirit, or how it is possible it should imprint any idea in the mind. Hence it is evident the production of ideas or sensations in our minds can be no reason why we should suppose matter or corporeal substances, since that is acknowledged to remain equally inexplicable with or without this supposition. If there-

fore it were possible for bodies to exist without the mind,
yet to hold they do so, must needs be a very precarious
opinion; since it is to suppose, without any reason at all,
that God has created innumerable beings that are entirely
useless, and serve to no manner of purpose.

20 In short, if there were external bodies, it is impossible
we should ever come to know it; and if there were not, we
might have the very same reasons to think there were that
we have now. Suppose, what no one can deny possible,
an intelligence, without the help of external bodies, to be
affected with the same train of sensations or ideas that you
are, imprinted in the same order and with like vividness
in his mind. I ask whether that intelligence hath not all
the reason to believe the existence of corporeal substances,
represented by his ideas, and exciting them in his mind,
that you can possibly have for believing the same thing?
Of this there can be no question; which one consideration
is enough to make any reasonable person suspect the
strength of whatever arguments he may think himself to
have for the existence of bodies without the mind.

21 Were it necessary to add any farther proof against
the existence of matter, after what has been said, I could
instance several of those errors and difficulties (not to
mention impieties) which have sprung from that tenet.
It has occasioned numberless controversies and disputes in
philosophy, and not a few of far greater moment in religion.
But I shall not enter into the detail of them in this place, as
well because I think arguments *a posteriori* are unnecessary
for confirming what has been, if I mistake not, sufficiently
demonstrated *a priori*,[1] as because I shall hereafter find
occasion to say somewhat of them.

22 I am afraid I have given cause to think me needlessly
prolix in handling this subject. For to what purpose is it

[1] [So also in Sect. 61 : *a priori* because following from the axiom
' *esse* is *percipi* '.—ED.]

59

to dilate on that which may be demonstrated with the utmost evidence in a line or two, to anyone that is capable of the least reflexion? It is but looking into your own thoughts, and so trying whether you can conceive it possible for a sound, or figure, or motion, or colour, to exist without the mind, or unperceived. This easy trial may make you see, that what you contend for is a downright contradiction. Insomuch that I am content to put the whole upon this issue; if you can but conceive it possible for one extended movable substance, or in general, for any one idea or anything like an idea, to exist otherwise than in a mind perceiving it, I shall readily give up the cause: and as for all that *compages* of external bodies which you contend for, I shall grant you its existence, though you cannot either give me any reason why you believe it exists, or assign any use to it when it is supposed to exist. I say, the bare possibility of your opinion's being true, shall pass for an argument that it is so.

23 But say you, surely there is nothing easier than to imagine trees, for instance, in a park, or books existing in a closet, and nobody by to perceive them. I answer, you may so, there is no difficulty in it: but what is all this, I beseech you, more than framing in your mind certain ideas which you call *books* and *trees*, and at the same time omitting to frame the idea of anyone that may perceive them? But do not you yourself perceive or think of them all the while? This therefore is nothing to the purpose: it only shows you have the power of imagining or forming ideas in your mind; but it doth not show that you can conceive it possible the objects of your thought may exist without the mind: to make out this, it is necessary that you conceive them existing unconceived or unthought of, which is a manifest repugnancy. When we do our utmost to conceive the existence of external bodies, we are all the while only contemplating our own ideas. But the

mind taking no notice of itself is deluded to think it can and doth conceive bodies existing unthought of or without the mind; though at the same time they are apprehended by or exist in itself. A little attention will discover to anyone the truth and evidence of what is here said, and make it unnecessary to insist on any other proofs against the existence of material substance.

24 It is very obvious, upon the least inquiry into our own thoughts, to know whether it be possible for us to understand what is meant by the *absolute existence of sensible objects in themselves, or without the mind.* To me it is evident those words mark out either a direct contradiction, or else nothing at all. And to convince others of this, I know no readier or fairer way than to entreat they would calmly attend to their own thoughts : and if by this attention, the emptiness or repugnancy of those expressions does appear, surely nothing more is requisite for their conviction. It is on this therefore that I insist, to wit, that the absolute existence of unthinking things are words without a meaning, or which include a contradiction. This is what I repeat and inculcate, and earnestly recommend to the attentive thoughts of the reader.

25 All our ideas, sensations, or the things which we perceive, by whatsoever names they may be distinguished, are visibly inactive ; there is nothing of power or agency included in them. So that one idea or object of thought cannot produce, or make any alteration in, another. To be satisfied of the truth of this, there is nothing else requisite but a bare observation of our ideas. For since they and every part of them exist only in the mind, it follows that there is nothing in them but what is perceived.[1] But whoever shall attend to his ideas, whether of sense or

---

[1] [There being nothing between the mind and its sensory objects, these are completely patent. This was the usual view, accepted by thinkers as diverse as the Cartesians, Locke, and Hume.—Ed.]

reflexion, will not perceive in them any power or activity; there is therefore no such thing contained in them. A little attention will discover to us that the very being of an idea implies passiveness and inertness in it, insomuch that it is impossible for an idea to do anything, or, strictly speaking, to be the cause of anything: neither can it be the resemblance or pattern of any active being, as is evident from Sect. 8. Whence it plainly follows that extension, figure and motion cannot be the cause of our sensations. To say, therefore, that these are the effects of powers resulting from the configuration, number, motion, and size of corpuscles, must certainly be false.

26 We perceive a continual succession of ideas, some are anew excited, others are changed or totally disappear. There is therefore some cause of these ideas whereon they depend, and which produces and changes them. That this cause cannot be any quality or idea or combination of ideas, is clear from the preceding section. It must therefore be a substance; but it has been shown that there is no corporeal or material substance: it remains therefore that the cause of ideas is an incorporeal active substance or spirit.

27 A spirit is one simple, undivided, active being: as it perceives ideas, it is called the *understanding*, and as it produces or otherwise operates about them, it is called the *will*. Hence there can be no idea formed of a soul or spirit: for all ideas whatever, being passive and inert (*vid.* Sect. 25), they cannot represent unto us, by way of image or likeness, that which acts. A little attention will make it plain to anyone, that to have an idea which shall be like that active principle of motion and change of ideas, is absolutely impossible. Such is the nature of *spirit* or that which acts, that it cannot be of itself perceived, but only by the effects which it produceth. If any man shall doubt of the truth of what is here delivered, let him but reflect

and try if he can frame the idea of any power or active being: and whether he hath ideas of two principal powers, marked by the names *will* and *understanding*, distinct from each other as well as from a third idea of substance or being in general, with a relative notion of its supporting or being the subject of the aforesaid powers, which is signified by the name *soul* or *spirit*. This is what some hold; but so far as I can see, the words *will*, *soul*, *spirit*, do not stand for different ideas, or in truth for any idea at all, but for something which is very different from ideas, and which being an agent cannot be like unto, or represented by, any idea whatsoever. Though it must be owned at the same time, that we have some notion of soul, spirit, and the operations of the mind, such as willing, loving, hating, inasmuch as we know or understand the meaning of those words.[1]

28 I find I can excite ideas in my mind at pleasure, and vary and shift the scene as oft as I think fit. It is no more than willing, and straightway this or that idea arises in my fancy: and by the same power it is obliterated, and makes way for another. This making and unmaking of ideas doth very properly denominate the mind active. Thus much is certain, and grounded on experience: but when we talk of unthinking agents, or of exciting ideas exclusive of volition, we only amuse ourselves with words.

29 But whatever power I may have over my own thoughts, I find the ideas actually perceived by sense have

---

[1] [This sentence was added in the second edition, and the term ' notion ' thus introduced in a technical sense was at the same time added to Sects. 89, 140 and 142. This simply makes the statement of his doctrine easier. He had said in 1710 that there are two kinds of realities, the one extended, passive and apprehended, the other unextended, active and apprehending. Considered as objects he had called the first kind ' ideas '. He now calls the second ' notions '. *Cf. Siris*, Sect. 308. In *De Motu*, Sect. 53, he uses the term ' pure intellect ' for the faculty of ' notions '.—Ed.]

not a like dependence on my will. When in broad day-light I open my eyes, it is not in my power to choose whether I shall see or no, or to determine what particular objects shall present themselves to my view; and so like-wise as to the hearing and other senses, the ideas imprinted on them are not creatures of my will. There is therefore some other will or spirit that produces them.

30 The ideas of sense are more strong, lively, and dis-tinct than those of the imagination; they have likewise a steadiness, order, and coherence, and are not excited at random, as those which are the effects of human wills often are, but in a regular train or series, the admirable connexion whereof sufficiently testifies the wisdom and benevolence of its Author. Now the set rules or established methods, wherein the mind we depend on excites in us the ideas of sense, are called the *Laws of Nature* : and these we learn by experience, which teaches us that such and such ideas are attended with such and such other ideas, in the ordinary course of things.

31 This gives us a sort of foresight, which enables us to regulate our actions for the benefit of life. And without this we should be eternally at a loss : we could not know how to act anything that might procure us the least pleasure, or remove the least pain, of sense. That food nourishes, sleep refreshes, and fire warms us, that to sow in the seed-time is the way to reap in the harvest, and, in general, that to obtain such or such ends, such or such means are conducive, all this we know, not by discovering any necessary connexion between our ideas, but only by the observation of the settled Laws of Nature, without which we should be all in uncertainty and confusion, and a grown man no more know how to manage himself in the affairs of life, than an infant just born.

32 And yet this consistent uniform working, which so evidently displays the goodness and wisdom of that govern-

ing spirit whose will constitutes the Laws of Nature, is so far from leading our thoughts to him, that it rather sends them a-wandering after second causes. For when we perceive certain ideas of sense constantly followed by other ideas, and we know this is not of our doing, we forthwith attribute power and agency to the ideas themselves, and make one the cause of another, than which nothing can be more absurd and unintelligible. Thus, for example, having observed that when we perceive by sight a certain round luminous figure, we at the same time perceive by touch the idea or sensation called *heat*, we do from thence conclude the sun to be the cause of heat. And in like manner perceiving the motion and collision of bodies to be attended with sound, we are inclined to think the latter an effect of the former.

33 The ideas imprinted on the senses by the Author of Nature are called *real things* : and those excited in the imagination, being less regular, vivid and constant, are more properly termed *ideas*, or *images of things*, which they copy and represent. But then our sensations, be they never so vivid and distinct, are nevertheless *ideas*, that is, they exist in the mind, or are perceived by it, as truly as the ideas of its own framing. The ideas of sense are allowed to have more reality in them, that is, to be more strong, orderly, and coherent than the creatures of the mind ; but this is no argument that they exist without the mind. They are also less dependent on the spirit or thinking substance which perceives them, in that they are excited by the will of another and more powerful spirit : yet still they are *ideas*, and certainly no *idea*, whether faint or strong, can exist otherwise than in a mind perceiving it.

34 Before we proceed any farther, it is necessary to spend some time in answering objections which may

probably be made against the principles hitherto laid down. In doing of which, if I seem too prolix to those of quick apprehensions, I hope it may be pardoned, since all men do not equally apprehend things of this nature; and I am willing to be understood by everyone. First then, it will be objected that by the foregoing principles, all that is real and substantial in Nature is banished out of the world: and instead thereof a chimerical scheme of ideas takes place. All things that exist, exist only in the mind, that is, they are purely notional. What therefore becomes of the sun, moon, and stars? What must we think of houses, rivers, mountains, trees, stones; nay, even of our bodies? Are all these but so many chimeras and illusions on the fancy? To all which, and whatever else of the same sort may be objected, I answer, that by the principles premised, we are not deprived of any one thing in Nature. Whatever we see, feel, hear, or any wise conceive or understand, remains as secure as ever, and is as real as ever. There is a *rerum natura*, and the distinction between realities and chimeras retains its full force. This is evident from Sects. 29, 30, and 33, where we have shown what is meant by *real things* in opposition to *chimeras*, or ideas of our own framing; but then they both equally exist in the mind, and in that sense are alike *ideas*.

35 I do not argue against the existence of any one thing that we can apprehend, either by sense or reflexion. That the things I see with mine eyes and touch with my hands do exist, really exist, I make not the least question. The only thing whose existence we deny, is that which philosophers call matter or corporeal substance. And in doing of this, there is no damage done to the rest of mankind, who, I dare say, will never miss it. The atheist indeed will want the colour of an empty name to support his impiety; and the philosophers may possibly find they have lost a great handle for trifling and disputation.

66

36 If any man thinks this detracts from the existence or reality of things, he is very far from understanding what hath been premised in the plainest terms I could think of. Take here an abstract of what has been said. There are spiritual substances, minds or human souls, which will or excite ideas in themselves at pleasure : but these are faint, weak, and unsteady in respect of others they perceive by sense, which being impressed upon them according to certain Rules or Laws of Nature, speak themselves the effects of a mind more powerful and wise than human spirits. These latter are said to have more *reality* in them than the former : by which is meant that they are more affecting, orderly, and distinct, and that they are not fictions of the mind perceiving them. And in this sense, the sun that I see by day is the real sun, and that which I imagine by night is the idea of the former. In the sense here given of *reality*, it is evident that every vegetable, star, mineral, and in general each part of the mundane system, is as much a *real being* by our principles as by any other. Whether others mean anything by the term *reality* different from what I do, I entreat them to look into their own thoughts and see.

37 It will be urged that thus much at least is true, to wit, that we take away all corporeal substances. To this my answer is, that if the word *substance* be taken in the vulgar sense, for a combination of sensible qualities, such as extension, solidity, weight, and the like : this we cannot be accused of taking away. But if it be taken in a philosophic sense, for the support of accidents or qualities without the mind : then indeed I acknowledge that we take it away, if one may be said to take away that which never had any existence, not even in the imagination.

38 But, say you, it sounds very harsh to say we eat and drink ideas, and are clothed with ideas. I acknowledge it does so, the word *idea* not being used in common discourse

67

to signify the several combinations of sensible qualities, which are called *things* : and it is certain that any expression which varies from the familiar use of language will seem harsh and ridiculous. But this doth not concern the truth of the proposition, which in other words is no more than to say, we are fed and clothed with those things which we perceive immediately by our senses. The hardness or softness, the colour, taste, warmth, figure, and suchlike qualities, which combined together constitute the several sorts of victuals and apparel, have been shown to exist only in the mind that perceives them ; and this is all that is meant by calling them *ideas ;* which word, if it was as ordinarily used as *thing*, would sound no harsher nor more ridiculous than it. I am not for disputing about the propriety, but the truth of the expression. If therefore you agree with me that we eat and drink, and are clad with the immediate objects of sense which cannot exist unperceived or without the mind, I shall readily grant it is more proper or conformable to custom, that they should be called things rather than ideas.

39 If it be demanded why I make use of the word *idea*, and do not rather in compliance with custom call them things, I answer, I do it for two reasons : first, because the term *thing*, in contradistinction to *idea*, is generally supposed to denote somewhat existing without the mind : secondly, because *thing* hath a more comprehensive signification than *idea*, including spirits or thinking things as well as ideas. Since therefore the objects of sense exist only in the mind, and are withal thoughtless and inactive, I chose to mark them by the word *idea*, which implies those properties.

41 Secondly, it will be objected that there is a great difference betwixt real fire, for instance, and the idea of fire, betwixt dreaming or imagining one's self burnt, and actually being so : this and the like may be urged in opposition to our tenets. To all which the answer is evident

from what hath been already said, and I shall only add in this place, that if real fire be very different from the idea of fire, so also is the real pain that it occasions very different from the idea of the same pain: and yet nobody will pretend that real pain either is, or can possibly be, in an unperceiving thing or without the mind, any more than its idea.

42 Thirdly, it will be objected that we see things actually without or at a distance from us, and which consequently do not exist in the mind, it being absurd that those things which are seen at the distance of several miles should be as near to us as our own thoughts. In answer to this, I desire it may be considered, that in a dream we do oft perceive things as existing at a great distance off, and yet for all that, those things are acknowledged to have their existence only in the mind.

43 But for the fuller clearing of this point, it may be worth while to consider, how it is that we perceive distance and things placed at a distance by sight. For that we should in truth see external space, and bodies actually existing in it, some nearer, others farther off, seems to carry with it some opposition to what hath been said, of their existing nowhere without the mind. The consideration of this difficulty it was that gave birth to my *Essay towards a new Theory of Vision*, which was published not long since, wherein it is shown that *distance* or outness is neither immediately of itself perceived by sight, nor yet apprehended or judged of by lines and angles, or anything that hath a necessary connexion with it: but that it is only suggested to our thoughts, by certain visible ideas and sensations attending vision, which in their own nature have no manner of similitude or relation, either with distance, or things placed at a distance. But by a connexion taught us by experience, they come to signify and suggest them to us, after the same manner that words of any language suggest the ideas they are made to stand for.

PRINCIPLES OF HUMAN KNOWLEDGE

Insomuch that a man born blind, and afterwards made to see, would not, at first sight, think the things he saw to be without his mind, or at any distance from him. See Sect. 41 of the forementioned treatise.

44 The ideas of sight and touch make two species, entirely distinct and heterogeneous. The former are marks and prognostics of the latter. That the proper objects of sight neither exist without the mind, nor are the images of external things, was shown even in that treatise. Though throughout the same, the contrary be supposed true of tangible objects: not that to suppose that vulgar error was necessary for establishing the notion therein laid down; but because it was beside my purpose to examine and refute it in a discourse concerning *vision*. So that in strict truth the ideas of sight, when we apprehend by them distance and things placed at a distance, do not suggest or mark out to us things actually existing at a distance, but only admonish us what ideas of touch will be imprinted in our minds at such and such distances of time, and in consequence of such and such actions. It is, I say, evident from what has been said in the foregoing parts of this treatise, and in Sect. 147 and elsewhere of the *Essay concerning Vision*, that visible ideas are the language whereby the governing spirit, on whom we depend, informs us what tangible ideas he is about to imprint upon us, in case we excite this or that motion in our own bodies. But for a fuller information on this point, I refer to the essay itself.

45 Fourthly, it will be objected that from the foregoing principles it follows, things are every moment annihilated and created anew. The objects of sense exist only when they are perceived: the trees therefore are in the garden, or the chairs in the parlour, no longer than while there is somebody by to perceive them. Upon shutting my eyes all the furniture in the room is reduced to nothing, and barely

upon opening them it is again created. In answer to all which, I refer the reader to what has been said in Sects. 3, 4, &c., and desire he will consider whether he means anything by the actual existence of an idea, distinct from its being perceived. For my part, after the nicest inquiry I could make, I am not able to discover that anything else is meant by those words. And I once more entreat the reader to sound his own thoughts, and not suffer himself to be imposed on by words. If he can conceive it possible either for his ideas or their archetypes[1] to exist without being perceived, then I give up the cause: but if he cannot, he will acknowledge it is unreasonable for him to stand up in defence of he knows not what, and pretend to charge on me as an absurdity the not assenting to those propositions which at bottom have no meaning in them.

46 It will not be amiss to observe how far the received principles of philosophy are themselves chargeable with those pretended absurdities. It is thought strangely absurd that upon closing my eyelids, all the visible objects round me should be reduced to nothing; and yet is not this what philosophers commonly acknowledge, when they agree on all hands, that light and colours, which alone are the proper and immediate objects of sight, are mere sensations that exist no longer than they are perceived? Again, it may to some perhaps seem very incredible, that things should be every moment creating, yet this very notion is commonly taught in the Schools. For the Schoolmen, though they acknowledge the existence of matter, and that the whole mundane fabric is framed out of it, are nevertheless of opinion that it cannot subsist without the divine conservation, which by them is expounded to be a continual creation.

---

[1] [The archetype of an idea is what the idea is alleged to copy. An idea of sense cannot copy anything insensible, and therefore cannot have a material archetype.—ED.]

48 If we consider it, the objection proposed in Sect. 45 will not be found reasonably charged on the principles we have premised, so as in truth to make any objection at all against our notions. For though we hold indeed the objects of sense to be nothing else but ideas which cannot exist unperceived; yet we may not hence conclude they have no existence except only while they are perceived by us, since there may be some other spirit that perceives them, though we do not. Wherever bodies are said to have no existence without the mind, I would not be understood to mean this or that particular mind, but all minds whatsoever.[1] It does not therefore follow from the foregoing principles, that bodies are annihilated and created every moment, or exist not at all during the intervals between our perception of them.

49 Fifthly, it may perhaps be objected, that if extension and figure exist only in the mind it follows that the mind is extended and figured; since extension is a mode or attribute, which (to speak with the Schools) is predicated of the subject in which it exists. I answer, those qualities are in the mind only as they are perceived by it, that is, not by way of *mode* or *attribute*, but only by way of *idea*[2]; and it no more follows that the soul or mind is extended because extension exists in it alone, than it does that it is red or blue, because those colours are on all hands acknowledged to exist in it, and no where else. As to what philosophers say of subject and mode, that seems very groundless and unintelligible. For instance, in this proposition, a die is hard, extended and square, they will have it that the word *die* denotes a subject or substance, distinct from the

---

[1] [Because Berkeley has argued not that each man's sensa are inseparable from him, but that sensa are essentially what can be sensed, and are therefore relative to some mind or other. *Cf.* Sect. 90.—ED.]

[2] [That sensa are modes of mind was the contemporary view. In denying it Berkeley was revolutionary.—ED.]

hardness, extension and figure, which are predicated of it, and in which they exist. This I cannot comprehend: to me a die seems to be nothing distinct from those things which are termed its modes or accidents. And to say a die is hard, extended and square, is not to attribute those qualities to a subject distinct from and supporting them, but only an explication of the meaning of the word *die*.

50 Sixthly, you will say there have been a great many things explained by matter and motion; take away these, and you destroy the whole corpuscular philosophy, and undermine those mechanical principles which have been applied with so much success to account for the phenomena. In short, whatever advances have been made, either by ancient or modern philosophers, in the study of Nature, do all proceed on the supposition, that corporeal substance or matter doth really exist. To this I answer, that there is not any one phenomenon explained on that supposition, which may not as well be explained without it, as might easily be made appear by an induction of particulars. To explain the phenomena is all one as to show why upon such and such occasions we are affected with such and such ideas. But how matter should operate on a spirit, or produce any idea in it, is what no philosopher will pretend to explain.[1] It is therefore evident, there can be no use of matter in natural philosophy. Besides, they who attempt to account for things, do it not by corporeal substance, but by figure, motion, and other qualities, which are in truth no more than mere ideas, and therefore cannot be the cause of any thing, as hath been already shown. See Sect. 25.

53 [Seventhly] As to the opinion that there are no corporeal causes, this has been heretofore maintained by some of the Schoolmen, as it is of late by others among the

[1] [Descartes had all but said, and Malebranche had said outright, that it is inexplicable.—Ed.]

modern philosophers,[1] who though they allow matter to exist, yet will have God alone to be the immediate efficient cause of all things. These men saw, that amongst all the objects of sense, there was none which had any power or activity included in it, and that by consequence this was likewise true of whatever bodies they supposed to exist without the mind like unto the immediate objects of sense. But then, that they should suppose an innumerable multitude of created beings, which they acknowledge are not capable of producing any one effect in Nature, and which therefore are made to no manner of purpose, since God might have done everything as well without them; this I say, though we should allow it possible, must yet be a very unaccountable and extravagant supposition.

58 Tenthly, it will be objected, that the notions we advance are inconsistent with several sound truths in philosophy and mathematics. For example, the motion of the earth is now universally admitted by astronomers, as a truth grounded on the clearest and most convincing reasons; but on the foregoing principles, there can be no such thing. For motion being only an idea, it follows that if it be not perceived, it exists not; but the motion of the earth is not perceived by sense. I answer, that tenet, if rightly understood, will be found to agree with the principles we have premised: for the question, whether the earth moves or no, amounts in reality to no more than this, to wit, whether we have reason to conclude from what hath been observed by astronomers, that if we were placed in such and such circumstances, and such or such a position and distance, both from the earth and sun, we should perceive the former to move among the choir of the planets, and appearing in all respects like one of them: and this,

---

[1] [*E.g.*, the Occasionalists. Even Locke inclined to this view: natural substances ' being not perhaps so truly active powers as our hasty thoughts are apt to represent them ' (*Essay* II, xxi, 2).—ED.]

by the established rules of Nature, which we have no reason to mistrust, is reasonably collected from the phenomena.

60 In the eleventh place, it will be demanded to what purpose serves that curious organisation of plants, and the admirable mechanism in the parts of animals; might not vegetables grow, and shoot forth leaves and blossoms, and animals perform all their motions, as well without as with all that variety of internal parts so elegantly contrived and put together, which being ideas have nothing powerful or operative in them, nor have any necessary connexion with the effects ascribed to them? If it be a spirit that immediately produces every effect by a *fiat*, or act of his will, we must think all that is fine and artificial in the works, whether of man or Nature, to be made in vain. By this doctrine, though an artist hath made the spring and wheels, and every movement of a watch, and adjusted them in such a manner as he knew would produce the motions he designed; yet he must think all this done to no purpose, and that it is an intelligence which directs the index, and points to the hour of the day. If so, why may not the intelligence do it, without his being at the pains of making the movements, and putting them together? Why does not an empty case serve as well as another? And how comes it to pass, that whenever there is any fault in the going of a watch, there is some corresponding disorder to be found in the movements, which being mended by a skilful hand, all is right again? The like may be said of all the clockwork of Nature, great part whereof is so wonderfully fine and subtle, as scarce to be discerned by the best microscope. In short, it will be asked, how upon our principles any tolerable account can be given, or any final cause assigned of an innumerable multitude of bodies and machines framed with the most exquisite art, which in the common philosophy have very apposite uses assigned them, and serve to explain abundance of phenomena.

75

61 To all which I answer, first, that though there were some difficulties relating to the administration of providence, and the uses by it assigned to the several parts of Nature, which I could not solve by the foregoing principles, yet this objection could be of small weight against the truth and certainty of those things which may be proved *a priori*, with the utmost evidence. Secondly, but neither are the received principles free from the like difficulties ; for it may still be demanded, to what end God should take those roundabout methods of effecting things by instruments and machines, which no one can deny might have been effected by the mere command of his will, without all that apparatus : nay, if we narrowly consider it, we shall find the objection may be retorted with greater force on those who hold the existence of those machines without the mind ; for it has been made evident, that solidity, bulk, figure, motion and the like, have no *activity* or *efficacy* in them, so as to be capable of producing any one effect in Nature. See Sect. 25. Whoever, therefore, supposes them to exist (allowing the supposition possible) when they are not perceived, does it manifestly to no purpose ; since the only use that is assigned to them, as they exist unperceived, is that they produce those perceivable effects, which in truth cannot be ascribed to anything but spirit.

62 But to come nearer the difficulty, it must be observed, that though the fabrication of all those parts and organs be not absolutely necessary to the producing any effect, yet it is necessary to the producing of things in a constant, regular way, according to the Laws of Nature.[1] There are certain general laws that run through the whole chain of natural effects : these are learned by the observation and study of Nature, and are by men applied as well to the

[1] [*Cf. Siris*, Sect. 160 : ' Instruments are necessary to assist not the governor but the governed'.—ED.]

framing artificial things for the use and ornament of life, as to the explaining the various phenomena: which explication consists only in showing the conformity any particular phenomenon hath to the general Laws of Nature, or, which is the same thing, in discovering the *uniformity* there is in the production of natural effects; as will be evident to whoever shall attend to the several instances, wherein philosophers pretend to account for appearances. That there is a great and conspicuous use in these regular constant methods of working observed by the Supreme Agent, hath been shown in Sect. 31. And it is no less visible, that a particular size, figure, motion and disposition of parts are necessary, though not absolutely to the producing any effect, yet to the producing it according to the standing mechanical Laws of Nature. Thus, for instance, it cannot be denied that God, or the intelligence which sustains and rules the ordinary course of things, might, if he were minded to produce a miracle, choose all the motions on the dial-plate of a watch, though nobody had ever made the movements, and put them in it: but yet if he will act agreeably to the rules of mechanism, by him for wise ends established and maintained in the Creation, it is necessary that those actions of the watchmaker, whereby he makes the movements and rightly adjusts them, precede the production of the aforesaid motions; as also that any disorder in them be attended with the perception of some corresponding disorder in the movements, which being once corrected all is right again.

64 To set this matter in a yet clearer light, I shall observe that what has been objected in Sect. 60 amounts in reality to no more than this: ideas are not anyhow and at random produced, there being a certain order and connexion between them, like to that of cause and effect: there are also several combinations of them, made in a very regular and artificial manner, which seem like so many instruments in

the hand of Nature, that being hid as it were behind the scenes, have a secret operation in producing those appearances which are seen on the theatre of the world, being themselves discernible only to the curious eye of the philosopher. But since one idea cannot be the cause of another, to what purpose is that connexion? And since those instruments, being barely *inefficacious perceptions* in the mind, are not subservient to the production of natural effects; it is demanded why they are made, or, in other words, what reason can be assigned why God should make us, upon a close inspection into his works, behold so great variety of ideas, so artfully laid together, and so much according to rule; it not being credible, that he would be at the expense (if one may so speak) of all that art and regularity to no purpose?

65 To all which my answer is, first, that the connexion of ideas does not imply the relation of *cause* and *effect*, but only of a mark or *sign* with the thing *signified*. The fire which I see is not the cause of the pain I suffer upon my approaching it, but the mark that forewarns me of it. In like manner, the noise that I hear is not the effect of this or that motion or collision of the ambient bodies, but the sign thereof. Secondly, the reason why ideas are formed into machines, that is, artificial and regular combinations, is the same with that for combining letters into words. That a few original ideas may be made to signify a great number of effects and actions, it is necessary they be variously combined together: and to the end their use be permanent and universal, these combinations must be made by *rule*, and with *wise contrivance*. By this means abundance of information is conveyed unto us, concerning what we are to expect from such and such actions, and what methods are proper to be taken, for the exciting such and such ideas: which in effect is all that I conceive to be distinctly meant, when it is said that by discerning the

figure, texture, and mechanism of the inward parts of bodies, whether natural or artificial, we may attain to know the several uses and properties depending thereon, or the nature of the thing.

66 Hence it is evident that those things which, under the notion of a cause co-operating or concurring to the production of effects, are altogether inexplicable and run us into great absurdities, may be very naturally explained, and have a proper and obvious use assigned them, when they are considered only as marks or signs for our information. And it is the searching after and endeavouring to understand those signs instituted by the Author of Nature, that ought to be the employment of the natural philosopher, and not the pretending to explain things by corporeal causes; which doctrine seems to have too much estranged the minds of men from that active principle, that supreme and wise spirit, *in whom we live, move, and have our being.*

67 In the twelfth place, it may perhaps be objected that though it be clear from what has been said, that there can be no such thing as an inert, senseless, extended, solid, figured, movable substance, existing without the mind, such as philosophers describe matter : yet if any man shall leave out of his idea of *matter*, the positive ideas of extension, figure, solidity and motion, and say that he means only by that word an inert senseless substance, that exists without the mind, or unperceived, which is the occasion of our ideas, or at the presence whereof God is pleased to excite ideas in us : it doth not appear, but that matter taken in this sense may possibly exist. In answer to which I say, first, that it seems no less absurd to suppose a substance without accidents, than it is to suppose accidents without a substance. But secondly, though we should grant this unknown substance may possibly exist, yet where can it be supposed to be ? That it exists not in the mind is agreed,

and that it exists not in place is no less certain; since all extension exists only in the mind, as hath been already proved. It remains therefore that it exists nowhere at all.

68 Let us examine a little the description that is here given us of *matter*. It neither acts, nor perceives, nor is perceived: for this is all that is meant by saying it is an inert, senseless, unknown substance; which is a definition entirely made up of negatives, excepting only the relative notion of its standing under or supporting: but then it must be observed, that it *supports* nothing at all; and how nearly this comes to the description of a *non-entity*, I desire may be considered. But, say you, it is the *unknown occasion*, at the presence of which ideas are excited in us by the will of God. Now I would fain know how anything can be present to us, which is neither perceivable by sense nor reflexion, nor capable of producing any idea in our minds, nor is at all extended, nor hath any form, nor exists in any place. The words *to be present*, when thus applied, must needs be taken in some abstract and strange meaning, and which I am not able to comprehend.

69 Again, let us examine what is meant by *occasion*: so far as I can gather from the common use of language, that word signifies, either the agent which produces any effect, or else something that is observed to accompany, or go before it, in the ordinary course of things. But when it is applied to matter as above described, it can be taken in neither of those senses. For matter is said to be passive and inert, and so cannot be an agent or efficient cause. It is also unperceivable, as being devoid of all sensible qualities, and so cannot be the occasion of our perceptions in the latter sense: as when the burning my finger is said to be the occasion of the pain that attends it. What therefore can be meant by calling matter an *occasion*? This term is either used in no sense at all, or else in some sense very distant from its received signification.

70 You will perhaps say that matter, though it be not perceived by us, is nevertheless perceived by God, to whom it is the occasion of exciting ideas in our minds. For, say you, since we observe our sensations to be imprinted in an orderly and constant manner, it is but reasonable to suppose there are certain constant and regular occasions of their being produced. That is to say, that there are certain permanent and distinct parcels of matter corresponding to our ideas, which, though they do not excite them in our minds, or any ways immediately affect us, as being altogether passive and unperceivable to us, they are nevertheless to God, by whom they are perceived, as it were so many occasions to remind him when and what ideas to imprint on our minds : that so things may go on in a constant uniform manner.

71 In answer to this I observe, that as the notion of matter is here stated, the question is no longer concerning the existence of a thing distinct from *spirit* and *idea*, from perceiving and being perceived : but whether there are not certain ideas, of I know not what sort, in the mind of God, which are so many marks or notes that direct Him how to produce sensations in our minds, in a constant and regular method : much after the same manner as a musician is directed by the notes of music to produce that harmonious train and composition of sound which is called a *tune ;* though they who hear the music do not perceive the notes, and may be entirely ignorant of them. But this notion of matter seems too extravagant to deserve a confutation. Besides, it is in effect no objection against what we have advanced, to wit, that there is no senseless, unperceived *substance.*

72 If we follow the light of reason, we shall, from the constant uniform method of our sensations, collect the goodness and wisdom of the *spirit* who excites them in our minds. But this is all that I can see reasonably concluded

PRINCIPLES OF HUMAN KNOWLEDGE

from thence. To me, I say, it is evident that the being of a *spirit infinitely wise, good, and powerful* is abundantly sufficient to explain all the appearances of Nature. But as for *inert senseless matter*, nothing that I perceive has any the least connexion with it, or leads to the thoughts of it. And I would fain see anyone explain any the meanest phenomenon in Nature by it, or show any manner of reason, though in the lowest rank of probability, that he can have for its existence; or even make any tolerable sense or meaning of that supposition. For as to its being an occasion, we have, I think, evidently shown that with regard to us it is no occasion: it remains therefore that it must be, if at all, the occasion to God of exciting ideas in us; and what this amounts to, we have just now seen.

85 Having done with the objections, which I endeavoured to propose in the clearest light, and gave them all the force and weight I could, we proceed in the next place to take a view of our tenets in their consequences. Some of these appear at first sight, as that several difficult and obscure questions, on which abundance of speculation hath been thrown away, are entirely banished from philosophy. Whether corporeal substance can think? Whether matter be infinitely divisible? And how it operates on spirit? these and the like inquiries have given infinite amusement to philosophers in all ages. But depending on the existence of *matter*, they have no longer any place on our principles. Many other advantages there are, as well with regard to *religion* as the *sciences*, which it is easy for any one to deduce from what hath been premised. But this will appear more plainly in the sequel.

86 From the principles we have laid down, it follows, human knowledge may naturally be reduced to two heads, that of *ideas*, and that of *spirits*. Of each of these I shall

treat in order. And first as to ideas or unthinking things, our knowledge of these hath been very much obscured and confounded, and we have been led into very dangerous errors, by supposing a twofold existence of the objects of sense, the one *intelligible*, or in the mind, the other *real* and without the mind: whereby unthinking things are thought to have a natural subsistence of their own, distinct from being perceived by spirits. This, which, if I mistake not, hath been shown to be a most groundless and absurd notion, is the very root of *scepticism ;* for so long as men thought that real things subsisted without the mind, and that their knowledge was only so far forth *real* as it was conformable to *real things*, it follows, they could not be certain that they had any real knowledge at all. For how can it be known that the things which are perceived are conformable to those which are not perceived, or exist without the mind ?

87 Colour, figure, motion, extension and the like, considered only as so many *sensations* in the mind, are perfectly known, there being nothing in them which is not perceived. But if they are looked on as notes or images, referred to *things* or *archetypes* existing without the mind, then are we involved all in *scepticism*. We see only the appearances, and not the real qualities of things. What may be the extension, figure, or motion of anything really and absolutely, or in itself, it is impossible for us to know, but only the proportion or the relation they bear to our senses. Things remaining the same, our ideas vary, and which of them, or even whether any of them at all represent the true quality really existing in the thing, it is out of our reach to determine. So that, for aught we know, all we see, hear, and feel, may be only phantom and vain chimera, and not at all agree with the real things existing in *rerum natura*. All this scepticism follows from our supposing a difference between *things* and *ideas*, and

that the former have a subsistence without the mind, or unperceived. It were easy to dilate on this subject, and show how the arguments urged by *sceptics* in all ages depend on the supposition of external objects.

88 So long as we attribute a real existence to unthinking things, distinct from their being perceived, it is not only impossible for us to know with evidence the nature of any real unthinking being, but even that it exists. Hence it is, that we see philosophers distrust their senses, and doubt of the existence of heaven and earth, of everything they see or feel, even of their own bodies. And after all their labour and struggle of thought, they are forced to own, we cannot attain to any self-evident or demonstrative knowledge of the existence of sensible things. But all this doubtfulness, which so bewilders and confounds the mind, and makes *philosophy* ridiculous in the eyes of the world, vanishes, if we annex a meaning to our words, and do not amuse ourselves with the terms *absolute, external, exist,* and such like, signifying we know not what. I can as well doubt of my own being, as of the being of those things which I actually perceive by sense : it being a manifest contradiction, that any sensible object should be immediately perceived by sight or touch, and at the same time have no existence in Nature, since the very existence of an unthinking being consists in *being perceived*.

89 Nothing seems of more importance, towards erecting a firm system of sound and real knowledge, which may be proof against the assaults of *scepticism,* than to lay the beginning in a distinct explication of what is meant by *thing, reality, existence*: for in vain shall we dispute concerning the real existence of things, or pretend to any knowledge thereof, so long as we have not fixed the meaning of those words. *Thing* or *being* is the most general name of all; it comprehends under it two kinds entirely distinct and heterogeneous, and which have nothing common but

the name, to wit, *spirits* and *ideas*. The former are *active, indivisible substances*: the latter are *inert, fleeting, dependent beings*, which subsist not by themselves, but are supported by, or exist in minds or spiritual substances. We comprehend our own existence by inward feeling or reflexion, and that of other spirits by reason. We may be said to have some knowledge or notion of our own minds, of spirits and active beings, whereof in a strict sense we have not ideas. In like manner we know and have a notion of relations between things or ideas, which relations are distinct from the ideas or things related, inasmuch as the latter may be perceived by us without our perceiving the former. To me it seems that ideas, spirits and relations are all in their respective kinds the object of human knowledge and subject of discourse: and that the term *idea* would be improperly extended to signify everything we know or have any notion of.

90 Ideas imprinted on the senses are real things, or do really exist; this we do not deny, but we deny they can subsist without the minds which perceive them, or that they are resemblances of any archetypes existing without the mind: since the very being of a sensation or idea consists in being perceived, and an idea can be like nothing but an idea. Again, the things perceived by sense may be termed *external*, with regard to their origin, in that they are not generated from within, by the mind itself, but imprinted by a spirit distinct from that which perceives them. Sensible objects may likewise be said to be without the mind, in another sense, namely when they exist in some other mind. Thus when I shut my eyes, the things I saw may still exist, but it must be in another mind.

91 It were a mistake to think, that what is here said derogates in the least from the reality of things. It is acknowledged on the received principles, that extension, motion, and in a word all sensible qualities, have need of a

support, as not being able to subsist by themselves. But the objects perceived by sense are allowed to be nothing but combinations of those qualities, and consequently cannot subsist by themselves. Thus far it is agreed on all hands. So that in denying the things perceived by sense an existence independent of a substance, or support wherein they may exist, we detract nothing from the received opinion of their *reality*, and are guilty of no innovation in that respect. All the difference is, that according to us the unthinking beings perceived by sense have no existence distinct from being perceived, and cannot therefore exist in any other substance than those unextended, indivisible substances, or *spirits*, which act, and think, and perceive them : whereas philosophers vulgarly hold that the sensible qualities exist in an inert, extended, unperceiving substance, which they call *matter*, to which they attribute a natural subsistence, exterior to all thinking beings, or distinct from being perceived by any mind whatsoever, even the eternal mind of the Creator, wherein they suppose only ideas of the corporeal substances created by Him : if indeed they allow them to be at all created.

92 For as we have shown the doctrine of matter or corporeal substance to have been the main pillar and support of *scepticism*, so likewise upon the same foundation have been raised all the impious schemes of *atheism* and irreligion. Nay, so great a difficulty hath it been thought to conceive matter produced out of nothing, that the most celebrated among the ancient philosophers, even of these who maintained the being of a God, have thought matter to be uncreated and coeternal with him. How great a friend material substance hath been to *atheists* in all ages, were needless to relate. All their monstrous systems have so visible and necessary a dependence on it, that when this corner-stone is once removed, the whole fabric cannot choose but fall to the ground ; insomuch that it is no longer

worth while to bestow a particular consideration on the absurdities of every wretched sect of *atheists*.

97 Beside the external existence of the objects of perception, another great source of errors and difficulties, with regard to ideal knowledge, is the doctrine of *abstract ideas*, such as it hath been set forth in the Introduction. The plainest things in the world, those we are most intimately acquainted with, and perfectly know, when they are considered in an abstract way, appear strangely difficult and incomprehensible. Time, place, and motion, taken in particular or concrete, are what everybody knows; but having passed through the hands of a metaphysician, they become too abstract and fine to be apprehended by men of ordinary sense. Bid your servant meet you at such a *time*, in such a *place*, and he shall never stay to deliberate on the meaning of those words: in conceiving that particular time and place, or the motion by which he is to get thither, he finds not the least difficulty. But if *time* be taken, exclusive of all those particular actions and ideas that diversify the day, merely for the continuation of existence, or duration in abstract, then it will perhaps gravel even a philosopher to comprehend it.

98 Whenever I attempt to frame a simple idea of *time*, abstracted from the succession of ideas in my mind, which flows uniformly, and is participated by all beings, I am lost and embrangled in inextricable difficulties. I have no notion of it at all, only I hear others say, it is infinitely divisible, and speak of it in such a manner as leads me to entertain odd thoughts of my existence: since that doctrine lays one under an absolute necessity of thinking, either that he passes away innumerable ages without a thought, or else that he is annihilated every moment of his life: both which seem equally absurd. Time therefore being nothing, abstracted from the succession of ideas in our minds, it follows that the duration of any finite spirit must be

estimated by the number of ideas or actions succeeding each other in that same spirit or mind. Hence it is a plain consequence that the soul always thinks:[1] and in truth whoever shall go about to divide in his thoughts, or abstract, the *existence* of a spirit from its *cogitation*, will, I believe, find it no easy task.

99 So likewise, when we attempt to abstract extension and motion from all other qualities, and consider them by themselves, we presently lose sight of them, and run into great extravagances. All which depend on a two-fold abstraction : first, it is supposed that extension, for example, may be abstracted from all other sensible qualities ; and secondly, that the entity of extension may be abstracted from its being perceived. But whoever shall reflect, and take care to understand what he says, will, if I mistake not, acknowledge that all sensible qualities are alike *sensations,* and alike *real;* that where the extension is, there is the colour too, to wit, in his mind, and that their archetypes can exist only in some other *mind :* and that the objects of sense are nothing but those sensations combined, blended, or (if one may so speak) concreted together : none of all which can be supposed to exist unperceived.

101 The two great provinces of speculative science, conversant about ideas received from sense and their relations, are *natural philosophy* and *mathematics*; with regard to each of these I shall make some observations. And first, I shall say somewhat of natural philosophy. On this subject it is, that the *sceptics* triumph : all that stock of arguments they produce to depreciate our faculties, and make mankind appear ignorant and low, are drawn principally from this head, to wit, that we are under an invincible blindness as to the *true* and *real* nature of things. This they exaggerate, and

---

[1] [As Descartes had said (Reply to Fifth Set of Objections to his *Meditations*), on the ground that mind is essentially consciousness ; Berkeley *also* on the ground of his empiricist view of time.—Ed.]

love to enlarge on. We are miserably bantered, say they, by our senses, and amused only with the outside and show of things. The real essence, the internal qualities, and constitution of every the meanest object, is hid from our view; something there is in every drop of water, every grain of sand, which it is beyond the power of human understanding to fathom or comprehend. But it is evident from what has been shown, that all this complaint is groundless, and that we are influenced by false principles to that degree as to mistrust our senses, and think we know nothing of those things which we perfectly comprehend.

102 One great inducement to our pronouncing ourselves ignorant of the nature of things, is the current opinion that everything includes within itself the cause of its properties: or that there is in each object an inward essence, which is the source whence its discernible qualities flow, and whereon they depend. Some have pretended to account for appearances by occult qualities, but of late they are mostly resolved into mechanical causes, to wit, the figure, motion, weight, and suchlike qualities of insensible particles: whereas in truth, there is no other agent or efficient cause than *spirit*, it being evident that motion, as well as all other *ideas*, is perfectly inert. See Sect. 25. Hence, to endeavour to explain the production of colours or sounds, by figure, motion, magnitude and the like, must needs be labour in vain. And accordingly, we see the attempts of that kind are not at all satisfactory. Which may be said, in general, of those instances, wherein one idea or quality is assigned for the cause of another. I need not say, how many *hypotheses* and speculations are left out, and how much the study of Nature is abridged by this doctrine.

103 The great mechanical principle now in vogue is *attraction*. That a stone falls to the earth, or the sea swells towards the moon, may to some appear sufficiently explained thereby. But how are we enlightened by being

told this is done by attraction? Is it that that word signifies the manner of the tendency, and that it is by the mutual drawing of bodies, instead of their being impelled or protruded towards each other? But nothing is determined of the manner or action, and it may as truly (for aught we know) be termed *impulse* or *protrusion* as *attraction*. Again, the parts of steel we see cohere firmly together, and this also is accounted for by attraction; but in this, as in the other instances, I do not perceive that anything is signified besides the effect itself; for as to the manner of the action whereby it is produced, or the cause which produces it, these are not so much as aimed at.

104 Indeed, if we take a view of the several phenomena, and compare them together, we may observe some likeness and conformity between them. For example, in the falling of a stone to the ground, in the rising of the sea towards the moon, in cohesion and crystallisation, there is something alike, namely an union or mutual approach of bodies. So that any one of these or the like phenomena may not seem strange or surprising to a man who hath nicely observed and compared the effects of Nature. For that only is thought so which is uncommon, or a thing by itself, and out of the ordinary course of our observation. That bodies should tend towards the centre of the earth, is not thought strange, because it is what we perceive every moment of our lives. But that they should have a like gravitation towards the centre of the moon, may seem odd and unaccountable to most men, because it is discerned only in the tides. But a philosopher, whose thoughts take in a larger compass of Nature, having observed a certain similitude of appearances, as well in the heavens as the earth, that argue innumerable bodies to have a mutual tendency towards each other, which he denotes by the general name *attraction*, whatever can be reduced to that, he thinks justly accounted for. Thus he

explains the tides by the attraction of the terraqueous globe towards the moon, which to him doth not appear odd or anomalous, but only a particular example of a general rule or law of Nature.

105 If therefore we consider the difference there is betwixt natural philosophers and other men, with regard to their knowledge of the phenomena, we shall find it consists, not in an exacter knowledge of the efficient cause that produces them, for that can be no other than the *will of a spirit*, but only in a greater largeness of comprehension, whereby analogies, harmonies, and agreements are discovered in the works of Nature, and the particular effects explained, that is, reduced to general rules, see Sect. 62, which rules grounded on the analogy, and uniformness observed in the production of natural effects, are most agreeable, and sought after by the mind; for that they extend our prospect beyond what is present, and near to us, and enable us to make very probable conjectures, touching things that may have happened at very great distances of time and place, as well as to predict things to come; which sort of endeavour towards omniscience is much affected by the mind.

106 But we should proceed warily in such things: for we are apt to lay too great a stress on analogies, and, to the prejudice of truth, humour that eagerness of the mind whereby it is carried to extend its knowledge into general theorems. For example, gravitation, or mutual attraction, because it appears in many instances, some are straightway for pronouncing *universal;* and that to *attract, and be attracted by every other body, is an essential quality inherent in all bodies whatsoever.* Whereas it appears the fixed stars have no such tendency towards each other: and so far is that gravitation from being *essential* to bodies, that in some instances a quite contrary principle seems to show itself: as in the perpendicular growth of plants, and the elasticity

of the air. There is nothing necessary or essential in the case, but it depends entirely on the will of the *governing spirit*, who causes certain bodies to cleave together, or tend towards each other, according to various laws, whilst he keeps others at a fixed distance; and to some he gives a quite contrary tendency to fly asunder, just as he sees convenient.

107 After what has been premised, I think we may lay down the following conclusions. First, it is plain philosophers amuse themselves in vain, when they inquire for any natural efficient cause, distinct from a *mind* or *spirit*. Secondly, considering the whole creation is the workmanship of a *wise and good agent*, it should seem to become philosophers, to employ their thoughts (contrary to what some hold) about the final causes of things : and I must confess, I see no reason, why pointing out the various ends, to which natural things are adapted, and for which they were originally with unspeakable wisdom contrived, should not be thought one good way of accounting for them and altogether worthy a philosopher. Thirdly, from what hath been premised no reason can be drawn, why the history of Nature should not still be studied, and observations and experiments made, which, that they are of use to mankind, and enable us to draw any general conclusions, is not the result of any immutable habitudes, or relations between things themselves, but only of God's goodness and kindness to men in the administration of the world. See Sects. 30 and 31. Fourthly, by a diligent observation of the phenomena within our view, we may discover the general laws of Nature, and from them deduce the other phenomena. I do not say *demonstrate ;* for all deductions of that kind depend on a supposition that the Author of Nature always operates uniformly, and in a constant observance of those rules we take for principles : which we cannot evidently know.

108 Those men who frame general rules from the phenomena, and afterwards derive the phenomena from those rules, seem to consider signs rather than causes. A man may well understand natural signs without knowing their analogy, or being able to say by what rule a thing is so or so. And as it is very possible to write improperly, through too strict an observance of general grammar rules : so in arguing from general rules of Nature, it is not impossible we may extend the analogy too far, and by that means run into mistakes.

110 The best key for the aforesaid analogy, or natural science, will be easily acknowledged to be a certain celebrated treatise of *mechanics*: [1] in the entrance of which justly admired treatise, time, space and motion are distinguished into *absolute* and *relative*, *true* and *apparent*, *mathematical* and *vulgar*: which distinction, as it is at large explained by the author, doth suppose those quantities to have an existence without the mind : and that they are ordinarily conceived with relation to sensible things, to which nevertheless in their own nature they bear no relation at all.

111 As for *time*, as it is there taken in an absolute or abstracted sense, for the duration or perseverance of the existence of things, I have nothing more to add concerning it, after what hath been already said on that subject, Sects. 97 and 98. For the rest, this celebrated author holds there is an *absolute space*, which, being unperceivable to sense, remains in itself similar and immovable : and relative space to be the measure thereof, which being movable and defined by its situation in respect of sensible bodies, is vulgarly taken for immovable space. *Place* he defines to be that part of space which is occupied by any body. And according as the space is absolute or relative, so also is the place. *Absolute motion* is said to be the translation of a body

[1] [Newton's *Principia Mathematica* (1687). On these sections see *De Motu.*—ED.]

from absolute place to absolute place, as relative motion is from one relative place to another. And because the parts of absolute space do not fall under our senses, instead of them we are obliged to use their sensible measures : and so define both place and motion with respect to bodies, which we regard as immovable. But, it is said, in philosophical matters we must abstract from our senses, since it may be, that none of those bodies which seem to be quiescent, are truly so : and the same thing which is moved relatively, may be really at rest. As likewise one and the same body may be in relative rest and motion, or even moved with contrary relative motions at the same time, according as its place is variously defined. All which ambiguity is to be found in the apparent motions, but not at all in the true or absolute, which should therefore be alone regarded in philosophy. And the true, we are told, are distinguished from apparent or relative motions by the following properties. First, in true or absolute motion, all parts which preserve the same position with respect to the whole, partake of the motions of the whole. Secondly, the place being moved, that which is placed therein is also moved : so that a body moving in a place which is in motion doth participate the motion of its place. Thirdly, true motion is never generated or changed, otherwise than by force impressed on the body itself. Fourthly, true motion is always changed by force impressed on the body moved. Fifthly, in circular motion barely relative, there is no centrifugal force, which nevertheless in that which is true or absolute, is proportional to the quantity of motion.

112 But notwithstanding what hath been said, it doth not appear to me, that there can be any motion other than *relative*: so that to conceive motion, there must be at least conceived two bodies, whereof the distance or position in regard to each other is varied. Hence if there was one only body in being, it could not possibly be moved. This

seems evident, in that the idea I have of motion doth necessarily include relation.

113 But though in every motion it be necessary to conceive more bodies than one, yet it may be that one only is moved, namely that on which the force causing the change of distance is impressed, or in other words, that to which the action is applied. For however some may define relative motion, so as to term that body *moved*, which changes its distance from some other body, whether the force or action causing that change were applied to it, or no: yet as relative motion is that which is perceived by sense, and regarded in the ordinary affairs of life, it should seem that every man of common sense knows what it is, as well as the best philosopher: now I ask any one, whether in his sense of motion as he walks along the streets, the stones he passes over may be said to *move*, because they change distance with his feet? To me it seems, that though motion includes a relation of one thing to another, yet it is not necessary that each term of the relation be denominated from it. As a man may think of somewhat which doth not think, so a body may be moved to or from another body, which is not therefore itself in motion.

114 As the place happens to be variously defined, the motion which is related to it varies. A man in a ship may be said to be quiescent, with relation to the sides of the vessel, and yet move with relation to the land. Or he may move eastward in respect of the one, and westward in respect of the other. In the common affairs of life, men never go beyond the earth to define the place of any body: and what is quiescent in respect of that, is accounted *absolutely* to be so. But philosophers, who have a greater extent of thought, and juster notions of the system of things, discover even the earth itself to be moved. In order therefore to fix their notions, they seem to conceive the corporeal world as finite, and the utmost unmoved walls or

shell thereof to be the place whereby they estimate true motions. If we sound our own conceptions, I believe we may find all the absolute motion we can frame an idea of to be at bottom no other than relative motion thus defined. For as hath been already observed, absolute motion exclusive of all external relation is incomprehensible: and to this kind of relative motion, all the above-mentioned properties, causes, and effects ascribed to absolute motion, will, if I mistake not, be found to agree. . . .

115 For to denominate a body *moved*, it is requisite, first, that it change its distance or situation with regard to some other body: and secondly, that the force or action occasioning that change be applied to it. If either of these be wanting, I do not think that agreeably to the sense of mankind, or the propriety of language, a body can be said to be in motion. I grant indeed, that it is possible for us to think a body, which we see change its distance from some other, to be moved, though it have no force applied to it (in which sense there may be apparent motion), but then it is because the force causing the change of distance is imagined by us to be applied or impressed on that body thought to move. Which indeed shows we are capable of mistaking a thing to be in motion which is not, and that is all.

116 From what hath been said, it follows that the philosophic consideration of motion doth not imply the being of an *absolute space*, distinct from that which is perceived by sense, and related to bodies: which that it cannot exist without the mind, is clear upon the same principles, that demonstrate the like of all other objects of sense. And perhaps, if we inquire narrowly, we shall find we cannot even frame an idea of *pure space*, exclusive of all body. This I must confess seems impossible, as being a most abstract idea. When I excite a motion in some part of my body, if it be free or without resistance, I say

there is *space*: but if I find a resistance, then I say there is *body*: and in proportion as the resistance to motion is lesser or greater, I say the *space* is more or less *pure*. So that when I speak of pure or empty space, it is not to be supposed that the word *space* stands for an idea distinct from, or conceivable without body and motion. Though indeed we are apt to think every noun substantive stands for a distinct idea, that may be separated from all others: which hath occasioned infinite mistakes. When therefore supposing all the world to be annihilated besides my own body, I say there still remains *pure space*: thereby nothing else is meant, but only that I conceive it possible for the limbs of my body to be moved on all sides without the least resistance: but if that too were annihilated, then there could be no motion, and consequently no space. Some perhaps may think the sense of seeing doth furnish them with the idea of pure space; but it is plain from what we have elsewhere shown, that the ideas of space and distance are not obtained by that sense. See the *Essay concerning Vision*.

118 Hitherto of natural philosophy: we come now to make some inquiry concerning that other great branch of speculative knowledge, to wit, *mathematics*. These, how celebrated soever they may be, for their clearness and certainty of demonstration, which is hardly anywhere else to be found, cannot nevertheless be supposed altogether free from mistakes; if in their principles there lurks some secret error, which is common to the professors of those sciences with the rest of mankind. Mathematicians, though they deduce their theorems from a great height of evidence, yet their first principles are limited by the consideration of quantity: and they do not ascend into any inquiry concerning those transcendental maxims, which influence all the particular sciences, each part whereof, mathematics not excepted, doth consequently participate of the errors

involved in them. That the principles laid down by mathematicians are true, and their way of deduction from those principles clear and incontestable, we do not deny. But we hold, there may be certain erroneous maxims of greater extent than the object of mathematics, and for that reason not expressly mentioned, though tacitly supposed throughout the whole progress of that science ; and that the ill effects of those secret unexamined errors are diffused through all the branches thereof. To be plain, we suspect the mathematicians are, as well as other men, concerned in the errors arising from the doctrine of abstract general ideas, and the existence of objects without the mind.

119 *Arithmetic* hath been thought to have for its object abstract ideas of *number*. Of which to understand the properties and mutual habitudes is supposed no mean part of speculative knowledge. The opinion of the pure and intellectual nature of numbers in abstract hath made them in esteem with those philosophers who seem to have affected an uncommon fineness and elevation of thought. It hath set a price on the most trifling numerical speculations which in practice are of no use, but serve only for amusement : and hath therefore so far infected the minds of some, that they have dreamt of mighty *mysteries* involved in numbers, and attempted the explication of natural things by them. But if we inquire into our own thoughts, and consider what hath been premised, we may perhaps entertain a low opinion of those high flights and abstractions, and look on all inquiries about numbers only as so many *difficiles nugæ*, so far as they are not subservient to practice, and promote the benefit of life.

120 Unity in abstract we have before considered in Sect. 13, from which and what hath been said in the Introduction, it plainly follows there is not any such idea. But number being defined a *collection of units*, we may conclude

that, if there be no such thing as unity or unit in abstract, there are no ideas of number in abstract denoted by the numerical names and figures. The theories therefore in arithmetic, if they are abstracted from the names and figures, as likewise from all use and practice, as well as from the particular things numbered, can be supposed to have nothing at all for their object. Hence we may see how entirely the science of numbers is subordinate to practice, and how jejune and trifling it becomes when considered as a matter of mere speculation.

121 However, since there may be some who, deluded by the specious show of discovering abstracted verities, waste their time in arithmetical theorems and problems, which have not any use: it will not be amiss, if we more fully consider and expose the vanity of that pretence; and this will plainly appear, by taking a view of arithmetic in its infancy, and observing what it was that originally put men on the study of that science, and to what scope they directed it. It is natural to think that at first men, for ease of memory and help of computation, made use of counters, or in writing of single strokes, points or the like, each whereof was made to signify an unit, that is, some one thing of whatever kind they had occasion to reckon. Afterwards they found out the more compendious ways of making one character stand in place of several strokes, or points. And lastly, the notation of the Arabians or Indians came into use, wherein by the repetition of a few characters or figures, and varying the signification of each figure according to the place it obtains, all numbers may be most aptly expressed: which seems to have been done in imitation of language, so that an exact analogy is observed betwixt the notation by figures and names, the nine simple figures answering the nine first numeral names, and places in the former corresponding to denominations in the latter. And agreeably to those conditions of the simple and local

value of figures, were contrived methods of finding from the given figures or marks of the parts, what figures and how placed, are proper to denote the whole or *vice versa*. And having found the sought figures, the same rule or analogy being observed throughout, it is easy to read them into words; and so the number becomes perfectly known. For then the number of any particular things is said to be known, when we know the name or figures (with their due arrangement) that according to the standing analogy belong to them. For these signs being known, we can by the operations of arithmetic know the signs of any part of the particular sums signified by them; and thus computing in signs (because of the connexion established betwixt them and the distinct multitudes of things, whereof one is taken for an unit), we may be able rightly to sum up, divide, and proportion the things themselves that we intend to number.

122 In *arithmetic* therefore we regard not the *things* but the *signs*, which nevertheless are not regarded for their own sake, but because they direct us how to act with relation to things, and dispose rightly of them. Now agreeably to what we have before observed, of words in general (Sect. 19. Introd.), it happens here likewise, that abstract ideas are thought to be signified by numeral names or characters, while they do not suggest ideas of particular things to our minds. I shall not at present enter into a more particular dissertation on this subject; but only observe that it is evident from what hath been said, those things which pass for abstract truths and theorems concerning numbers, are, in reality, conversant about no object distinct from particular numerable things, except only names and characters; which originally came to be considered, on no other account but their being *signs*, or capable to represent aptly whatever particular things men had need to compute. Whence it follows, that to study

them for their own sake would be just as wise, and to as good purpose, as if a man, neglecting the true use or original intention and subserviency of language, should spend his time in impertinent criticisms upon words, or reasonings and controversies purely verbal.

123 From numbers we proceed to speak of *extension*, which considered as relative is the object of geometry. The *infinite* divisibility of *finite* extension, though it is not expressly laid down, either as an axiom or theorem in the elements of that science, yet is throughout the same everywhere supposed, and thought to have so inseparable and essential a connexion with the principles and demonstrations in geometry, that mathematicians never admit it into doubt, or make the least question of it. And as this notion is the source from whence do spring all those amusing geometrical paradoxes, which have such a direct repugnancy to the plain common sense of mankind, and are admitted with so much reluctance into a mind not yet debauched by learning: so is it the principal occasion of all that nice and extreme subtlety, which renders the study of *mathematics* so difficult and tedious. Hence if we can make it appear, that no finite extension contains innumerable parts, or is infinitely divisible, it follows that we shall at once clear the science of geometry from a great number of difficulties and contradictions, which have ever been esteemed a reproach to human reason, and withal make the attainment thereof a business of much less time and pains than it hitherto hath been.

124 Every particular finite extension, which may possibly be the object of our thought, is an *idea* existing only in the mind, and consequently each part thereof must be perceived. If therefore I cannot perceive innumerable parts in any finite extension that I consider, it is certain they are not contained in it: but it is evident, that I cannot distinguish innumerable parts in any particular

PRINCIPLES OF HUMAN KNOWLEDGE

line, surface, or solid, which I either perceive by sense, or figure to myself in my mind : wherefore I conclude they are not contained in it. Nothing can be plainer to me, than that the extensions I have in view are no other than my own ideas, and it is no less plain, that I cannot resolve any one of my ideas into an infinite number of other ideas, that is, that they are not infinitely divisible. If by *finite extension* be meant something distinct from a finite idea, I declare I do not know what that is, and so cannot affirm or deny anything of it. But if the terms *extension*, *parts*, and the like, are taken in any sense conceivable, that is, for ideas, then to say a finite quantity or extension consists of parts infinite in number, is so manifest a contradiction, that every one at first sight acknowledges it to be so. And it is impossible it should ever gain the assent of any reasonable creature, who is not brought to it by gentle and slow degrees, as a converted Gentile to the belief of *transubstantiation*. Ancient and rooted prejudices do often pass into principles : and those propositions which once obtain the force and credit of a *principle*, are not only themselves, but likewise whatever is deducible from them, thought privileged from all examination. And there is no absurdity so gross, which by this means the mind of man may not be prepared to swallow.

126 It hath been observed in another place, that the theorems and demonstrations in geometry are conversant about universal ideas. Sect. 15. Introd. Where it is explained in what sense this ought to be understood, to wit, that the particular lines and figures included in the diagram are supposed to stand for innumerable others of different sizes : or in other words, the geometer considers them abstracting from their magnitude : which doth not imply that he forms an abstract idea, but only that he cares not what the particular magnitude is, whether great or small, but looks on that as a thing indifferent to the

demonstration: hence it follows, that a line in the scheme, but an inch long, must be spoken of as though it contained ten thousand parts, since it is regarded not in itself, but as it is universal; and it is universal only in its signification, whereby it represents innumerable lines greater than itself, in which may be distinguished ten thousand parts or more, though there may not be above an inch in it. After this manner the properties of the lines signified are (by a very usual figure) transferred to the sign, and thence through mistake thought to appertain to it considered in its own nature.

127 Because there is no number of parts so great, but it is possible there may be a line containing more, the inch-line is said to contain parts more than any assignable number; which is true, not of the inch taken absolutely, but only for the things signified by it. But men not retaining that distinction in their thoughts, slide into a belief that the small particular line described on paper contains in itself parts innumerable. There is no such thing as the ten-thousandth part of an *inch;* but there is of a *mile* or *diameter of the earth*, which may be signified by that inch. When therefore I delineate a triangle on paper, and take one side not above an inch, for example, in length to be the *radius :* this I consider as divided into ten thousand or an hundred thousand parts, or more. For though the ten-thousandth part of that line considered in itself is nothing at all, and consequently may be neglected without any error or inconveniency; yet these described lines being only marks standing for greater quantities, whereof it may be the ten-thousandth part is very considerable, it follows, that to prevent notable errors in practice, the *radius* must be taken of ten thousand parts, or more.

128 From what hath been said the reason is plain why, to the end any theorem may become universal in its use, it is necessary we speak of the lines described on paper as

though they contained parts which really they do not. In doing of which, if we examine the matter thoroughly, we shall perhaps discover that we cannot conceive an inch itself as consisting of, or being divisible into a thousand parts, but only some other line which is far greater than an inch, and represented by it. And that when we say a line is *infinitely divisible*, we must mean a line which is *infinitely great*. What we have here observed seems to be the chief cause, why to suppose the infinite divisibility of finite extension hath been thought necessary in geometry.

135 Having dispatched what we intended to say concerning the knowledge of *ideas*, the method we proposed leads us, in the next place, to treat of *spirits*: with regard to which, perhaps human knowledge is not so deficient as is vulgarly imagined. The great reason that is assigned for our being thought ignorant of the nature of spirits is our not having an idea of it. But surely it ought not to be looked on as a defect in a human understanding, that it does not perceive the idea of *spirit*, if it is manifestly impossible there should be any such *idea*. And this, if I mistake not, has been demonstrated in Sect. 27: to which I shall here add that a spirit has been shown to be the only substance or support wherein the unthinking beings or ideas can exist: but that this *substance* which supports or perceives ideas should itself be an *idea* or like an *idea*, is evidently absurd.

136 It will perhaps be said that we want a sense (as some have imagined) proper to know substances withal, which if we had, we might know our own soul, as we do a triangle. To this I answer, that in case we had a new sense bestowed upon us, we could only receive thereby some new sensations of ideas of sense. But I believe nobody will say, that what he means by the terms *soul* and *substance* is only some particular sort of idea or sensation.

We may therefore infer, that all things duly considered, it is not more reasonable to think our faculties defective, in that they do not furnish us with an idea of spirit or active thinking substance, than it would be if we should blame them for not being able to comprehend a *round square*.

137 From the opinion that spirits are to be known after the manner of an idea or sensation, have risen many absurd and heterodox tenets, and much scepticism about the nature of the soul. It is even probable, that this opinion may have produced a doubt in some, whether they had any soul at all distinct from their body, since upon inquiry they could not find they had an idea of it. That an *idea* which is inactive, and the existence whereof consists in being perceived, should be the image or likeness of an agent subsisting by itself, seems to need no other refutation, than barely attending to what is meant by those words. But perhaps you will say, that though an *idea* cannot resemble a *spirit*, in its thinking, acting, or subsisting by itself, yet it may in some other respects: and it is not necessary that an idea or image be in all respects like the original.

138 I answer, if it does not in those mentioned, it is impossible it should represent it in any other thing. Do but leave out the power of willing, thinking, and perceiving ideas, and there remains nothing else wherein the idea can be like a spirit. For by the word *spirit* we mean only that which thinks, wills, and perceives; this, and this alone, constitutes the signification of that term. If therefore it is impossible that any degree of those powers should be represented in an idea, it is evident there can be no idea of a spirit.

139 But it will be objected, that if there is no idea signified by the terms *soul*, *spirit*, and *substance*, they are wholly insignificant, or have no meaning in them. I answer, those words do mean or signify a real thing, which is

neither an idea nor like an idea, but that which perceives ideas, and wills, and reasons about them. What I am myself, that which I denote by the term *I*, is the same with what is meant by *soul* or *spiritual substance*. If it be said that this is only quarrelling at a word, and that since the immediate significations of other names are by common consent called *ideas*, no reason can be assigned, why that which is signified by the name *spirit* or *soul* may not partake in the same appellation, I answer, all the unthinking objects of the mind agree, in that they are entirely passive, and their existence consists only in being perceived : whereas a soul or spirit is an active being, whose existence consists not in being perceived, but in perceiving ideas and thinking. It is therefore necessary, in order to prevent equivocation and confounding natures perfectly disagreeing and unlike, that we distinguish between *spirit* and *idea*. See Sect. 27.

140 In a large sense indeed, we may be said to have an idea, or rather a notion,[1] of *spirit*, that is, we understand the meaning of the word, otherwise we could not affirm or deny anything of it. Moreover, as we conceive the ideas that are in the minds of other spirits by means of our own, which we suppose to be resemblances of them : so we know other spirits by means of our own soul, which in that sense is the image or idea of them, it having a like respect to other spirits, that blueness or heat by me perceived hath to those ideas perceived by another.

141 It must not be supposed, that they who assert the natural immortality of the soul are of opinion that it is absolutely incapable of annihilation even by the infinite power of the Creator who first gave it being : but only that it is not liable to be broken or dissolved by the ordinary

---

[1] [' or rather a notion ' was added in second ed. ; so also was the second half of Sect. 142 (from ' We may not, I think '). See insertion of ' or notion ' in facsimile (p. vi) and note on Sect. 27.—ED.]

Laws of Nature or motion. They indeed, who hold the soul of man to be only a thin vital flame, or system of animal spirits, make it perishing and corruptible as the body, since there is nothing more easily dissipated than such a being, which it is naturally impossible should survive the ruin of the tabernacle wherein it is enclosed. And this notion hath been greedily embraced and cherished by the worst part of mankind, as the most effectual antidote against all impressions of virtue and religion. But it hath been made evident, that bodies of what frame or texture soever are barely passive ideas in the mind, which is more distant and heterogeneous from them, than light is from darkness. We have shown that the soul is indivisible, incorporeal, unextended, and it is consequently incorruptible. Nothing can be plainer, than that the motions, changes, decays, and dissolutions which we hourly see befall natural bodies (and which is what we mean by the *course of Nature*) cannot possibly affect an active, simple, uncompounded substance : such a being therefore is indissoluble by the force of Nature, that is to say, *the soul of man is naturally immortal.*

142 After what hath been said, it is, I suppose, plain that our souls are not to be known in the same manner as senseless inactive objects, or by way of *idea*. *Spirits* and *ideas* are things so wholly different, that when we say, *they exist, they are known,* or the like, these words must not be thought to signify anything common to both natures. There is nothing alike or common in them : and to expect that by any multiplication or enlargement of our faculties, we may be enabled to know a spirit as we do a triangle, seems as absurd as if we should hope to *see a sound*. This is inculcated because I imagine it may be of moment towards clearing several important questions, and preventing some very dangerous errors concerning the nature of the soul. We may not, I think, strictly be said to have an idea of an

active being, or of an action, although we may be said to have a notion of them. I have some knowledge or notion of my mind, and its acts about ideas, inasmuch as I know or understand what is meant by those words. What I know, that I have some notion of. I will not say, that the terms *idea* and *notion* may not be used convertibly, if the world will have it so. But yet it conduceth to clearness and propriety, that we distinguish things very different by different names. It is also to be remarked, that all relations including an act of the mind, we cannot so properly be said to have an idea, but rather a notion of the relations or habitudes between things. But if in the modern way the word *idea* is extended to spirits, and relations and acts; this is after all an affair of verbal concern.

143 It will not be amiss to add, that the doctrine of *abstract ideas* hath had no small share in rendering those sciences intricate and obscure, which are particularly conversant about spiritual things. Men have imagined they could frame abstract notions of the powers and acts of the mind, and consider them prescinded, as well from the mind or spirit itself, as from their respective objects and effects. Hence a great number of dark and ambiguous terms, presumed to stand for abstract notions, have been introduced into metaphysics and morality, and from these have grown infinite distractions and disputes amongst the learned.

144 But nothing seems more to have contributed towards engaging men in controversies and mistakes, with regard to the nature and operations of the mind, than the being used to speak of those things in terms borrowed from sensible ideas. For example, the will is termed the *motion* of the soul: this infuses a belief, that the mind of man is as a ball in motion, impelled and determined by the objects of sense, as necessarily as that is by the stroke of a racket. Hence arise endless scruples and errors of dangerous

consequence in morality. All which I doubt not may be cleared, and truth appear plain, uniform, and consistent, could but philosophers be prevailed on to retire into themselves, and attentively consider their own meaning.

145 From what hath been said, it is plain that we cannot know the existence of other spirits, otherwise than by their operations, or the ideas by them excited in us. I perceive several motions, changes, and combinations of ideas, that inform me there are certain particular agents like myself, which accompany them, and concur in their production. Hence the knowledge I have of other spirits is not immediate as is the knowledge of my ideas ; but depending on the intervention of ideas, by me referred to agents or spirits distinct from myself, as effects or concomitant signs.

146 But though there be some things which convince us, human agents are concerned in producing them ; yet it is evident to everyone, that those things which are called the works of Nature, that is, the far greater part of the ideas or sensations perceived by us, are not produced by, or dependent on the wills of men. There is therefore some other spirit that causes them, since it is repugnant that they should subsist by themselves. See Sect. 29. But if we attentively consider the constant regularity, order, and concatenation of natural things, the surprising magnificence, beauty, and perfection of the larger, and the exquisite contrivance of the smaller parts of the creation, together with the exact harmony and correspondence of the whole, but above all, the never enough admired laws of pain and pleasure, and the instincts or natural inclinations, appetites and passions of animals ; I say if we consider all these things, and at the same time attend to the meaning and import of the attributes, one, eternal, infinitely wise, good, and perfect, we shall clearly perceive that they belong to the aforesaid spirit, *who works all in all*, and *by whom all things consist*.

147 Hence it is evident, that God is known as certainly and immediately as any other mind or spirit whatsoever, distinct from ourselves. We may even assert, that the existence of God is far more evidently perceived than the existence of men; because the effects of Nature are infinitely more numerous and considerable than those ascribed to human agents. There is not any one mark that denotes a man, or effect produced by him, which doth not more strongly evince the being of that spirit who is the *Author of Nature*. For it is evident that in affecting other persons, the will of man hath no other object, than barely the motion of the limbs of his body; but that such a motion should be attended by or excite any idea in the mind of another, depends wholly on the will of the Creator. He alone it is who, *upholding all things by the Word of his Power*, maintains that intercourse between spirits whereby they are able to perceive the existence of each other. And yet this pure and clear light which enlightens every one is itself invisible.

148 It seems to be a general pretence of the unthinking herd, that they cannot see God. Could we but see him, say they, as we see a man, we should believe that he is, and believing obey his commands. But alas, we need only open our eyes to see the sovereign Lord of all things with a more full and clear view than we do any one of our fellow creatures. Not that I imagine we see God (as some will have it) by a direct and immediate view, or see corporeal things, not by themselves, but by seeing that which represents them in the essence of God, which doctrine is I must confess to me incomprehensible.[1] But I shall explain my meaning. A human spirit or person is not perceived

---

[1] [Malebranche : matter being cut off from our minds, we know it only in the Ideas of it in God's mind, into which, by reason, we look directly. For Berkeley, knowledge of the corporeal is immediate, of God mediate or inferential. See below, pp. 167–9.—ED.]

by sense, as not being an idea; when therefore we see the colour, size, figure, and motions of a man, we perceive only certain sensations or ideas excited in our own minds: and these being exhibited to our view in sundry distinct collections, serve to mark out unto us the existence of finite and created spirits like ourselves. Hence it is plain we do not see a man, if by *man* is meant that which lives, moves, perceives, and thinks as we do: but only such a certain collection of ideas, as directs us to think there is a distinct principle of thought and motion like to ourselves, accompanying and represented by it. And after the same manner we see God; all the difference is, that whereas some one finite and narrow assemblage of ideas denotes a particular human mind, whithersoever we direct our view we do at all times and in all places perceive manifest tokens of the divinity: everything we see, hear, feel, or anywise perceive by sense, being a sign or effect of the Power of God; as is our perception of those very motions, which are produced by men.

150 But you will say, hath Nature no share in the production of natural things, and must they be all ascribed to the immediate and sole operation of God? I answer, if by *Nature* is meant only the visible *series* of effects, or sensations imprinted on our minds according to certain fixed and general laws: then it is plain, that Nature taken in this sense cannot produce anything at all. But if by *Nature* is meant some being distinct from God, as well as from the Laws of Nature, and things perceived by sense, I must confess that word is to me an empty sound, without any intelligible meaning annexed to it. . . .

151 It will I doubt not be objected that the slow and gradual methods observed in the production of natural things do not seem to have for their cause the immediate hand of an *almighty Agent*. Besides, monsters, untimely births, fruits blasted in the blossom, rains falling in desert

places, miseries incident to human life, are so many arguments that the whole frame of Nature is not immediately actuated and superintended by a spirit of infinite wisdom and goodness. But the answer to this objection is in a good measure plain from Sect. 62, it being visible, that the aforesaid methods of Nature are absolutely necessary, in order to working by the most simple and general rules, and after a steady and consistent manner; which argues both the *wisdom* and *goodness* of God. . . It is clear from what we have elsewhere observed, that the operating according to general and stated laws is so necessary for our guidance in the affairs of life, and letting us into the secret of Nature, that without it all reach and compass of thought, all human sagacity and design, could serve to no manner of purpose: it were even impossible there should be any such faculties or powers in the mind. See Sect. 31. Which one consideration abundantly out-balances whatever particular inconveniences may thence arise.

152 We should further consider, that the very blemishes and defects of Nature are not without their use, in that they make an agreeable sort of variety, and augment the beauty of the rest of the creation, as shades in a picture serve to set off the brighter and more enlightened parts. We would likewise do well to examine, whether our taxing the waste of seeds and embryos, and accidental destruction of plants and animals, before they come to full maturity, as an imprudence in the Author of Nature, be not the effect of prejudice contracted by our familiarity with impotent and saving mortals. In *man* indeed a thrifty management of those things, which he cannot procure without much pains and industry, may be esteemed *wisdom*. But we must not imagine that the inexplicably fine machine of an animal or vegetable costs the great Creator any more pains or trouble in its production than a pebble doth: nothing being more evident than that an omnipotent

spirit can indifferently produce everything by a mere *fiat* or act of his will. Hence it is plain, that the splendid profusion of natural things should not be interpreted weakness or prodigality in the agent who produces them, but rather be looked on as an argument of the riches of his power.

153 As for the mixture of pain or uneasiness which is in the world, pursuant to the general Laws of Nature, and the actions of finite imperfect spirits : this, in the state we are in at present, is indispensably necessary to our well-being. But our prospects are too narrow : we take, for instance, the idea of some one particular pain into our thoughts, and account it *evil ;* whereas if we enlarge our view, so as to comprehend the various ends, connexions, and dependencies of things, on what occasions and in what proportions we are affected with pain and pleasure, the nature of human freedom, and the design with which we are put into the world ; we shall be forced to acknowledge that those particular things, which considered in themselves appear to be *evil*, have the nature of *good*, when considered as linked with the whole system of beings.

154 From what hath been said it will be manifest to any considering person, that it is merely for want of attention and comprehensiveness of mind, that there are any favourers of *atheism* or the *Manichean heresy* to be found. Little and unreflecting souls may indeed burlesque the works of Providence, the beauty and order whereof they have not capacity, or will not be at the pains, to comprehend. But those who are masters of any justness and extent of thought, and are withal used to reflect, can never sufficiently admire the divine traces of wisdom and goodness that shine throughout the economy of Nature. But what truth is there which shineth so strongly on the mind, that by an aversion of thought, a wilful shutting of the eyes, we may not escape seeing it ? Is it therefore to be wondered

at, if the generality of men, who are ever intent on business or pleasure, and little used to fix or open the eye of their mind, should not have all that conviction and evidence of the being of God which might be expected in reasonable creatures?

156 For after all, what deserves the first place in our studies is the consideration of *God*, and our *duty ;* which to promote, as it was the main drift and design of my labours, so shall I esteem them altogether useless and in-effectual, if by what I have said I cannot inspire my readers with a pious sense of the presence of God: and having shown the falseness or vanity of those barren speculations which make the chief employment of learned men, the better dispose them to reverence and embrace the salutary truths of the Gospel, which to know and to practise is the highest perfection of human nature.

[FINIS]

THREE DIALOGUES
BETWEEN
HYLAS AND PHILONOUS

The design of which is plainly to demonstrate
the reality and perfection of human knowledge,
the incorporeal nature of the soul, and the
immediate providence of a Deity : in opposition
to sceptics and atheists.   Also to open a method
for rendering the sciences more easy, useful,
and compendious.

First published 1713   Second Edition 1734

EDITOR'S NOTE

The work shows a rare mastery of philosophical dialogue. There are two characters: Hylas, a believer in matter, and Philonous, who represents Berkeley. The doctrines of the *Principles* are re-expressed for a wider public, with a consequent expansion of some points and contraction or omission of others, e.g. the argument against abstract 'ideas' is given more briefly, and that against the distinction of sensory qualities into primary and secondary more fully. That the denial of material substance does not entail the denial of mental substance is brought out with special clearness.

DIAL. I. *Supposing two sensory orders, one sensible and one beyond sense, results in scepticism.* Primary and secondary qualities, alike sensa, are tied to mind (pp. 119-46). Distinction of object and thing untenable (146-57). Sensa cannot resemble the insensible (157-62).

DIAL. II. *On the cause of sensa.* Sensa can be explained only by reference to a cosmic mind (163-7). Immaterialism distinguished from Malebranche's theory (167-70). Material substance, being a self-contradictory idea, cannot be inferred or postulated (170-8).

DIAL. III. *Objections against immaterialism considered.* Mental substance must be denied with material substance (181-5). To call corporeal things 'ideas' is queer (185). To deny material causality is to impute all evil bodily deeds to God (185-7). Optical illusions prove the inveracity of sense (187 f.). Pain being an object to God, He must be imperfect (188 f.). If sense is always true, the same thing should always appear the same (189-92). If sensa are the corporeal things, no two minds can perceive the same thing (192-4). Conclusion —the advantages of immaterialism, and the fallacies to be guarded against in considering it (194-9).

. . . HYLAS. You were represented in last night's conversation as one who maintained the most extravagant opinion that ever entered into the mind of man, to wit, that there is no such thing as *material substance* in the world.

PHILONOUS. That there is no such thing as what philosophers call *material substance*, I am seriously persuaded : but if I were made to see anything absurd or sceptical in this, I should then have the same reason to renounce this, that I imagine I have now to reject the contrary opinion.

HYLAS. What! can anything be more fantastical, more repugnant to common sense, or a more manifest piece of scepticism, than to believe there is no such thing as *matter?*

PHILONOUS. Softly, good Hylas. What if it should prove that you, who hold there is, are by virtue of that opinion a greater *sceptic*, and maintain more paradoxes and repugnancies to common sense, than I who believe no such thing ?

HYLAS. You may as soon persuade me, the part is greater than the whole, as that, in order to avoid absurdity and scepticism, I should ever be obliged to give up my opinion in this point.

PHILONOUS. Well, then, are you content to admit that opinion for true, which upon examination shall appear most agreeable to common sense, and remote from scepticism ?

HYLAS. With all my heart. Since you are for raising disputes about the plainest things in Nature, I am content for once to hear what you have to say.

PHILONOUS. Pray, Hylas, what do you mean by a *sceptic ?*

HYLAS. I mean what all men mean, one that doubts of everything.

PHILONOUS. He then who entertains no doubt concerning some particular point, with regard to that point cannot be thought a *sceptic*.

HYLAS. I agree with you.

PHILONOUS. Whether doth doubting consist in embracing the affirmative or negative side of a question?

HYLAS. In neither; for whoever understands English, cannot but know that *doubting* signifies a suspense between both.

PHILONOUS. He then that denieth any point, can no more be said to doubt of it, than he who affirmeth it with the same degree of assurance.

HYLAS. True.

PHILONOUS. And consequently, for such his denial is no more to be esteemed a *sceptic* than the other.

HYLAS. I acknowledge it.

PHILONOUS. How cometh it to pass then, Hylas, that you pronounce me a *sceptic*, because I deny what you affiirm, to wit, the existence of matter? Since, for aught you can tell, I am as peremptory in my denial, as you in your affirmation.

HYLAS. Hold, Philonous, I have been a little out in my definition; but every false step a man makes in discourse is not to be insisted on. I said indeed, that a *sceptic* was one who doubted of everything; but I should have added, or who denies the reality and truth of things.

PHILONOUS. What things? Do you mean the principles and theorems of sciences? But these you know are universal intellectual notions, and consequently independent of matter; the denial therefore of this doth not imply the denying them.

HYLAS. I grant it. But are there no other things? What think you of distrusting the senses, of denying the real existence of sensible things, or pretending to know nothing of them.   Is not this sufficient to denominate a man a *sceptic* ?

PHILONOUS.   Shall we therefore examine which of us it is that denies the reality of sensible things, or professes the greatest ignorance of them ; since, if I take you rightly, he is to be esteemed the greatest *sceptic* ?

HYLAS.   That is what I desire.

PHILONOUS.   What do you mean by sensible things ?

HYLAS.   Those things which are perceived by the senses. Can you imagine that I mean anything else ?

PHILONOUS.   Pardon me, Hylas, if I am desirous clearly to apprehend your notions, since this may much shorten our inquiry.   Suffer me then to ask you this farther question. Are those things only perceived by the senses which are perceived immediately ?   Or may those things properly be said to be *sensible*, which are perceived mediately, or not without the intervention of others ?

HYLAS.   I do not sufficiently understand you.

PHILONOUS.   In reading a book, what I immediately perceive are the letters, but mediately, or by means of these, are suggested to my mind the notions of God, virtue, truth, etc.   Now, that the letters are truly sensible things, or perceived by sense, there is no doubt : but I would know whether you take the things suggested by them to be so too.

HYLAS.   No certainly, it were absurd to think *God* or *virtue* sensible things, though they may be signified and suggested to the mind by sensible marks, with which they have an arbitrary connexion.

PHILONOUS.   It seems then, that by *sensible things* you mean those only which can be perceived immediately by sense.

HYLAS.   Right.

PHILONOUS.   Doth it not follow from this, that though I see one part of the sky red, and another blue, and that my reason doth thence evidently conclude there must be some cause of that diversity of colours, yet that cause cannot be said to be a sensible thing, or perceived by the sense of seeing?

HYLAS. It doth.

PHILONOUS. In like manner, though I hear variety of sounds, yet I cannot be said to hear the causes of those sounds.

HYLAS. You cannot.

PHILONOUS. And when by my touch I perceive a thing to be hot and heavy, I cannot say with any truth or propriety, that I feel the cause of its heat or weight.

HYLAS. To prevent any more questions of this kind, I tell you once for all, that by *sensible things* I mean those only which are perceived by sense, and that in truth the senses perceive nothing which they do not perceive immediately: for they make no inferences. The deducing therefore of causes or occasions from effects and appearances, which alone are perceived by sense, entirely relates to reason.

PHILONOUS. This point then is agreed between us, that *sensible things are those only which are immediately perceived by sense*. You will farther inform me, whether we immediately perceive by sight anything beside light, and colours, and figures: or by hearing, anything but sounds: by the palate, anything beside tastes: by the smell, beside odours: or by the touch, more than tangible qualities.

HYLAS. We do not.

PHILONOUS. It seems therefore, that if you take away all sensible qualities, there remains nothing sensible.

HYLAS. I grant it.

PHILONOUS. Sensible things therefore are nothing else but so many sensible qualities, or combinations of sensible qualities.

HYLAS. Nothing else.

PHILONOUS. Heat then is a sensible thing.

HYLAS. Certainly.

PHILONOUS. Doth the reality of sensible things consist in being perceived ? or, is it something distinct from their being perceived, and that bears no relation to the mind ?

HYLAS. To *exist* is one thing, and to be *perceived* is another.

PHILONOUS. I speak with regard to sensible things only : and of these I ask, whether by their real existence you mean a subsistence exterior to the mind, and distinct from their being perceived ?

HYLAS. I mean a real absolute being, distinct from, and without any relation to their being perceived.

PHILONOUS. Heat therefore, if it be allowed a real being, must exist without the mind.

HYLAS. It must.

PHILONOUS. Tell me, Hylas, is this real existence equally compatible to all degrees of heat which we perceive : or is there any reason why we should attribute it to some, and deny it others ? And if there be, pray let me know that reason.

HYLAS. Whatever degree of heat we perceive by sense, we may be sure the same exists in the object that occasions it.

PHILONOUS. What, the greatest as well as the least ?

HYLAS. I tell you, the reason is plainly the same in respect of both : they are both perceived by sense ; nay, the greater degree of heat is more sensibly perceived ; and consequently, if there is any difference, we are more certain of its real existence than we can be of the reality of a lesser degree.

PHILONOUS. But is not the most vehement and intense degree of heat a very great pain ?

HYLAS. No one can deny it.

PHILONOUS. And is any unperceiving thing capable of pain or pleasure ?

HYLAS. No certainly.

PHILONOUS. Is your material substance a senseless being, or a being endowed with sense and perception?

HYLAS. It is senseless without doubt.

PHILONOUS. It cannot therefore be the subject of pain.

HYLAS. By no means.

PHILONOUS. Nor consequently of the greatest heat perceived by sense, since you acknowledge this to be no small pain.

HYLAS. I grant it.

PHILONOUS. What shall we say then of your external object; is it a material substance or no?

HYLAS. It is a material substance with the sensible qualities inhering in it.

PHILONOUS. How then can a great heat exist in it, since you own it cannot in a material substance? I desire you would clear this point.

HYLAS. Hold, Philonous, I fear I was out in yielding intense heat to be a pain. It should seem rather, that pain is something distinct from heat, and the consequence or effect of it.

PHILONOUS. Upon putting your hand near the fire, do you perceive one simple uniform sensation, or two distinct sensations?

HYLAS. But one simple sensation.

PHILONOUS. Is not the heat immediately perceived?

HYLAS. It is.

PHILONOUS. And the pain?

HYLAS. True.

PHILONOUS. Seeing therefore they are both immediately perceived at the same time, and the fire affects you only with one simple, or uncompounded idea, it follows that this same simple idea is both the intense heat immediately perceived, and the pain; and consequently, that the intense heat immediately perceived is nothing distinct from a particular sort of pain.

HYLAS. It seems so.

PHILONOUS. Again, try in your thoughts, Hylas, if you can conceive a vehement sensation to be without pain, or pleasure.

HYLAS. I cannot.

PHILONOUS. Or can you frame to yourself an idea of sensible pain or pleasure in general, abstracted from every particular idea of heat, cold, tastes, smells, etc. ?

HYLAS. I do not find that I can.

PHILONOUS. Doth it not therefore follow, that sensible pain is nothing distinct from those sensations or ideas, in an intense degree ?

HYLAS. It is undeniable; and to speak the truth, I begin to suspect a very great heat cannot exist but in a mind perceiving it.

PHILONOUS. What ! are you then in that *sceptical* state of suspense, between affirming and denying ?

HYLAS. I think I may be positive in the point. A very violent and painful heat cannot exist without the mind.

PHILONOUS. It hath not therefore, according to you, any real being.

HYLAS. I own it.

PHILONOUS. Is it therefore certain, that there is no body in nature really hot ?

HYLAS. I have not denied there is any real heat in bodies. I only say, there is no such thing as an intense real heat.

PHILONOUS. But did you not say before, that all degrees of heat were equally real: or if there was any difference, that the greater were more undoubtedly real than the lesser.

HYLAS. True: but it was because I did not then consider the ground there is for distinguishing between them, which I now plainly see. And it is this: because intense heat is nothing else but a particular kind of painful sensation; and pain cannot exist but in a perceiving being; it follows that no intense heat can really exist in an unperceiving corporeal substance. But this is no reason why we should deny heat in an inferior degree to exist in such a substance.

PHILONOUS. But how shall we be able to discern those degrees of heat which exist only in the mind, from those which exist without it?

HYLAS. That is no difficult matter. You know, the least pain cannot exist unperceived; whatever therefore degree of heat is a pain, exists only in the mind. But as for all other degrees of heat, nothing obliges us to think the same of them.

PHILONOUS. I think you granted before, that no unperceiving being was capable of pleasure, any more than of pain.

HYLAS. I did.

PHILONOUS. And is not warmth, or a more gentle degree of heat than what causes uneasiness, a pleasure?

HYLAS. What then?

PHILONOUS. Consequently it cannot exist without the mind in any unperceiving substance, or body.

HYLAS. So it seems.

PHILONOUS. Since therefore as well those degrees of heat that are not painful, as those that are, can exist only in a thinking substance; may we not conclude that external bodies are absolutely incapable of any degree of heat whatever?

HYLAS. On second thoughts, I do not think it so evident that warmth is a pleasure, as that a great degree of heat is a pain.

PHILONOUS. I do not pretend that warmth is as great a pleasure as heat is a pain. But if you grant it to be even a small pleasure, it serves to make good my conclusion.

HYLAS. I could rather call it an *indolence*. It seems to be nothing more than a privation of both pain and pleasure. And that such a quality or state as this may agree to an unthinking substance, I hope you will not deny.

PHILONOUS. If you are resolved to maintain that warmth, or a gentle degree of heat, is no pleasure, I know not how to convince you otherwise, than by appealing to your own sense. But what think you of cold?

HYLAS. The same that I do of heat. An intense degree of cold is a pain: for to feel a very great cold, is to perceive a great uneasiness: it cannot therefore exist without the mind; but a lesser degree of cold may, as well as a lesser degree of heat.

PHILONOUS. Those bodies, therefore, upon whose application to our own we perceive a moderate degree of heat, must be concluded to have a moderate degree of heat or warmth in them: and those upon whose application we feel a like degree of cold, must be thought to have cold in them.

HYLAS. They must.

PHILONOUS. Can any doctrine be true that necessarily leads a man into an absurdity?

HYLAS. Without doubt it cannot.

PHILONOUS. Is it not an absurdity to think that the same thing should be at the same time both cold and warm?

HYLAS. It is.

PHILONOUS. Suppose now one of your hands hot, and the other cold, and that they are both at once put into the same vessel of water in an intermediate state; will not the water seem cold to one hand, and warm to the other?

HYLAS. It will.

PHILONOUS. Ought we not therefore by your principles to conclude, it is really both cold and warm at the same time, that is, according to your own concession, to believe an absurdity?

HYLAS. I confess it seems so.

PHILONOUS. Consequently, the principles themselves are false, since you have granted that no true principle leads to an absurdity.

HYLAS. But after all, can anything be more absurd than to say, *there is no heat in the fire?*

PHILONOUS. To make the point still clearer; tell me, whether in two cases exactly alike, we ought not to make the same judgment?

HYLAS. We ought.

PHILONOUS. When a pin pricks your finger, doth it not rend the fibres of your flesh?

HYLAS. It doth.

PHILONOUS. And when a coal burns your finger, doth it any more?

HYLAS. It doth not.

PHILONOUS. Since therefore you neither judge the sensation itself occasioned by the pin, nor anything like it, to be in the pin; you should not, conformably to what you have now granted, judge the sensation occasioned by the fire, or anything like it, to be in the fire.

HYLAS. Well, since it must be so, I am content to yield this point, and acknowledge, that heat and cold are only sensations existing in our minds: but there still remain qualities enough to secure the reality of external things.

PHILONOUS. But what will you say, Hylas, if it shall appear that the case is the same with regard to all other sensible qualities, and that they can no more be supposed to exist without the mind, than heat and cold?

HYLAS. Then indeed you will have done something to the purpose; but that is what I despair of seeing proved.

PHILONOUS. Let us examine them in order. What think you of tastes, do they exist without the mind or no?

HYLAS. Can any man in his senses doubt whether sugar is sweet, or wormwood bitter?

PHILONOUS. Inform me, Hylas. Is a sweet taste a particular kind of pleasure or pleasant sensation, or is it not?

HYLAS. It is.

PHILONOUS. And is not bitterness some kind of uneasiness or pain?

HYLAS. I grant it.

PHILONOUS. If therefore sugar and wormwood are unthinking corporeal substances existing without the mind, how can sweetness and bitterness, that is, pleasure and pain, agree to them?

HYLAS. Hold, Philonous, I now see what it was deluded me all this time. You asked whether heat and cold, sweetness and bitterness, were not particular sorts of pleasure and pain; to which I answered simply, that they were. Whereas I should have thus distinguished: those qualities, as perceived by us, are pleasures or pains, but not as existing in the external objects. We must not, therefore, conclude absolutely, that there is no heat in the fire, or sweetness in the sugar, but only that heat or sweetness, as perceived by us, are not in the fire or sugar. What say you to this?

PHILONOUS. I say it is nothing to the purpose. Our discourse proceeded altogether concerning sensible things, which you defined to be the things we *immediately perceive by our senses*. Whatever other qualities therefore you speak of, as distinct from these, I know nothing of them, neither do they at all belong to the point in dispute. You may indeed pretend to have discovered certain qualities which you do not perceive, and assert those insensible qualities exist in fire and sugar. But what use can be made of this to your present purpose, I am at a loss to conceive. Tell me then once more, do you acknowledge that heat and cold, sweetness and bitterness (meaning those qualities which are perceived by the senses) do not exist without the mind ?

HYLAS. I see it is to no purpose to hold out, so I give up the cause as to those mentioned qualities. Though I profess it sounds oddly, to say that sugar is not sweet.

PHILONOUS. But for your farther satisfaction, take this along with you : that which at other times seems sweet, shall to a distempered palate appear bitter. And nothing can be plainer, than that divers persons perceive different tastes in the same food, since that which one man delights in, another abhors. And how could this be, if the taste was something really inherent in the food ?

HYLAS. I acknowledge I know not how.

PHILONOUS. In the next place, odours are to be considered. And with regard to these, I would fain know, whether what hath been said of tastes doth not exactly agree to them ? Are they not so many pleasing or displeasing sensations ?

HYLAS. They are.

PHILONOUS. Can you then conceive it possible that they should exist in an unperceiving thing ?

HYLAS. I cannot.

PHILONOUS. Or can you imagine, that filth and ordure affect those brute animals that feed on them out of choice, with the same smells which we perceive in them ?

HYLAS. By no means.

PHILONOUS. May we not therefore conclude of smells, as of the other forementioned qualities, that they cannot exist in any but a perceiving substance or mind ?

HYLAS. I think so.

PHILONOUS. Then as to sounds, what must we think of them : are they accidents really inherent in external bodies, or not ?

HYLAS. That they inhere not in the sonorous bodies, is plain from hence ; because a bell struck in the exhausted receiver of an air-pump sends forth no sound. The air therefore must be thought the subject of sound.

PHILONOUS. What reason is there for that, Hylas?

HYLAS. Because when any motion is raised in the air, we perceive a sound greater or lesser, in proportion to the air's motion; but without some motion in the air, we never hear any sound at all.

PHILONOUS. And granting that we never hear a sound but when some motion is produced in the air, yet I do not see how you can infer from thence, that the sound itself is in the air.

HYLAS. It is this very motion in the external air, that produces in the mind the sensation of *sound*. For, striking on the drum of the ear, it causeth a vibration, which by the auditory nerves being communicated to the brain, the soul is thereupon affected with the sensation called *sound*.

PHILONOUS. What! is sound then a sensation?

HYLAS. I tell you, as perceived by us, it is a particular sensation in the mind.

PHILONOUS. And can any sensation exist without the mind?

HYLAS. No certainly.

PHILONOUS. How then can sound, being a sensation, exist in the air, if by the *air* you mean a senseless substance existing without the mind?

HYLAS. You must distinguish, Philonous, between sound as it is perceived by us, and as it is in itself; or (which is the same thing) between the sound we immediately perceive, and that which exists without us. The former indeed is a particular kind of sensation, but the latter is merely a vibrative or undulatory motion in the air.

PHILONOUS. I thought I had already obviated that distinction by the answer I gave when you were applying it in a like case before. But to say no more of that; are you sure then that sound is really nothing but motion?

HYLAS. I am.

PHILONOUS. Whatever therefore agrees to real sound, may with truth be attributed to motion.

HYLAS. It may.

PHILONOUS. It is then good sense to speak of *motion*, as of a thing that is *loud, sweet, acute,* or *grave.*

HYLAS. I see that you are resolved not to understand me. Is it not evident, those accidents or modes belong only to sensible sound, or *sound* in the common acceptation of the word, but not to *sound* in the real and philosophic sense, which, as I just now told you, is nothing but a certain motion of the air?

PHILONOUS. It seems then there are two sorts of sound, the one vulgar, or that which is heard, the other philosophical and real.

HYLAS. Even so.

PHILONOUS. And the latter consists in motion.

HYLAS. I told you so before.

PHILONOUS. Tell me, Hylas, to which of the senses, think you, the idea of motion belongs: to the hearing?

HYLAS. No certainly, but to the sight and touch.

PHILONOUS. It should follow then, that according to you, real sounds may possibly be *seen* or *felt,* but never *heard.*

HYLAS. Look you, Philonous, you may if you please make a jest of my opinion, but that will not alter the truth of things. I own indeed, the inferences you draw me into, sound something oddly; but common language, you know, is framed by, and for the use of the vulgar: we must not therefore wonder, if expressions adapted to exact philosophic notions seem uncouth and out of the way.

PHILONOUS. Is it come to that? I assure you, I imagine myself to have gained no small point, since you make so light of departing from common phrases and opinions; it being a main part of our inquiry, to examine whose notions are widest of the common road, and most repugnant to the general sense of the world. But can you think it no more than a philosophical paradox, to say that *real sounds are never heard*, and that the idea of them is obtained by some other sense. And is there nothing in this contrary to nature and the truth of things?

HYLAS. To deal ingenuously, I do not like it. And after the concessions already made, I had as well grant that sounds too have no real being without the mind.

PHILONOUS. And I hope you will make no difficulty to acknowledge the same of colours.

HYLAS. Pardon me: the case of colours is very different. Can anything be plainer than that we see them on the objects?

PHILONOUS. The objects you speak of are, I suppose, corporeal substances, existing without the mind.

HYLAS. They are.

PHILONOUS. And have true and real colours inhering in them?

HYLAS. Each visible object hath that colour which we see in it.

PHILONOUS. How! Is there anything visible but what we perceive by sight?

HYLAS. There is not.

PHILONOUS. And do we perceive anything by sense, which we do not perceive immediately?

HYLAS. How often must I be obliged to repeat the same thing? I tell you, we do not.

PHILONOUS. Have patience, good Hylas; and tell me once more, whether there is anything immediately perceived by the senses, except sensible qualities. I know you asserted there was not: but I would now be informed, whether you still persist in the same opinion.

HYLAS. I do.

PHILONOUS. Pray, is your corporeal substance either a sensible quality, or made up of sensible qualities?

HYLAS. What a question that is ! Who ever thought it was ?

PHILONOUS. My reason for asking was, because in saying, *each visible object hath that colour which we see in it*, you make visible objects to be corporeal substances ; which implies either that corporeal substances are sensible qualities, or else that there is something beside sensible qualities perceived by sight : but as this point was formerly agreed between us, and is still maintained by you, it is a clear consequence that your corporeal substance is nothing distinct from sensible qualities.

HYLAS. You may draw as many absurd consequences as you please, and endeavour to perplex the plainest things ; but you shall never persuade me out of my senses. I clearly understand my own meaning.

PHILONOUS. I wish you would make me understand it too. But since you are unwilling to have your notion of corporeal substance examined, I shall urge that point no farther. Only be pleased to let me know, whether the same colours which we see exist in external bodies, or some other.

HYLAS. The very same.

PHILONOUS. What ! are then the beautiful red and purple we see on yonder clouds, really in them ? Or do you imagine they have in themselves any other form, than that of a dark mist or vapour ?

HYLAS. I must own, Philonous, those colours are not really in the clouds as they seem to be at this distance. They are only apparent colours.

PHILONOUS. *Apparent* call you them ? How shall we distinguish these apparent colours from real ?

HYLAS. Very easily. Those are to be thought apparent, which appearing only at a distance, vanish upon a nearer approach.

PHILONOUS. And those, I suppose, are to be thought real, which are discovered by the most near and exact survey.

HYLAS. Right.

PHILONOUS. Is the nearest and exactest survey made by the help of a microscope, or by the naked eye?

HYLAS. By a microscope, doubtless.

PHILONOUS. But a microscope often discovers **colours** in an object different from those perceived by the unassisted sight. And in case we had microscopes magnifying to any assigned degree, it is certain that no object whatsoever viewed through them, would appear in the same colour which it exhibits to the naked eye.

HYLAS. And what will you conclude from all this? You cannot argue that there are really and naturally no colours on objects: because by artificial managements they may be altered, or made to vanish.

PHILONOUS. I think it may evidently be concluded from your own concessions, that all the colours we see with our naked eyes are only apparent as those on the clouds, since they vanish upon a more close and accurate inspection, which is afforded us by a microscope. Then as to what you say by way of prevention: I ask you, whether the real and natural state of an object is better discovered by a very sharp and piercing sight, or by one which is less sharp?

HYLAS. By the former without doubt.

PHILONOUS. Is it not plain from *dioptrics*, that microscopes make the sight more penetrating, and represent objects as they would appear to the eye, in case it were naturally endowed with a most exquisite sharpness?

HYLAS. It is.

PHILONOUS. Consequently the microscopical representation is to be thought that which best sets forth the real nature of the thing, or what it is in itself. The colours therefore by it perceived are more genuine and real than those perceived otherwise.

HYLAS. I confess there is something in what you say.

PHILONOUS. Besides, it is not only possible but manifest, that there actually are animals whose eyes are by Nature framed to perceive those things which by reason of their minuteness escape our sight. What think you of those inconceivably small animals perceived by glasses ? Must we suppose they are all stark blind ? Or, in case they see, can it be imagined their sight hath not the same use in preserving their bodies from injuries, which appears in that of all other animals ? And if it hath, is it not evident, they must see particles less than their own bodies, which will present them with a far different view in each object, from that which strikes our senses ? Even our own eyes do not always represent objects to us after the same manner. In the *jaundice*, every one knows that all things seem yellow. Is it not therefore highly probable, those animals in whose eyes we discern a very different texture from that of ours, and whose bodies abound with different humours, do not see the same colours in every object that we do ? From all which should it not seem to follow, that all colours are equally apparent, and that none of those which we perceive are really inherent in any outward object ?

HYLAS. It should.

PHILONOUS. The point will be past all doubt, if you consider, that in case colours were real properties or affections inherent in external bodies, they could admit of no alteration, without some change wrought in the very bodies themselves : but is it not evident from what hath been said, that upon the use of microscopes, upon a change happening in the humours of the eye, or a variation of distance, without any manner of real alteration in the thing itself, the colours of any object are either changed, or totally disappear ? Nay all other circumstances remaining the same, change but the situation of some objects, and they shall present different colours to the eye. The same thing happens upon viewing an object in various degrees of light. And what is more known, than that the same bodies appear differently coloured by candle-light, from what they do in the open day? Add to these the experiment of a prism, which, separating the heterogeneous rays of light, alters the colour of any object; and will cause the whitest to appear of a deep blue or red to the naked eye. And now tell me, whether you are still of opinion, that every body hath its true real colour inhering in it; and if you think it hath, I would fain know farther from you, what certain distance and position of the object, what peculiar texture and formation of the eye, what degree or kind of light is necessary for ascertaining that true colour, and distinguishing it from apparent ones.

HYLAS. I own myself entirely satisfied, that they are all equally apparent; and that there is no such thing as colour really inhering in external bodies, but that it is altogether in the light. And what confirms me in this opinion is, that in proportion to the light, colours are still more or less vivid; and if there be no light, then are there no colours perceived. Besides, allowing there are colours on external objects, yet how is it possible for us to perceive them? For no external body affects the mind, unless it act first on our organs of sense. But the only action of bodies is motion; and motion cannot be communicated otherwise than by impulse. A distant object therefore cannot act on the eye, nor consequently make itself or its properties perceivable to the soul. Whence it plainly follows, that it is immediately some contiguous substance, which operating on the eye occasions a perception of colours : and such is light.

PHILONOUS. How ! is light then a substance ?

HYLAS. I tell you, Philonous, external light is nothing but a thin fluid substance, whose minute particles, being agitated with a brisk motion, and in various manners reflected from the different surfaces of outward objects to the eyes, communicate different motions to the optic nerves ; which being propagated to the brain, cause therein various impressions : and these are attended with the sensations of red, blue, yellow, etc.

PHILONOUS. It seems then, the light doth no more than shake the optic nerves.

HYLAS. Nothing else.

PHILONOUS. And consequent to each particular motion of the nerves the mind is affected with a sensation, which is some particular colour.

HYLAS. Right.

PHILONOUS. And these sensations have no existence without the mind.

HYLAS. They have not.

PHILONOUS. How then do you affirm that colours are in the light, since by *light* you understand a corporeal substance external to the mind ?

HYLAS. Light and colours, as immediately perceived by us, I grant cannot exist without the mind. But in themselves they are only the motions and configurations of certain insensible particles of matter.

PHILONOUS. Colours then in the vulgar sense, or taken for the immediate objects of sight, cannot agree to any but a perceiving substance.

HYLAS. That is what I say.

PHILONOUS. Well then, since you give up the point as to those sensible qualities, which are alone thought colours by all mankind beside, you may hold what you please with regard to those invisible ones of the philosophers. It is not my business to dispute about them ; only I would advise you to bethink yourself, whether considering the inquiry we are upon, it be prudent for you to affirm, *the red and blue which we see are not real colours, but certain un-*

known motions and figures, which no man ever did or can see, are truly so. Are not these shocking notions, and are not they subject to as many ridiculous inferences, as those you were obliged to renounce before in the case of sounds ?

HYLAS. I frankly own, Philonous, that it is in vain to stand out any longer. Colours, sounds, tastes, in a word, all those termed *secondary qualities*, have certainly no existence without the mind. But by this acknowledgment I must not be supposed to derogate anything from the reality of matter or external objects, seeing it is no more than several philosophers maintain, who nevertheless are the farthest imaginable from denying matter. For the clearer understanding of this, you must know sensible qualities are by philosophers divided into *primary* and *secondary*. The former are extension, figure, solidity, gravity, motion, and rest. And these they hold exist really in bodies. The latter are those above enumerated ; or briefly, all sensible qualities beside the primary, which they assert are only so many sensations or ideas existing nowhere but in the mind. But all this, I doubt not, you are already apprised of. For my part, I have been a long time sensible there was such an opinion current among philosophers, but was never thoroughly convinced of its truth till now.

PHILONOUS. You are still then of opinion that extension and figures are inherent in external unthinking substances.

HYLAS. I am.

PHILONOUS. But what if the same arguments which are brought against secondary qualities, will hold good against these also ?

HYLAS. Why then I shall be obliged to think, they too exist only in the mind.

PHILONOUS. Is it your opinion, the very figure and

extension which you perceive by sense exist in the outward object or material substance?

HYLAS. It is.

PHILONOUS. Have all other animals as good grounds to think the same of the figure and extension which they see and feel?

HYLAS. Without doubt, if they have any thought at all.

PHILONOUS. Answer me, Hylas. Think you the senses were bestowed upon all animals for their preservation and well-being in life? Or were they given to men alone for this end?

HYLAS. I make no question but they have the same use in all other animals.

PHILONOUS. If so, is it not necessary they should be enabled by them to perceive their own limbs, and those bodies which are capable of harming them?

HYLAS. Certainly.

PHILONOUS. A mite therefore must be supposed to see his own foot, and things equal or even less than it, as bodies of some considerable dimension; though at the same time they appear to you scarce discernible, or at best as so many visible points.

HYLAS. I cannot deny it.

PHILONOUS. And to creatures less than the mite they will seem yet larger.

HYLAS. They will.

PHILONOUS. Insomuch that what you can hardly discern, will to another extremely minute animal appear as some huge mountain.

HYLAS. All this I grant.

PHILONOUS. Can one and the same thing be at the same time in itself of different dimensions?

HYLAS. That were absurd to imagine.

PHILONOUS. But from what you have laid down it follows, that both the extension by you perceived, and that perceived by the mite itself, as likewise all those perceived by lesser animals, are each of them the true extension of the mite's foot, that is to say, by your own principles you are led into an absurdity.

HYLAS. There seems to be some difficulty in the point.

PHILONOUS. Again, have you not acknowledged that no real inherent property of any object can be changed, without some change in the thing itself?

HYLAS. I have.

PHILONOUS. But as we approach to or recede from an object, the visible extension varies, being at one distance ten or an hundred times greater than at another. Doth it not therefore follow from hence likewise, that it is not really inherent in the object?

HYLAS. I own I am at a loss what to think.

PHILONOUS. Your judgment will soon be determined, if you will venture to think as freely concerning this quality, as you have done concerning the rest. Was it not admitted as a good argument, that neither heat nor cold was in the water, because it seemed warm to one hand, and cold to the other?

HYLAS. It was.

PHILONOUS. Is it not the very same reasoning to conclude, there is no extension or figure in an object, because to one eye it shall seem little, smooth, and round, when at the same time it appears to the other, great, uneven, and angular?

HYLAS. The very same. But doth this latter fact ever happen?

PHILONOUS. You may at any time make the experiment, by looking with one eye bare, and with the other through a microscope.

HYLAS. I know not how to maintain it, and yet I am loth to give up *extension*; I see so many odd consequences following upon such a concession.

PHILONOUS. Odd, say you? After the concessions already
made, I hope you will stick at nothing for its oddness.
But on the other hand should it not seem very odd, if
the general reasoning which includes all other sensible
qualities did not also include extension? If it be allowed
that no idea nor anything like an idea can exist in an
unperceiving substance, then surely it follows that no
figure or mode of extension which we can either perceive or imagine, or have any idea of, can be really
inherent in matter; not to mention the peculiar difficulty
there must be in conceiving a material substance, prior
to and distinct from extension, to be the *substratum* of
extension. Be the sensible quality what it will, figure,
or sound, or colour; it seems alike impossible it should
subsist in that which doth not perceive it.

HYLAS. I give up the point for the present, reserving still
a right to retract my opinion, in case I shall hereafter
discover any false step in my progress to it.

PHILONOUS. That is a right you cannot be denied. Figures
and extension being dispatched, we proceed next to
motion. Can a real motion in any external body be at
the same time both very swift and very slow?

HYLAS. It cannot.

PHILONOUS. Is not the motion of a body swift in a re-
ciprocal proportion to the time it takes up in describing
any given space? Thus a body that describes a mile
in an hour, moves three times faster than it would in
case it described only a mile in three hours.

HYLAS. I agree with you.

PHILONOUS. And is not time measured by the succession
of ideas in our minds?

HYLAS. It is.

PHILONOUS. And is it not possible ideas should succeed one
another twice as fast in your mind, as they do in mine,
or in that of some spirit of another kind.

HYLAS. I own it.

PHILONOUS. Consequently the same body may to another seem to perform its motion over any space in half the time that it doth to you. And the same reasoning will hold as to any other proportion : that is to say, according to your principles (since the motions perceived are both really in the object) it is possible one and the same body shall be really moved the same way at once, both very swift and very slow. How is this consistent either with common sense, or with what you just now granted ?

HYLAS. I have nothing to say to it.

PHILONOUS. Then as for *solidity ;* either you do not mean any sensible quality by that word, and so it is beside our inquiry : or if you do, it must be either hardness or resistance. But both the one and the other are plainly relative to our senses : it being evident that what seems hard to one animal, may appear soft to another, who hath greater force and firmness of limbs. Nor is it less plain that the resistance I feel is not in the body.

HYLAS. I own the very sensation of resistance, which is all you immediately perceive, is not in the *body*, but the cause of that sensation is.

PHILONOUS. But the causes of our sensations are not things immediately perceived, and therefore not sensible. This point I thought had been already determined.[1]

HYLAS. I own it was ; but you will pardon me if I seem a little embarrassed : I know not how to quit my old notions.

PHILONOUS. To help you out, do but consider, that if extension be once acknowledged to have no existence without the mind, the same must necessarily be granted

[1] [It had been agreed that at this stage only what is sensed shall be considered. The question of the causation of this is deferred to the second dialogue.—Ed.]

of motion, solidity, and gravity, since they all evidently suppose extension. It is therefore superfluous to inquire particularly concerning each of them. In denying extension, you have denied them all to have any real existence.

HYLAS. I wonder, Philonous, if what you say be true, why those philosophers who deny the secondary qualities any real existence should yet attribute it to the primary. If there is no difference between them, how can this be accounted for ?

PHILONOUS. It is not my business to account for every opinion of the philosophers. But among other reasons which may be assigned for this, it seems probable that pleasure and pain being rather annexed to the former than the latter, may be one. Heat and cold, tastes and smells, have something more vividly pleasing or disagreeable than the ideas of extension, figure, and motion affect us with. And it being too visibly absurd to hold, that pain or pleasure can be in an unperceiving substance, men are more easily weaned from believing the external existence of the secondary, than the primary qualities. You will be satisfied there is something in this, if you recollect the difference you made between an intense and more moderate degree of heat, allowing the one a real existence, while you denied it to the other. But after all, there is no rational ground for that distinction; for surely an indifferent sensation is as truly *a sensation*, as one more pleasing or painful ; and consequently should not any more than they be supposed to exist in an unthinking subject.

HYLAS. It is just come into my head, Philonous, that I have somewhere heard of a distinction between absolute and sensible extension. Now though it be acknowledged that *great* and *small*, consisting merely in the relation which other extended beings have to the parts of our own bodies, do not really inhere in the substances themselves; yet nothing obliges us to hold the same with regard to *absolute extension*,[1] which is something abstracted from *great* and *small*, from this or that particular magnitude or figure. So likewise as to motion, *swift* and *slow* are altogether relative to the succession of ideas in our own minds. But it doth not follow, because those modifications of motion exist not without the mind, that therefore absolute motion abstracted from them doth not.

PHILONOUS. Pray what is it that distinguishes one motion or one part of extension from another? Is it not something sensible, as some degree of swiftness or slowness, some certain magnitude or figure peculiar to each?

HYLAS. I think so.

PHILONOUS. These qualities therefore stripped of all sensible properties, are without all specific and numerical differences, as the Schools call them.

HYLAS. They are.

PHILONOUS. That is to say, they are extension in general, and motion in general.

HYLAS. Let it be so.

PHILONOUS. But it is an universally received maxim, that *everything which exists is particular*. How then can motion in general, or extension in general, exist in any corporeal substance?

HYLAS. I will take time to solve your difficulty.

PHILONOUS. But I think the point may be speedily decided. Without doubt you can tell whether you are able to frame this or that idea. Now I am content to put our dispute on this issue. If you can frame in your thoughts a distinct abstract idea of motion or extension, divested of all those sensible modes, as swift and slow, great and small, round and square, and the like, which are acknowledged to exist only in the mind, I will then

[1] [*Cf. Princ.*, Sects. 99, 111, 116, and *De Motu*, 53.—Ed.]

yield the point you contend for. But if you cannot, it will be unreasonable on your side to insist any longer upon what you have no notion of.

HYLAS. To confess ingenuously, I cannot.

PHILONOUS. Can you even separate the ideas of extension and motion from the ideas of all those qualities which they who make the distinction term *secondary*?

HYLAS. What! is it not an easy matter to consider extension and motion by themselves, abstracted from all other sensible qualities? Pray how do the mathematicians treat of them?

PHILONOUS. I acknowledge, Hylas, it is not difficult to form general propositions and reasonings about those qualities, without mentioning any other; and in this sense to consider or treat of them abstractedly. But how doth it follow that because I can pronounce the word *motion* by itself, I can form the idea of it in my mind exclusive of body? Or because theorems may be made of extension and figures, without any mention of *great* or *small*, or any other sensible mode or quality; that therefore it is possible such an abstract idea of extension, without any particular size or figure, or sensible quality, should be distinctly formed, and apprehended by the mind? Mathematicians treat of quantity, without regarding what other sensible qualities it is attended with, as being altogether indifferent to their demonstrations. But when, laying aside the words, they contemplate the bare ideas, I believe you will find they are not the pure abstracted ideas of extension.

HYLAS. But what say you to *pure intellect*? May not abstracted ideas be framed by that faculty?

PHILONOUS. Since I cannot frame abstract ideas at all, it is plain, I cannot frame them by the help of *pure intellect*, whatsoever faculty you understand by those words. Besides, not to inquire into the nature of pure intellect and its spiritual objects, as *virtue, reason, God,* or the like; thus much seems manifest, that sensible things are only to be perceived by sense, or represented by the imagination. Figures, therefore, and extension being originally perceived by sense, do not belong to pure intellect.[1] But for your farther satisfaction, try if you can frame the idea of any figure, abstracted from all particularities of size, or even from other sensible qualities.

HYLAS. Let me think a little—I do not find that I can.

PHILONOUS. And can you think it possible, that should really exist in Nature which implies a repugnancy in its conception?

HYLAS. By no means.

PHILONOUS. Since therefore it is impossible even for the mind to disunite the ideas of extension and motion from all other sensible qualities, doth it not follow, that where the one exist, there necessarily the other exist likewise?

HYLAS. It should seem so.

PHILONOUS. Consequently the very same arguments which you admitted, as conclusive against the secondary qualities, are without any farther application of force against the primary too. Besides, if you will trust your senses, is it not plain all sensible qualities coexist, or to them appear as being in the same place? Do they ever represent a motion, or figure, as being divested of all other visible and tangible qualities?

HYLAS. You need say no more on this head. I am free to own, if there be no secret error or oversight in our proceedings hitherto, that all sensible qualities are alike to be denied existence without the mind. But my fear is, that I have been too liberal in my former concessions,

---

[1] [This is the heart of Berkeley's denial of the possibility of abstract concepts of the sensory. The sensory can *only* be sensed or imagined. To think away its particularities is to think it away entirely.—ED.]

or overlooked some fallacy or other. In short, I did
not take time to think.

PHILONOUS. For that matter, Hylas, you may take what
time you please in reviewing the progress of our inquiry.
You are at liberty to recover any slips you might have
made, or offer whatever you have omitted, which
makes for your first opinion.

HYLAS. One great oversight I take to be this: that I did
not sufficiently distinguish the *object* from the *sensation*.
Now though this latter may not exist without the mind,
yet it will not thence follow that the former cannot.

PHILONOUS. What object do you mean? The object of the
senses?

HYLAS. The same.

PHILONOUS. It is then immediately perceived.

HYLAS. Right.

PHILONOUS. Make me to understand the difference
between what is immediately perceived, and a sensation.

HYLAS. The sensation I take to be an act of the mind
perceiving; beside which, there is something perceived;
and this I call the *object*. For example, there is red and
yellow on that tulip. But then the act of perceiving
those colours is in me only, and not in the tulip.

PHILONOUS. What tulip do you speak of? Is it that which
you see?

HYLAS. The same.

PHILONOUS. And what do you see beside colour, figure,
and extension?

HYLAS. Nothing.

PHILONOUS. What would you say then is, that the red and
yellow are coexistent with the extension; is it not?

HYLAS. That is not all; I would say, they have a real
existence without the mind, in some unthinking substance.

PHILONOUS. That the colours are really in the tulip which I see, is manifest. Neither can it be denied that this tulip may exist independent of your mind or mine; but that any immediate object of the senses, that is, any idea, or combination of ideas, should exist in an unthinking substance, or exterior to all minds, is in itself an evident contradiction. Nor can I imagine how this follows from what you said just now, to wit that the red and yellow were on the tulip *you saw*, since you do not pretend to *see* that unthinking substance.[1]

HYLAS. You have an artful way, Philonous, of diverting our inquiry from the subject.

PHILONOUS. I see you have no mind to be pressed that way. To return then to your distinction between *sensation* and *object*; if I take you right, you distinguish in every perception two things, the one an action of the mind, the other not.

HYLAS. True.

PHILONOUS. And this action cannot exist in, or belong to any unthinking thing; but whatever beside is implied in a perception, may.

HYLAS. That is my meaning.

PHILONOUS. So that if there was a perception without any act of the mind, it were possible such a perception should exist in an unthinking substance.

HYLAS. I grant it. But it is impossible there should be such a perception.

PHILONOUS. When is the mind said to be active?

HYLAS. When it produces, puts an end to, or changes anything.

---

[1] [Hylas is assuming that there are two tulips, one seen and a ' real ' one that is never seen. For Berkeley, a tulip beyond sense could not have the sensory qualities of a tulip, and therefore could not be a tulip. —Ed.]

PHILONOUS. Can the mind produce, discontinue, or change anything but by an act of the will?

HYLAS. It cannot.

PHILONOUS. The mind therefore is to be accounted active in its perceptions, so far forth as volition is included in them.

HYLAS. It is.

PHILONOUS. In plucking this flower, I am active, because I do it by the motion of my hand, which was consequent upon my volition; so likewise in applying it to my nose. But is either of these smelling?

HYLAS. No.

PHILONOUS. I act too in drawing the air through my nose; because my breathing so rather than otherwise, is the effect of my volition. But neither can this be called *smelling*: for if it were, I should smell every time I breathed in that manner.

HYLAS. True.

PHILONOUS. Smelling then is somewhat consequent to all this.

HYLAS. It is.

PHILONOUS. But I do not find my will concerned any farther. Whatever more there is, as that I perceive such a particular smell or any smell at all, this is independent of my will, and therein I am altogether passive. Do you find it otherwise with you, Hylas?

HYLAS. No, the very same.

PHILONOUS. Then as to seeing, is it not in your power to open your eyes, or keep them shut; to turn them this or that way?

HYLAS. Without doubt.

PHILONOUS. But doth it in like manner depend on your will, that in looking on this flower, you perceive *white* rather than any other colour? Or directing your open eyes toward yonder part of the heaven, can you avoid seeing the sun ? Or is light or darkness the effect of your volition ?

HYLAS. No certainly.

PHILONOUS. You are then in these respects altogether passive.

HYLAS. I am.

PHILONOUS. Tell me now, whether *seeing* consists in perceiving light and colours, or in opening and turning the eyes ?

HYLAS. Without doubt, in the former.

PHILONOUS. Since therefore you are in the very perception of light and colours altogether passive, what is become of that action you were speaking of, as an ingredient in every sensation ? And doth it not follow from your own concessions that the perception of light and colours, including no action in it, may exist in an unperceiving substance ? And is not this a plain contradiction ?

HYLAS. I know not what to think of it.

PHILONOUS. Besides, since you distinguish the *active* and *passive* in every perception, you must do it in that of pain. But how is it possible that pain, be it as little active as you please, should exist in an unperceiving substance ? In short, do but consider the point, and then confess ingenuously, whether light and colours, tastes, sounds, etc., are not all equally passions or sensations in the soul. You may indeed call them *external objects*, and give them in words what subsistence you please. But examine your own thoughts, and then tell me whether it be not as I say ?

HYLAS. I acknowledge, Philonous, that upon a fair observation of what passes in my mind, I can discover nothing else, but that I am a thinking being, affected with variety of sensations ; neither is it possible to conceive how a sensation should exist in an unperceiving substance. But then on the other hand, when I look on sensible things in a different view, considering them as so many modes and qualities, I find it necessary to suppose a material *substratum*, without which they cannot be conceived to exist.

PHILONOUS. *Material substratum* call you it? Pray, by which of your senses came you acquainted with that being?

HYLAS. It is not itself sensible; its modes and qualities only being perceived by the senses.

PHILONOUS. I presume then, it was by reflexion and reason you obtained the idea of it.

HYLAS. I do not pretend to any proper positive idea of it. However, I conclude it exists, because qualities cannot be conceived to exist without a support.

PHILONOUS. It seems then you have only a relative notion of it, or that you conceive it not otherwise than by conceiving the relation it bears to sensible qualities.

HYLAS. Right.

PHILONOUS. Be pleased therefore to let me know wherein that relation consists.

HYLAS. Is it not sufficiently expressed in the term *substratum*, or *substance*?

PHILONOUS. If so, the word *substratum* should import that it is spread under the sensible qualities or accidents.

HYLAS. True.

PHILONOUS. And consequently under extension.

HYLAS. I own it.

PHILONOUS. It is therefore somewhat in its own nature entirely distinct from extension.

HYLAS. I tell you, extension is only a mode, and matter is something that supports modes. And is it not evident the thing supported is different from the thing supporting?

PHILONOUS. So that something distinct from, and exclusive of extension, is supposed to be the *substratum* of extension.

HYLAS. Just so.

PHILONOUS. Answer me, Hylas. Can a thing be spread without extension? Or is not the idea of extension necessarily included in *spreading*?

HYLAS. It is.

PHILONOUS. Whatsoever therefore you suppose spread under anything, must have in itself an extension distinct from the extension of that thing under which it is spread.

HYLAS. It must.

PHILONOUS. Consequently every corporeal substance being the *substratum* of extension, must have in itself another extension by which it is qualified to be a *substratum* : and so on to infinity. And I ask whether this be not absurd in itself, and repugnant to what you granted just now, to wit, that the *substratum* was something distinct from, and exclusive of extension.

HYLAS. Ay but, Philonous, you take me wrong. I do not mean that matter is *spread* in a gross literal sense under extension. The word *substratum* is used only to express in general the same thing with *substance*.

PHILONOUS. Well then, let us examine the relation implied in the term *substance*. Is it not that it stands under accidents?

HYLAS. The very same.

PHILONOUS. But that one thing may stand under or support another, must it not be extended?

HYLAS. It must.

PHILONOUS. Is not therefore this supposition liable to the same absurdity with the former?

HYLAS. You still take things in a strict literal sense : that is not fair, Philonous.

PHILONOUS. I am not for imposing any sense on your words : you are at liberty to explain them as you please.

Only I beseech you, make me understand something by them. You tell me, matter supports or stands under accidents. How ! is it as your legs support your body ?

HYLAS. No ; that is the literal sense.

PHILONOUS. Pray let me know any sense, literal or not literal, that you understand it in.—— How long must I wait for an answer, Hylas ?

HYLAS. I declare I know not what to say. I once thought I understood well enough what was meant by matter's supporting accidents. But now the more I think on it, the less can I comprehend it; in short, I find that I know nothing of it.

PHILONOUS. It seems then you have no idea at all, neither relative nor positive, of matter ; you know neither what it is in itself, nor what relation it bears to accidents.

HYLAS. I acknowledge it.

PHILONOUS. And yet you asserted, that you could not conceive how qualities or accidents should really exist, without conceiving at the same time a material support of them.

HYLAS. I did.

PHILONOUS. That is to say, when you conceive the real existence of qualities, you do withal conceive something which you cannot conceive.

HYLAS. It was wrong, I own. But still I fear there is some fallacy or other. Pray what think you of this ? It is just come into my head, that the ground of all our mistakes lies in your treating of each quality by itself. Now, I grant that each quality cannot singly subsist without the mind. Colour cannot without extension, neither can figure without some other sensible quality. But as the several qualities united or blended together form entire sensible things, nothing hinders why such things may not be supposed to exist without the mind.

PHILONOUS. Either, Hylas, you are jesting, or have a very

bad memory. Though indeed we went through all the qualities by name one after another; yet my arguments, or rather your concessions, nowhere tended to prove that the secondary qualities did not subsist each alone by itself; but that they were not *at all* without the mind. Indeed in treating of figure and motion, we concluded they could not exist without the mind, because it was impossible even in thought to separate them from all secondary qualities, so as to conceive them existing by themselves. But then this was not the only argument made use of upon that occasion. But (to pass by all that hath been hitherto said, and reckon it for nothing, if you will have it so) I am content to put the whole upon this issue. If you can conceive it possible for any mixture or combination of qualities, or any sensible object whatever, to exist without the mind, then I will grant it actually to be so.

HYLAS. If it comes to that, the point will soon be decided. What more easy than to conceive a tree or house existing by itself, independent of, and unperceived by any mind whatsoever? I do at this present time conceive them existing after that manner.

PHILONOUS. How say you, Hylas, can you see a thing which is at the same time unseen?

HYLAS. No, that were a contradiction.

PHILONOUS. Is it not as great a contradiction to talk of *conceiving* a thing which is *unconceived?*

HYLAS. It is.

PHILONOUS. The tree or house therefore which you think of is conceived by you.

HYLAS. How should it be otherwise?

PHILONOUS. And what is conceived, is surely in the mind.

HYLAS. Without question, that which is conceived is in the mind.

PHILONOUS. How then came you to say, you conceived

a house or tree existing independent and out of all minds whatsoever?

HYLAS. That was, I own, an oversight; but stay, let me consider what led me into it. It is a pleasant mistake enough. As I was thinking of a tree in a solitary place, where no one was present to see it, methought that was to conceive a tree as existing unperceived or unthought of, not considering that I myself conceived it all the while. But now I plainly see, that all I can do is to frame ideas in my own mind. I may indeed conceive in my own thoughts the idea of a tree, or a house, or a mountain, but that is all. And this is far from proving that I can conceive them *existing out of the minds of all spirits*.[1]

PHILONOUS. You acknowledge then that you cannot possibly conceive how any one corporeal sensible thing should exist otherwise than in a mind.

HYLAS. I do.

PHILONOUS. And yet you will earnestly contend for the truth of that which you cannot so much as conceive.

HYLAS. I profess I know not what to think, but still there are some scruples remain with me. Is it not certain I see things at a distance?[2] Do we not perceive the stars and moon, for example, to be a great way off? Is not this, I say, manifest to the senses?

PHILONOUS. Do you not in a dream too perceive those or the like objects?

HYLAS. I do.

PHILONOUS. And have they not then the same appearance of being distant?

HYLAS. They have.

---

[1] [See the corresponding passage in *Princ.*, Sect. 23.—ED.]

[2] [See *Essay on Vision*, Sects. 1 ff. But note that in the dialogue Berkeley goes on to point out that even if ' outness ' were a visual datum, it would fall under the principle ' *esse* is *percipi* '.—ED.]

PHILONOUS. But you do not thence conclude the apparitions in a dream to be without the mind?

HYLAS. By no means.

PHILONOUS. You ought not therefore to conclude that sensible objects are without the mind, from their appearance or manner wherein they are perceived.

HYLAS. I acknowledge it. But doth not my sense deceive me in those cases?

PHILONOUS. By no means. The idea or thing which you immediately perceive, neither sense nor reason inform you that it actually exists without the mind. By sense you only know that you are affected with such certain sensations of light and colours, &c. And these you will not say are without the mind.

HYLAS. True: but beside all that, do you not think the sight suggests something of *outness* or *distance?*

PHILONOUS. Upon approaching a distant object, do the visible size and figure change perpetually, or do they appear the same at all distances?

HYLAS. They are in a continual change.

PHILONOUS. Sight therefore doth not suggest or any way inform you that the visible object you immediately perceive exists at a distance, or will be perceived when you advance farther onward, there being a continued series of visible objects succeeding each other, during the whole time of your approach.

HYLAS. It doth not; but still I know, upon seeing an object, what object I shall perceive after having passed over a certain distance: no matter whether it be exactly the same or no: there is still something of distance suggested in the case.

PHILONOUS. Good Hylas, do but reflect a little on the point, and then tell me whether there be any more in it than this. From the ideas you actually perceive by sight, you have by experience learned to collect what other

ideas you will (according to the standing order of Nature)
be affected with, after such a certain succession of time
and motion.

HYLAS.   Upon the whole, I take it to be nothing else.

PHILONOUS.   Now is it not plain, that if we suppose a man
born blind was on a sudden made to see, he could at
first have no experience of what may be suggested
by sight.

HYLAS.   It is.

PHILONOUS.   He would not then according to you have
any notion of distance annexed to the things he saw;
but would take them for a new set of sensations existing
only in his mind.

HYLAS.   It is undeniable.

PHILONOUS.   But to make it still more plain: is not
distance a line turned endwise to the eye?

HYLAS.   It is.

PHILONOUS.   And can a line so situated be perceived by
sight?

HYLAS.   It cannot.

PHILONOUS.   Doth it not therefore follow that distance is
not properly and immediately perceived by sight?

HYLAS.   It should seem so.

PHILONOUS.   Again, is it your opinion that colours are at a
distance?

HYLAS.   It must be acknowledged, they are only in the
mind.

PHILONOUS.   But do not colours appear to the eye as
coexisting in the same place with extension and figures?

HYLAS.   They do.

PHILONOUS.   How can you then conclude from sight that
figures exist without, when you acknowledge colours do
not; the sensible appearance being the very same with
regard to both?

HYLAS.   I know not what to answer.

PHILONOUS. But allowing that distance was truly and immediately perceived by the mind, yet it would not thence follow it existed out of the mind. For whatever is immediately perceived is an idea; and can any *idea* exist out of the mind?

HYLAS. To suppose that were absurd: but inform me, Philonous, can we perceive or know nothing beside our ideas?

PHILONOUS. As for the rational deducing of causes from effects, that is beside our inquiry.[1] And by the senses you can best tell whether you perceive any thing which is not immediately perceived. And I ask you, whether the things immediately perceived are other than your own sensations or ideas? You have indeed more than once, in the course of this conversation, declared yourself on those points; but you seem by this last question to have departed from what you then thought.

HYLAS. To speak the truth, Philonous, I think there are two kinds of objects, the one perceived immediately, which are likewise called *ideas;* the other are real things or external objects perceived by the mediation of ideas, which are their images and representations. Now I own, ideas do not exist without the mind; but the latter sort of objects do. I am sorry I did not think of this distinction sooner; it would probably have cut short your discourse.

PHILONOUS. Are those external objects perceived by sense, or by some other faculty?

HYLAS. They are perceived by sense.

PHILONOUS. How! is there anything perceived by sense, which is not immediately perceived?

HYLAS. Yes, Philonous, in some sort there is. For

[5] [*I.e.*, in this first dialogue.—ED.]

example, when I look on a picture or statue of Julius Cæsar, I may be said after a manner to perceive him (though not immediately) by my senses.

PHILONOUS. It seems then, you will have our ideas, which alone are immediately perceived, to be pictures of external things: and that these also are perceived by sense, inasmuch as they have a conformity or resemblance to our ideas.

HYLAS. That is my meaning.

PHILONOUS. And in the same way that Julius Cæsar, in himself invisible, is nevertheless perceived by sight; real things in themselves imperceptible are perceived by sense.

HYLAS. In the very same.

PHILONOUS. Tell me, Hylas, when you behold the picture of Julius Cæsar, do you see with your eyes any more than some colours and figures with a certain symmetry and composition of the whole?

HYLAS. Nothing else.

PHILONOUS. And would not a man, who had never known anything of Julius Cæsar, see as much?

HYLAS. He would.

PHILONOUS. Consequently he hath his sight, and the use of it, in as perfect a degree as you.

HYLAS. I agree with you.

PHILONOUS. Whence comes it then that your thoughts are directed to the Roman Emperor, and his are not? This cannot proceed from the sensations or ideas of sense by you then perceived; since you acknowledge you have no advantage over him in that respect. It should seem therefore to proceed from reason and memory: should it not?

HYLAS. It should.

PHILONOUS. Consequently it will not follow from that instance, that anything is perceived by sense which is not immediately perceived. Though I grant we may in one acceptation be said to perceive sensible things mediately by sense: that is, when from a frequently perceived connexion, the immediate perception of ideas by one sense suggests to the mind others perhaps belonging to another sense, which are wont to be connected with them. For instance, when I hear a coach drive along the streets, immediately I perceive only the sound; but from the experience I have had that such a sound is connected with a coach, I am said to hear the coach. It is nevertheless evident, that in truth and strictness, nothing can be *heard* but *sound :* and the coach is not then properly perceived by sense, but suggested from experience. So likewise when we are said to see a red-hot bar of iron; the solidity and heat of the iron are not the objects of sight, but suggested to the imagination by the colour and figure, which are properly perceived by that sense. In short, those things alone are actually and strictly perceived by any sense, which would have been perceived, in case that same sense had then been first conferred on us. As for other things, it is plain they are only suggested to the mind by experience grounded on former perceptions. But to return to your comparison of Cæsar's picture, it is plain, if you keep to that, you must hold the real things or archetypes of our ideas are not perceived by sense, but by some internal faculty of the soul, as reason or memory. I would therefore fain know, what arguments you can draw from reason for the existence of what you call *real things* or *material objects*. Or whether you re-member to have seen them formerly as they are in them-selves? Or if you have heard or read of anyone that did?

HYLAS. I see, Philonous, you are disposed to raillery; but that will never convince me.

PHILONOUS. My aim is only to learn from you the way to come at the knowledge of *material beings*. Whatever we perceive, is perceived either immediately or mediately: by sense, or by reason and reflexion. But as you have excluded sense, pray show me what reason you have to believe their existence; or what *medium* you can possibly make use of, to prove it either to mine or your own understanding.

HYLAS. To deal ingenuously, Philonous, now I consider the point, I do not find I can give you any good reason for it. But thus much seems pretty plain, that it is at least possible such things may really exist. And as long as there is no absurdity in supposing them, I am resolved to believe as I did, till you bring good reasons to the contrary.

PHILONOUS. What! is it come to this, that you only believe the existence of material objects, and that your belief is founded barely on the possibility of its being true? Then you will have me bring reasons against it: though another would think it reasonable, the proof should lie on him who holds the affirmative. And after all, this very point which you are now resolved to maintain without any reason, is in effect what you have more than once during this discourse seen good reason to give up. But to pass over all this; if I understand you rightly, you say our ideas do not exist without the mind; but that they are copies, images, or representations of certain originals that do.

HYLAS. You take me right.

PHILONOUS. They are then like external things.

HYLAS. They are.

PHILONOUS. Have those things a stable and permanent nature independent of our senses; or are they in a perpetual change, upon our producing any motions in our bodies, suspending, exerting, or altering our faculties or organs of sense ?

HYLAS. Real things, it is plain, have a fixed and real nature, which remains the same, notwithstanding any change in our senses, or in the posture and motion of our bodies ; which indeed may affect the ideas in our minds, but it were absurd to think they had the same effect on things existing without the mind.

PHILONOUS. How then is it possible, that things perpetually fleeting and variable as our ideas, should be copies or images of anything fixed and constant ? Or in other words, since all sensible qualities, as size, figure, colour, etc., that is, our ideas, are continually changing upon every alteration in the distance, medium, or instruments of sensation ; how can any determinate material objects be properly represented or painted forth by several distinct things, each of which is so different from and unlike the rest ? Or if you say it resembles some one only of our ideas, how shall we be able to distinguish the true copy from all the false ones ?

HYLAS. I profess, Philonous, I am at a loss. I know not what to say to this.

PHILONOUS. But neither is this all. Which are material objects in themselves, perceptible or imperceptible ?

HYLAS. Properly and immediately nothing can be perceived but ideas. All material things therefore are in themselves insensible, and to be perceived only by their ideas.

PHILONOUS. Ideas then are sensible, and their archetypes or originals insensible.

HYLAS. Right.

PHILONOUS. But how can that which is sensible be like that which is insensible ? Can a real thing in itself *invisible* be like a *colour* ; or a real thing which is not *audible*, be like a *sound* ? In a word, can anything be like a sensation or idea, but another sensation or idea ?

HYLAS. I must own, I think not.

PHILONOUS. Is it possible there should be any doubt in the point? Do you not perfectly know your own ideas?

HYLAS. I know them perfectly; since what I do not perceive or know, can be no part of my idea.

PHILONOUS. Consider therefore, and examine them, and then tell me if there be anything in them which can exist without the mind: or if you can conceive anything like them existing without the mind.

HYLAS. Upon inquiry, I find it is impossible for me to conceive or understand how anything but an idea can be like an idea. And it is most evident that *no idea can exist without the mind.*

PHILONOUS. You are therefore by your principles forced to deny the reality of sensible things, since you made it to consist in an absolute existence exterior to the mind. That is to say, you are a downright *sceptic.* So I have gained my point, which was to show your principles led to scepticism.

HYLAS. For the present I am, if not entirely convinced, at least silenced.

PHILONOUS. I would fain know what more you would require in order to a perfect conviction. Have you not had the liberty of explaining yourself all manner of ways? Were any little slips in discourse laid hold and insisted on? Or were you not allowed to retract or reinforce anything you had offered, as best served your purpose? Hath not everything you could say been heard and examined with all the fairness imaginable? In a word, have you not in every point been convinced out of your own mouth? And if you can at present discover any flaw in any of your former concessions, or think of any remaining subterfuge, any new distinction, colour, or comment whatsoever, why do you not produce it? . . .

THE SECOND DIALOGUE

... HYLAS. I own there is a great deal in what you say. Nor can anyone be more entirely satisfied of the truth of those odd consequences, so long as I have in view the reasonings that lead to them. But when these are out of my thoughts, there seems on the other hand something so satisfactory, so natural and intelligible in the modern way of explaining things, that I profess I know not how to reject it.

PHILONOUS. I know not what way you mean.

HYLAS. I mean the way of accounting for our sensations or ideas.

PHILONOUS. How is that?

HYLAS. It is supposed the soul makes her residence in some part of the brain, from which the nerves take their rise, and are thence extended to all parts of the body: and that outward objects by the different impressions they make on the organs of sense, communicate certain vibrative motions to the nerves; and these being filled with spirits, propagate them to the brain or seat of the soul, which according to the various impressions or traces thereby made in the brain, is variously affected with ideas.

PHILONOUS. And call you this an explication of the manner whereby we are affected with ideas?

HYLAS. Why not, Philonous, have you anything to object against it?

PHILONOUS. I would first know whether I rightly understand your hypothesis. You make certain traces in the brain to be the causes or occasions of our ideas. Pray tell me, whether by the *brain* you mean any sensible thing?

HYLAS. What else think you I could mean?

PHILONOUS. Sensible things are all immediately perceivable; and those things which are immediately perceivable are ideas; and these exist only in the mind. Thus much you have, if I mistake not, long since agreed to.

HYLAS. I do not deny it.

PHILONOUS. The brain therefore you speak of, being a sensible thing, exists only in the mind. Now, I would fain know whether you think it reasonable to suppose, that one idea or thing existing in the mind, occasions all other ideas. And if you think so, pray how do you account for the origin of that primary idea or brain itself?

HYLAS. I do not explain the origin of our ideas by that brain which is perceivable to sense, this being itself only a combination of sensible ideas, but by another which I imagine.

PHILONOUS. But are not things imagined as truly in the mind as things perceived?

HYLAS. I must confess they are.

PHILONOUS. It comes therefore to the same thing; and you have been all this while accounting for ideas, by certain motions or impressions in the brain, that is, by some alterations in an idea, whether sensible or imaginable it matters not.

HYLAS. I begin to suspect my hypothesis.

PHILONOUS. Beside spirits, all that we know or conceive are our own ideas. When therefore you say, all ideas are occasioned by impressions in the brain, do you conceive this brain or no? If you do, then you talk of ideas imprinted in an idea, causing that same idea, which is absurd. If you do not conceive it, you talk unintelligibly, instead of forming a reasonable hypothesis.

HYLAS. I now clearly see it was a mere dream. There is nothing in it.

PHILONOUS. You need not be much concerned at it: for after all, this way of explaining things, as you called it, could never have satisfied any reasonable man. What connexion is there between a motion in the nerves, and the sensations of sound or colour in the mind? Or how is it possible these should be the effect of that?

HYLAS. But I could never think it had so little in it, as now it seems to have.

PHILONOUS. Well then, are you at length satisfied that no sensible things have a real existence; and that you are in truth an arrant *sceptic?*

HYLAS. It is too plain to be denied. . . My comfort is, you are as much a *sceptic* as I am.

PHILONOUS. There Hylas, I must beg leave to differ from you.

HYLAS. What! have you all along agreed to the premises, and do you now deny the conclusion, and leave me to maintain those paradoxes by myself which you led me into? This surely is not fair.

PHILONOUS. I deny that I agreed with you in those notions that led to scepticism. You indeed said, the reality of sensible things consisted in an *absolute existence* out of the minds of spirits, or distinct from their being perceived. And pursuant to this notion of reality, you are obliged to deny sensible things any real existence: that is, according to your own definition, you profess yourself a *sceptic*. But I neither said nor thought the reality of sensible things was to be defined after that manner. To me it is evident, for the reasons you allow of, that sensible things cannot exist otherwise than in a mind or spirit. Whence I conclude, not that they have no real existence, but that seeing they depend not on my thought, and have an existence distinct from being perceived by me, *there must be some other mind wherein they exist.* As sure therefore as the sensible world really exists, so sure is there an infinite omnipresent spirit who contains and supports it.

HYLAS. What ! this is no more than I and all Christians hold; nay, and all others too who believe there is a God and that he knows and comprehends all things.

PHILONOUS. Ay, but here lies the difference. Men commonly believe that all things are known or perceived by God, because they believe the being of a God, whereas I on the other side immediately and necessarily conclude the being of a God, because all sensible things must be perceived by him.

HYLAS. But so long as we all believe the same thing, what matter is it how we come by that belief ?

PHILONOUS. But neither do we agree in the same opinion. For philosophers, though they acknowledge all corporeal beings to be perceived by God, yet they attribute to them an absolute subsistence distinct from their being perceived by any mind whatever, which I do not. Besides, is there no difference between saying, *there is a God, therefore he perceives all things*: and saying, *sensible things do really exist: and if they really exist, they are necessarily perceived by an infinite mind : therefore there is an infinite mind, or God.* This furnishes you with a direct and immediate demonstration, from a most evident principle, of the *being of a God.* Divines and philosophers had proved beyond all controversy, from the beauty and usefulness of the several parts of the creation, that it was the workmanship of God. But that setting aside all help of astronomy and natural philosophy, all contemplation of the contrivance, order, and adjustment of things, an infinite mind should be necessarily inferred from the bare existence of the sensible world, is an advantage peculiar to them only who have made this easy reflexion : that the sensible world is that which we perceive by our several senses; and that nothing is perceived by the senses beside ideas ; and that no idea or archetype of an idea can exist otherwise than in a mind. You may now, without any laborious search into the sciences, without any subtlety of reason, or tedious length of discourse, oppose and baffle the most strenuous advocate for atheism. Those miserable refuges, whether in an eternal succession of unthinking causes and effects, or in a fortuitous concourse of atoms ; those wild imaginations of Vanini, Hobbes, and Spinoza ; in a word the whole system of atheism : is it not entirely overthrown by this single reflexion on the repugnancy included in supposing the whole, or any part, even the most rude and shapeless, of the visible world, to exist without a mind ? Let any one of those abettors of impiety but look into his own thoughts, and there try if he can conceive how so much as a rock, a desert, a chaos, or confused jumble of atoms, how anything at all, either sensible or imaginable, can exist independent of a mind; and he need go no farther to be convinced of his folly. Can anything be fairer than to put a dispute on such an issue, and leave it to a man himself to see if he can conceive, even in thought, what he holds to be true in fact, and from a notional to allow it a real existence ?

HYLAS. It cannot be denied, there is something highly serviceable to religion in what you advance. But do you not think it looks very like a notion entertained by some eminent moderns, of *seeing all things in God ?*

PHILONOUS. I would gladly know that opinion ; pray explain it to me.

HYLAS. They conceive that the soul, being immaterial, is incapable of being united with material things, so as to perceive them in themselves, but that she perceives them by her union with the substance of God, which being spiritual is therefore purely intelligible, or capable of being the immediate object of a spirit's thought. Besides, the divine essence contains in it perfections correspondent to each created being; and which are for that reason proper to exhibit or represent them to the mind.

PHILONOUS. I do not understand how our ideas, which are things altogether passive and inert, can be the essence, or any part (or like any part) of the essence or substance of God, who is an impassive, indivisible, purely active being. Many more difficulties and objections there are, which occur at first view against this hypothesis; but I shall only add that it is liable to all the absurdities of the common hypotheses, in making a created world exist otherwise than in the mind of a spirit. Beside all which it hath this peculiar to itself; that it makes that material world serve to no purpose. And if it pass for a good argument against other hypotheses in the sciences, that they suppose Nature or the divine wisdom to make something in vain, or do that by tedious roundabout methods, which might have been performed in a much more easy and compendious way, what shall we think of that hypothesis which supposes the whole world made in vain?

HYLAS. But what say you, are not you too of opinion that we see all things in God? If I mistake not, what you advance comes near it.

PHILONOUS. Few men think, yet all will have opinions. Hence men's opinions are superficial and confused. It is nothing strange that tenets which in themselves are ever so different should nevertheless be confounded with each other by those who do not consider them attentively. I shall not therefore be surprised, if some men imagine that I run into the enthusiasm of Malebranche, though in truth I am very remote from it. He builds on the most abstract general ideas, which I entirely disclaim.

He asserts an absolute external world, which I deny. He maintains that we are deceived by our senses, and know not the real natures or the true forms and figures of extended beings; of all which I hold the direct contrary. So that upon the whole there are no principles more fundamentally opposite than his and mine. It must be owned I entirely agree with what the holy Scripture saith, *that in God we live, and move, and have our being.* But that we see things in his essence after the manner above set forth, I am far from believing. Take here in brief my meaning. It is evident that the things I perceive are my own ideas, and that no idea can exist unless it be in a mind. Nor is it less plain that these ideas or things by me perceived, either themselves or their archetypes, exist independently of my mind, since I know myself not to be their author, it being out of my power to determine at pleasure, what particular ideas I shall be affected with upon opening my eyes or ears. They must therefore exist in some other mind, whose will it is they should be exhibited to me. The things, I say, immediately perceived, are ideas or sensations, call them which you will. But how can any idea or sensation exist in, or be produced by, anything but a mind or spirit? This indeed is inconceivable; and to assert that which is inconceivable, is to talk nonsense: is it not?

HYLAS. Without doubt.

PHILONOUS. But on the other hand, it is very conceivable that they should exist in, and be produced by, a spirit; since this is no more than I daily experience in myself, inasmuch as I perceive numberless ideas; and by an act of my will can form a great variety of them, and raise them up in my imagination: though it must be confessed, these creatures of the fancy are not altogether so distinct, so strong, vivid, and permanent, as those perceived by my senses, which latter are called *real things*. From all which I conclude, *there is a mind which affects me every moment with all the sensible impressions I perceive.* And from the variety, order, and manner of these, I conclude the Author of them to be *wise, powerful, and good, beyond comprehension.* Mark it well: I do not say, I see things by perceiving that which represents them in the intelligible substance of God. This I do not understand; but I say, the things by me perceived are known by the understanding, and produced by the will, of an infinite spirit. And is not all this most plain and evident? Is there any more in it, than what a little observation of our own minds and that which passes in them not only enableth us to conceive, but also obligeth us to acknowledge?

HYLAS. I think I understand you very clearly; and own the proof you give of a Deity seems no less evident, than it is surprising. But allowing that God is the Supreme and Universal Cause of all things, yet may not there be still a third nature besides spirits and ideas? May we not admit a subordinate and limited cause of our ideas? In a word, may there not for all that be *matter?*

PHILONOUS. How often must I inculcate the same thing? You allow the things immediately perceived by sense to exist nowhere without the mind: but there is nothing perceived by sense, which is not perceived immediately: therefore there is nothing sensible that exists without the mind. The matter therefore which you still insist on, is something intelligible, I suppose; something that may be discovered by reason, and not by sense.

HYLAS. You are in the right.

PHILONOUS. Pray let me know what reasoning your belief

of matter is grounded on; and what this matter is in your present sense of it.

HYLAS. I find myself affected with various ideas, whereof I know I am not the cause; neither are they the cause of themselves, or of one another, or capable of subsisting by themselves, as being altogether inactive, fleeting, dependent beings. They have therefore some cause distinct from me and them: of which I pretend to know no more, than that it is *the cause of my ideas*. And this thing, whatever it be, I call matter.

PHILONOUS. Tell me, Hylas, hath every one a liberty to change the current proper signification annexed to a common name in any language? For example, suppose a traveller should tell you, that in a certain country men might pass unhurt through the fire; and, upon explaining himself, you found he meant by the word *fire* that which others call *water* : or if he should assert there are trees which walk upon two legs, meaning men by the term *trees*. Would you think this reasonable?

HYLAS. No; I should think it very absurd. Common custom is the standard of propriety in language. And for any man to affect speaking improperly, is to pervert the use of speech, and can never serve to a better purpose than to protract and multiply disputes where there is no difference in opinion.

PHILONOUS. And doth not *matter*, in the common current acceptation of the word, signify an extended, solid, movable, unthinking, inactive substance?

HYLAS. It doth.

PHILONOUS. And hath it not been made evident, that no such substance can possibly exist? And though it should be allowed to exist, yet how can that which is *inactive* be a *cause ;* or that which is *unthinking* be a *cause of thought ?* You may indeed, if you please, annex to the word *matter* a contrary meaning to what is vulgarly received ; and tell me you understand by it an unextended, thinking, active being, which is the cause of our ideas. But what else is this, than to play with words, and run into that very fault you just now condemned with so much reason ? I do by no means find fault with your reasoning, in that you collect a cause from the phenomena : but I deny that the cause deducible by reason can properly be termed *matter*.

HYLAS. There is indeed something in what you say. But I am afraid you do not thoroughly comprehend my meaning. I would by no means be thought to deny that God or an Infinite Spirit is the supreme cause of all things. All I contend for is that subordinate to the supreme agent there is a cause of a limited and inferior nature, which concurs in the production of our ideas, not by any act of will or spiritual efficiency, but by that kind of action which belongs to matter, viz. *motion*.

PHILONOUS. I find you are at every turn relapsing into your old exploded conceit, of a movable and consequently an extended substance existing without the mind. What ! Have you already forgot you were convinced, or are you willing I should repeat what has been said on that head ? In truth this is not fair dealing in you, still to suppose the being of that which you have so often acknowledged to have no being. But not to insist farther on what has been so largely handled, I ask whether all your ideas are not perfectly passive and inert, including nothing of action in them ?

HYLAS. They are.

PHILONOUS. And are sensible qualities anything else but ideas ?

HYLAS. How often have I acknowledged that they are not ?

PHILONOUS. But is not motion a sensible quality ?

HYLAS. It is.

PHILONOUS. Consequently it is no action.

HYLAS. I agree with you. And indeed it is very plain, that when I stir my finger, it remains passive ; but my will which produced the motion is active.

PHILONOUS. Now I desire to know in the first place, whether motion being allowed to be no action, you can conceive any action besides volition : and in the second place, whether to say something and conceive nothing be not to talk nonsense : and lastly, whether having considered the premises, you do not perceive that to suppose any efficient or active cause of our ideas, other than *spirit*, is highly absurd and unreasonable ?

HYLAS. I give up the point entirely. But though matter may not be a cause, yet what hinders its being an *instrument* subservient to the supreme agent in the production of our ideas ?

PHILONOUS. An instrument, say you ; pray what may be the figure, springs, wheels, and motions of that instrument ?

HYLAS. Those I pretend to determine nothing of, both the substance and its qualities being entirely unknown to me.

PHILONOUS. What ? You are then of opinion, it is made up of unknown parts, that it hath unknown motions, and an unknown shape.

HYLAS. I do not believe it hath any figure or motion at all, being already convinced, that no sensible qualities can exist in an unperceiving substance.

PHILONOUS. But what notion is it possible to frame of an instrument void of all sensible qualities, even extension itself ?

HYLAS. I do not pretend to have any notion of it.

PHILONOUS. And what reason have you to think, this unknown, this inconceivable somewhat doth exist ? Is it that you imagine God cannot act as well without it, or that you find by experience the use of some such thing, when you form ideas in your own mind ?

HYLAS. You are always teasing me for reasons of my belief. Pray, what reasons have you not to believe it?

PHILONOUS. It is to me a sufficient reason not to believe the existence of anything, if I see no reason for believing it. But not to insist on reasons for believing, you will not so much as let me know what it is you would have me believe, since you say you have no manner of notion of it. After all, let me entreat you to consider whether it be like a philosopher, or even like a man of common sense, to pretend to believe you know not what, and you know not why.

HYLAS. Hold, Philonous. When I tell you matter is an *instrument*, I do not mean altogether nothing. It is true, I know not the particular kind of instrument; but however I have some notion of *instrument in general*, which I apply to it.

PHILONOUS. But what if it should prove that there is something, even in the most general notion of *instrument*, as taken in a distinct sense from *cause*, which makes the use of it inconsistent with the divine attributes?

HYLAS. Make that appear, and I shall give up the point.

PHILONOUS. What mean you by the general nature or notion of *instrument*?

HYLAS. That which is common to all particular instruments, composeth the general notion.

PHILONOUS. Is it not common to all instruments, that they are applied to the doing those things only, which cannot be performed by the mere act of our wills? Thus for instance, I never use an instrument to move my finger, because it is done by a volition. But I should use one, if I were to remove part of a rock, or tear up a tree by the roots. Are you of the same mind? Or can you show any example where an instrument is made use of in producing an effect immediately depending on the will of the agent?

HYLAS. I own I cannot.

PHILONOUS. How therefore can you suppose that an all-perfect spirit, on whose will all things have an absolute and immediate dependence, should need an instrument in his operations, or not needing it make use of it? Thus it seems to me that you are obliged to own the use of a lifeless inactive instrument to be incompatible with the infinite perfection of God; that is, by your own confession, to give up the point.

HYLAS. It doth not readily occur what I can answer you.

PHILONOUS. But methinks you should be ready to own the truth, when it hath been fairly proved to you. We indeed, who are beings of finite powers, are forced to make use of instruments. And the use of an instrument showeth the agent to be limited by rules of another's prescription, and that he cannot obtain his end, but in such a way and by such conditions. Whence it seems a clear consequence, that the supreme unlimited agent useth no tool or instrument at all. The will of an omnipotent spirit is no sooner exerted than executed, without the application of means, which, if they are employed by inferior agents, it is not upon account of any real efficacy that is in them, or necessary aptitude to produce any effect, but merely in compliance with the Laws of Nature, or those conditions prescribed to them by the first cause, who is himself above all limitation or prescription whatsoever.

HYLAS. I will no longer maintain that matter is an instrument. However, I would not be understood to give up its existence neither; since, notwithstanding what hath been said, it may still be an *occasion*.

PHILONOUS. How many shapes is your matter to take? Or how often must it be proved not to exist, before you are content to part with it? But to say no more of this (though by all the laws of disputation I may justly blame you for so frequently changing the signification of the principal term) I would fain know what you mean by affirming that matter is an occasion, having already denied it to be a cause. And when you have shown in what sense you understand *occasion*, pray in the next place be pleased to show me what reason induceth you to believe there is such an occasion of our ideas.

HYLAS. As to the first point: by *occasion* I mean an inactive unthinking being, at the presence whereof God excites ideas in our minds.

PHILONOUS. And what may be the nature of that inactive unthinking being?

HYLAS. I know nothing of its nature.

PHILONOUS. Proceed then to the second point, and assign some reason why we should allow an existence to this inactive, unthinking, unknown thing.

HYLAS. When we see ideas produced in our minds after an orderly and constant manner, it is natural to think they have some fixed and regular occasions, at the presence of which they are excited.

PHILONOUS. You acknowledge then God alone to be the cause of our ideas, and that he causes them at the presence of those occasions.

HYLAS. That is my opinion.

PHILONOUS. Those things which you say are present to God, without doubt he perceives.

HYLAS. Certainly; otherwise they could not be to him an occasion of acting.

PHILONOUS. Not to insist now on your making sense of this hypothesis, or answering all the puzzling questions and difficulties it is liable to: I only ask whether the order and regularity observable in the series of our ideas, or the course of Nature, be not sufficiently accounted for by the wisdom and power of God; and whether it doth not derogate from those attributes, to suppose he is influenced, directed, or put in mind, when and what he is to act, by any unthinking substance. And lastly whether, in case I granted all you contend for, it would make anything to your purpose, it not being easy to conceive how the external or absolute existence of an unthinking substance, distinct from its being perceived, can be inferred from my allowing that there are certain things perceived by the mind of God, which are to him the occasion of producing ideas in us.

HYLAS. I am perfectly at a loss what to think, this notion of *occasion* seeming now altogether as groundless as the rest.

PHILONOUS. Do you not at length perceive, that in all these different acceptations of *matter*, you have been only supposing you know not what, for no manner of reason, and to no kind of use ? . . .

HYLAS. The reality of things cannot be maintained without supposing the existence of matter. And is not this, think you, a good reason why I should be earnest in its defence ?

PHILONOUS. The reality of things ! What things, sensible or intelligible ?

HYLAS. Sensible things.

PHILONOUS. My glove, for instance.

HYLAS. That or any other thing perceived by the senses.

PHILONOUS. But to fix on some particular thing; is it not a sufficient evidence to me of the existence of this *glove*, that I see it, and feel it, and wear it ? Or if this will not do, how is it possible I should be assured of the reality of this thing, which I actually see in this place, by supposing that some unknown thing which I never did or can see, exists after an unknown manner, in an unknown place, or in no place at all ? How can the supposed reality of that which is intangible, be a proof that anything tangible really exists ? or of that

which is invisible, that any visible thing, or in general
of anything which is imperceptible, that a perceptible
exists? Do but explain this, and I shall think nothing
too hard for you.

HYLAS. Upon the whole I am content to own the existence
of matter is highly improbable; but the direct and
absolute impossibility of it does not appear to me.

PHILONOUS. But granting matter to be possible, yet upon
that account merely it can have no more claim to existence than a golden mountain or a centaur.

HYLAS. I acknowledge it; but still you do not deny it is
possible; and that which is possible, for aught you know,
may actually exist.

PHILONOUS. I deny it to be possible; and have, if I
mistake not, evidently proved from your own concessions
that it is not. In the common sense of the word *matter*, is
there any more implied, than an extended, solid, figured,
movable substance existing without the mind? And
have not you acknowledged over and over, that you have
seen evident reason for denying the possibility of such a
substance?

HYLAS. True, but that is only one sense of the term *matter*.

PHILONOUS. But is it not the only proper genuine received
sense? And if matter in such a sense be proved impossible, may it not be thought with good grounds
absolutely impossible? Else how could anything be
proved impossible? Or indeed how could there be
any proof at all one way or other, to a man who
takes the liberty to unsettle and change the common
signification of words? . . .

. . . HYLAS. . . . *Material substance* was no more than an hypothesis, and a false and groundless one too. I will no longer spend my breath in defence of it. But whatever hypothesis you advance, or whatsoever scheme of things you introduce in its stead, I doubt not it will appear every whit as false : let me but be allowed to question you upon it. That is, suffer me to serve you in your own kind, and I warrant it shall conduct you through as many perplexities and contradictions, to the very same state of scepticism that I myself am in at present.

PHILONOUS. I assure you, Hylas, I do not pretend to frame any hypothesis at all. I am of a vulgar cast, simple enough to believe my senses, and leave things as I find them. To be plain, it is my opinion that the real things are those very things I see and feel, and perceive by my senses. These I know, and finding they answer all the necessities and purposes of life, have no reason to be solicitous about any other unknown beings. A piece of sensible bread, for instance, would stay my stomach better than ten thousand times as much of that insensible, unintelligible, real bread you speak of. It is likewise my opinion that colours and other sensible qualities are on the objects. I cannot for my life help thinking that snow is white, and fire hot. You indeed, who by *snow* and *fire* mean certain external, unperceived, unperceiving substances, are in the right to deny whiteness or heat to be affections inherent in them. But I, who understand by those words the things I see and feel, am obliged to think like other folks. And as I am no sceptic with regard to the nature of things, so neither am I as to their existence. That a thing should be really perceived by my senses, and at the same time not really exist, is to me a plain contradiction; since I cannot prescind or abstract, even in thought, the existence of a sensible thing from its being perceived. Wood, stones, fire, water, flesh, iron, and the like things, which I name and discourse of, are things that I know. And I should not have known them, but that I perceived them by my senses; and things perceived by the senses are immediately perceived; and things immediately perceived are ideas; and ideas cannot exist without the mind; their existence therefore consists in being perceived; when therefore they are actually perceived, there can be no doubt of their existence. Away then with all that scepticism, all those ridiculous philosophical doubts. What a jest is it for a philosopher to question the existence of sensible things, till he hath it proved to him from the veracity of God; or to pretend our knowledge in this point falls short of intuition or demonstration! I might as well doubt of my own being as of the being of those things I actually see and feel.

HYLAS. Not so fast, Philonous: you say you cannot conceive how sensible things should exist without the mind. Do you not?

PHILONOUS. I do.

HYLAS. Supposing you were annihilated, cannot you conceive it possible, that things perceivable by sense may still exist?

PHILONOUS. I can; but then it must be in another mind. When I deny sensible things an existence out of the mind, I do not mean my mind in particular, but all minds. Now it is plain they have an existence exterior to my mind, since I find them by experience to be independent of it. There is therefore some other mind wherein they exist, during the intervals between the times of my perceiving them: as likewise they did before my birth, and would do after my supposed annihilation. And as the same is true, with regard to all other finite created spirits; it necessarily follows, there is an *omnipresent eternal Mind*, which knows and comprehends all things and exhibits them to our view in such a manner, and according to such rules as he himself hath ordained, and are by us termed the *Laws of Nature*.

HYLAS. Answer me, Philonous. Are all our ideas perfectly inert beings? Or have they any agency included in them?

PHILONOUS. They are altogether passive and inert.

HYLAS. And is not God an agent, a being purely active?

PHILONOUS. I acknowledge it.

HYLAS. No idea therefore can be like unto, or represent the nature of God.

PHILONOUS. It cannot.

HYLAS. Since therefore you have no idea of the mind of God, how can you conceive it possible, that things should exist in his mind? Or, if you can conceive the mind of God without having an idea of it, why may not I not be allowed to conceive the existence of matter, notwithstanding that I have no idea of it?

PHILONOUS. As to your first question: I own I have properly no idea, either of God or any other spirit; for these being active, cannot be represented by things perfectly inert, as our ideas are. I do nevertheless know that I who am a spirit or thinking substance, exist as certainly as I know my ideas exist. Farther, I know what I mean by the terms *I* and *myself*; and I know this immediately, or intuitively, though I do not perceive it as I perceive a triangle, a colour, or a sound. The mind, spirit or soul, is that indivisible unextended thing, which thinks, acts, and perceives. I say *indivisible*, because unextended; and *unextended*, because extended, figured, movable things, are ideas; and that which

perceives ideas, which thinks and wills, is plainly itself
no idea, nor like an idea. Ideas are things inactive,
and perceived: and spirits a sort of beings altogether
different from them. I do not therefore say my soul
is an idea, or like an idea. However, taking the word
idea in a large sense, my soul may be said to furnish me
with an idea, that is, an image or likeness of God,
though indeed extremely inadequate. For all the notion
I have of God is obtained by reflecting on my own soul,
heightening its powers, and removing its imperfections.
I have therefore, though not an inactive idea, yet
in myself some sort of an active thinking image of the
Deity. And though I perceive him not by sense, yet
I have a notion of him, or know him by reflexion and
reasoning. My own mind and my own ideas I have an
immediate knowledge of; and by the help of these, do
mediately apprehend the possibility of the existence of
other spirits and ideas. Farther, from my own being,
and from the dependency I find in myself and my ideas,
I do, by an act of reason, necessarily infer the existence of
a God, and of all created things in the mind of God.
So much for your first question. For the second: I
suppose by this time you can answer it yourself. For
you neither perceive matter objectively, as you do an
inactive being or idea, nor know it, as you do yourself
by a reflex act: neither do you mediately apprehend
it by similitude of the one or the other : nor yet collect
it by reasoning from that which you know immediately.
All which makes the case of *matter* widely different from
that of the *Deity*.

HYLAS. You say your own soul supplies you with some sort
of an idea or image of God. But at the same time you
acknowledge you have, properly speaking, no idea of
your own soul. You even affirm that spirits are a sort
of beings altogether different from ideas. Consequently

that no idea can be like a spirit. We have therefore no idea of any spirit. You admit nevertheless that there is spiritual substance, although you have no idea of it; while you deny there can be such a thing as material substance, because you have no notion or idea of it. Is this fair dealing? To act consistently, you must either admit matter or reject spirit. What say you to this?

PHILONOUS. I say in the first place, that I do not deny the existence of material substance, merely because I have no notion of it, but because the notion of it is inconsistent, or in other words, because it is repugnant that there should be a notion of it. Many things, for aught I know, may exist, whereof neither I nor any other man hath or can have any idea or notion whatsoever. But then those things must be possible, that is, nothing inconsistent must be included in their definition. I say secondly, that although we believe things to exist which we do not perceive; yet we may not believe that any particular thing exists, without some reason for such belief: but I have no reason for believing the existence of matter. I have no immediate intuition thereof: neither can I mediately from my sensations, ideas, notions, actions or passions, infer an unthinking, unperceiving, inactive substance, either by probable deduction, or necessary consequence. Whereas the being of myself, that is, my own soul, mind or thinking principle, I evidently know by reflexion. You will forgive me if I repeat the same things in answer to the same objections. In the very notion or definition of material substance, there is included a manifest repugnance and inconsistency. But this cannot be said of the notion of spirit. That ideas should exist in what doth not perceive, or be produced by what doth not act, is repugnant. But it is no repugnancy to say that a perceiving thing should be the subject of ideas, or an active thing the cause of them. It is granted we have neither an immediate evidence nor a demonstrative knowledge of the existence of other finite spirits ; but it will not thence follow that such spirits are on a foot with material substances—if to suppose the one be inconsistent, and it be not inconsistent to suppose the other ; if the one can be inferred by no argument, and there is a probability for the other ; if we see signs and effects indicating distinct finite agents like ourselves, and see no sign or symptom whatever that leads to a rational belief of matter. I say lastly, that I have a notion [1] of spirit, though I have not, strictly speaking, an idea of it. I do not perceive it as an idea or by means of an idea, but know it by reflection.

HYLAS. Notwithstanding all you have said, to me it seems, that according to your own way of thinking, and in consequence of your own principles, it should follow that you are only a system of floating ideas, without any substance to support them. Words are not to be used without a meaning. And as there is no more meaning in spiritual substance than in material substance, the one is to be exploded as well as the other.

PHILONOUS. How often must I repeat, that I know or am conscious of my own being ; and that I myself am not my ideas, but somewhat else, a thinking active principle that perceives, knows, wills, and operates about ideas? I know that I, one and the same self, perceive both colours and sounds : that a colour cannot perceive a sound, nor a sound a colour : that I am therefore one individual principle, distinct from colour and sound ; and, for the same reason, from all other sensible things and inert ideas. But I am not in like manner conscious either of the existence or essence of matter. On the contrary, I know that nothing inconsistent can exist,

---

[1] [See note on *Princ.*, Sect. 27.—ED.]

and that the existence of matter implies an inconsistency. Farther, I know what I mean, when I affirm that there is a spiritual substance or support of ideas, that is, that a spirit knows and perceives ideas. But I do not know what is meant when it is said that an unperceiving substance hath inherent in it and supports either ideas or the archetypes of ideas. There is therefore upon the whole no parity of case between spirit and matter . . .

HYLAS. But still, Philonous, you hold there is nothing in the world but spirits and ideas. And this, you must needs acknowledge, sounds very oddly.

PHILONOUS. I own the word *idea*, not being commonly used for *thing*, sounds something out of the way. My reason for using it was, because a necessary relation to the mind is understood to be implied by that term; and it is now commonly used by philosophers, to denote the immediate objects of the understanding. But however oddly the proposition may sound in words, yet it includes nothing so very strange or shocking in its sense, which in effect amounts to no more than this, to wit, that there are only things perceiving, and things perceived; or that every unthinking being is necessarily, and from the very nature of its existence, perceived by some mind; if not by any finite created mind, yet certainly by the infinite mind of God, in whom *we live, and move, and have our being*. Is this as strange as to say, the sensible qualities are not on the objects: or, that we cannot be sure of the existence of things, or know anything of their real natures, though we both see and feel them, and perceive them by all our senses?

HYLAS. And in consequence of this, must we not think there are no such things as physical or corporeal causes; but that a spirit is the immediate cause of all the phenomena in Nature? Can there be anything more extravagant than this?

PHILONOUS. Yes, it is infinitely more extravagant to say, a thing which is inert, operates on the mind, and which is unperceiving, is the cause of our perceptions. Besides, that which to you, I know not for what reason, seems so extravagant, is no more than the Holy Scriptures assert in a hundred places. In them God is represented as the sole and immediate Author of all those effects, which some heathens and philosophers are wont to ascribe to Nature, matter, fate, or the like unthinking principle. This is so much the constant language of Scripture, that it were needless to confirm it by citations.

HYLAS. You are not aware, Philonous, that in making God the immediate author of all the motions in Nature, you make him the author of murder, sacrilege, adultery, and the like heinous sins.

PHILONOUS. In answer to that, I observe first, that the imputation of guilt is the same, whether a person commits an action with or without an instrument. In case therefore you suppose God to act by the mediation of an instrument, or occasion, called *matter*, you as truly make Him the author of sin as I, who think Him the immediate agent in all those operations vulgarly ascribed to Nature. I farther observe, that sin or moral turpitude doth not consist in the outward physical action or motion, but in the internal deviation of the will from the laws of reason and religion. This is plain, in that the killing an enemy in a battle, or putting a criminal legally to death, is not thought sinful, though the outward act be the very same with that in the case of murder. Since therefore sin doth not consist in the physical action, the making God an immediate cause of all such actions, is not making him the author of sin. Lastly, I have nowhere said that God is the only agent who produces all the motions in bodies. It is true, I have denied there are any other agents beside spirits: but this is very consistent with allowing to thinking rational beings, in the production of motions, the use of limited powers, ultimately indeed derived from God, but immediately under the direction of their own wills, which is sufficient to entitle them to all the guilt of their actions. . . .

HYLAS. What say you to this? Since, according to you, men judge of the reality of things by their senses, how can a man be mistaken in thinking the moon a plain lucid surface, about a foot in diameter; or a square tower, seen at a distance, round; or an oar, with one end in the water, crooked?

PHILONOUS. He is not mistaken with regard to the ideas he actually perceives; but in the inferences he makes from his present perceptions. Thus in the case of the oar, what he immediately perceives by sight is certainly crooked; and so far he is in the right. But if he thence conclude, that upon taking the oar out of the water he shall perceive the same crookedness; or that it would affect his touch as crooked things are wont to do: in that he is mistaken. In like manner if he shall conclude from what he perceives in one station, that in case he advances toward the moon or tower, he should still be affected with the like ideas, he is mistaken. But his mistake lies not in what he perceives immediately and at present (it being a manifest contradiction to suppose he should err in respect of that) but in the wrong judgment he makes concerning the idea he apprehends to be connected with those immediately perceived; or concerning the ideas that, from what he perceives at present, he imagines would be perceived in other circumstances. The case is the same with regard to the Copernican system. We do not here perceive any motion of the earth : but it were erroneous thence to conclude, that in case we were placed at as great a distance from that, as we are now from the other planets, we should not then perceive its motion . . .

HYLAS. And now I warrant you think you have made the point very clear, little suspecting that what you advance leads directly to a contradiction. Is it not an absurdity to imagine any imperfection in God ?

PHILONOUS. Without doubt.

HYLAS. To suffer pain is an imperfection.

PHILONOUS. It is.

HYLAS. Are we not sometimes affected with pain and uneasiness by some other being?

PHILONOUS. We are.

HYLAS. And have you not said that being is a spirit, and is not that spirit God ?

PHILONOUS. I grant it.

HYLAS. But you have asserted, that whatever ideas we perceive from without, are in the mind which affects us. The ideas therefore of pain and uneasiness are in God ; or in other words, God suffers pain : that is to say, there is an imperfection in the Divine Nature, which you acknowledged was absurd. So you are caught in a plain contradiction.

PHILONOUS. That God knows or understands all things, and that he knows among other things what pain is, even every sort of painful sensation, and what it is for his creatures to suffer pain, I make no question. But that God, though he knows and sometimes causes painful sensations in us, can himself suffer pain, I positively deny. We who are limited and dependent spirits, are liable to impressions of sense, the effects of an external agent, which being produced against our wills, are sometimes painful and uneasy. But God, whom no external being can affect, who perceives nothing by sense as we do, whose will is absolute and independent, causing all things, and liable to be thwarted or resisted by nothing; it is evident such a being as this can suffer nothing, nor be affected with any painful sensation, or indeed any sensation at all. We are chained to a body, that is to say, our perceptions are connected with corporeal motions. By the law of our nature we are affected upon every alteration in the nervous parts of our sensible body: which sensible body, rightly considered, is nothing but a complexion of such qualities or ideas as have no existence distinct from being perceived by a mind: so that this connexion of sensations with corporeal motions, means no more than a correspondence in the order of Nature between two sets of ideas, or things immediately perceivable. But God is a pure spirit, disengaged from all such sympathy or natural ties. No corporeal motions are attended with the sensations of pain or pleasure in his mind. To know everything knowable is certainly a perfection; but to endure, or suffer, or feel anything by sense, is an imperfection. The former, I say, agrees to God, but not the latter. God knows or hath ideas; but his ideas are not conveyed to him by sense, as ours are. Your not distinguishing where there is so manifest a difference, makes you fancy you see an absurdity where there is none . . .

HYLAS. You say you believe your senses; and seem to applaud yourself that in this you agree with the vulgar. According to you therefore, the true nature of a thing is discovered by the senses. If so, whence comes that disagreement? Why is not the same figure, and other sensible qualities, perceived all manner of ways? And why should we use a microscope, the better to discover the true nature of a body, if it were discoverable to the naked eye?

PHILONOUS. Strictly speaking, Hylas, we do not see the same object that we feel; neither is the same object perceived by the microscope, which was by the naked eye. But in case every variation was thought sufficient to constitute a new kind or individual, the endless number or confusion of names would render language impracticable. Therefore to avoid this as well as other inconveniencies which are obvious upon a little thought, men combine together several ideas, apprehended by divers senses, or by the same sense at different times, or in different circumstances, but observed however to have some connexion in Nature, either with respect to co-existence or succession; all which they refer to one name, and consider as one thing. Hence it follows that when I examine by my other senses a thing I have seen, it is not in order to understand better the same object which I had perceived by sight, the object of one sense not being perceived by the other senses. And when I look through a microscope, it is not that I may perceive more clearly what I perceived already with my bare eyes, the object perceived by the glass being quite different from the former. But in both cases my aim is only to know what ideas are connected together; and the more a man knows of the connexion of ideas, the more he is said to know of the nature of things. What therefore if our ideas are variable; what if our senses are not in all circumstances affected with the same appearances? It will not thence follow, they are not to be trusted, or that they are inconsistent either with themselves or anything else, except it be with your preconceived notion of (I know not what) one single, unchanged, unperceivable, real nature, marked by each name: which prejudice seems to have taken its rise from not rightly understanding the common language of men speaking of several distinct ideas, as united into one thing by the mind. And indeed there is cause to suspect several erroneous conceits of the philosophers are owing to the same original : while they began to build their schemes, not so much on notions as words, which were framed by the vulgar, merely for conveniency and dispatch in the common actions of life, without any regard to speculation.

HYLAS. Methinks I apprehend your meaning.

PHILONOUS. It is your opinion, the ideas we perceive by our senses are not real things, but images, or copies of them. Our knowledge therefore is no farther real, than as our ideas are the true representations of those originals. But as these supposed originals are in themselves unknown, it is impossible to know how far our ideas resemble them ; or whether they resemble them at all. We cannot therefore be sure we have any real knowledge. Farther, as our ideas are perpetually varied, without any change in the supposed real things, it necessarily follows they cannot all be true copies of them : or if some are, and others are not, it is impossible to distinguish the former from the latter. And this plunges us yet deeper in uncertainty. Again, when we consider the point, we cannot conceive how any idea, or anything like an idea, should have an absolute existence out of a mind : nor consequently, according to you, how there should be any real thing in Nature. The result of all which is, that we are thrown into the most hopeless and abandoned *scepticism.* Now give me leave to ask you, *first,* whether your referring ideas to certain absolutely existing unperceived substances, as their originals, be not the source of all this *scepticism ? Secondly,* whether you are informed, either by sense or reason, of the existence of those unknown originals ? And in case you are not, whether it be not absurd to suppose them ? *Thirdly,* whether, upon inquiry, you find there is anything distinctly conceived or meant by the *absolute or external existence of unperceiving substances* ? *Lastly*, whether the premises considered, it be not the wisest way to follow Nature, trust your senses, and laying aside all anxious thought about unknown natures or substances, admit with the vulgar those for real things, which are perceived by the senses ?

HYLAS. For the present, I have no inclination to the answering part. I would much rather see how you can get over what follows. Pray are not the objects perceived by the senses of one likewise perceivable to others present ? If there were an hundred more here, they would all see the garden, the trees, and flowers as I see them. But they are not in the same manner affected with the ideas I frame in my imagination. Does not this make a difference between the former sort of objects and the latter ?

PHILONOUS. I grant it does. Nor have I ever denied a difference between the objects of sense and those of imagination. But what would you infer from thence ? You cannot say that sensible objects exist unperceived, because they are perceived by many.

HYLAS. I own I can make nothing of that objection : but it hath led me into another. Is it not your opinion that by our senses we perceive only the ideas existing in our minds ?

PHILONOUS. It is.

HYLAS. But the same idea which is in my mind, cannot be in yours, or in any other mind. Doth it not therefore follow from your principles, that no two can see the same thing ? And is not this highly absurd ?

PHILONOUS. If the term *same* be taken in the vulgar acceptation, it is certain (and not at all repugnant to the principles I maintain) that different persons may perceive the same thing ; or the same thing or idea exist in different minds. Words are of arbitrary imposition ;

and since men are used to apply the word *same* where no distinction or variety is perceived, and I do not pretend to alter their perceptions, it follows, that as men have said before, *several saw the same thing*, so they may upon like occasions still continue to use the same phrase, without any deviation either from propriety of language, or the truth of things. But if the term *same* be used in the acceptation of *philosophers*, who pretend to an abstracted notion of identity, then, according to their sundry definitions of this notion (for it is not yet agreed wherein that philosophic identity consists), it may or may not be possible for divers persons to perceive the same thing. But whether philosophers shall think fit to call a thing the *same* or no, is, I conceive, of small importance. Let us suppose several men together, all endued with the same faculties, and consequently affected in like sort by their senses, and who had yet never known the use of language; they would without question agree in their perceptions. Though perhaps, when they came to the use of speech, some regarding the uniformness of what was perceived, might call it the *same* thing: others especially regarding the diversity of persons who perceived, might choose the denomination of different things. But who sees not that all the dispute is about a word? to wit, whether what is perceived by different persons, may yet have the term *same* applied to it? Or suppose a house, whose walls or outward shell remaining unaltered, the chambers are all pulled down, and new ones built in their place; and that you should call this the *same*, and I should say it was not the *same* house: would we not for all this perfectly agree in our thoughts of the house, considered in itself? And would not all the difference consist in a sound? If you should say, we differed in our notions; for that you superadded to your idea of the house the simple abstracted idea of identity, whereas I did not: I would tell you I know not what you mean by that *abstracted idea of identity* ; and should desire you to look into your own thoughts, and be sure you understood yourself.—Why so silent, Hylas ? Are you not yet satisfied, men may dispute about identity and diversity, without any real difference in their thoughts and opinions, abstracted from names ? Take this farther reflexion with you : that whether matter be allowed to exist or no, the case is exactly the same as to the point in hand. For the materialists themselves acknowledge what we immediately perceive by our senses, to be our own ideas. Your difficulty therefore, that no two see the same thing, makes equally against the materialists and me . . .

PHILONOUS. When a man is swayed, he knows not why, to one side of a question ; can this, think you, be anything else but the effect of prejudice, which never fails to attend old and rooted notions ? And indeed in this respect I cannot deny the belief of matter to have very much the advantage over the contrary opinion, with men of a learned education.

HYLAS. I confess it seems to be as you say.

PHILONOUS. As a balance therefore to this weight of prejudice, let us throw into the scale the great advantages that arise from the belief of immaterialism, both in regard to religion and human learning. The being of a God, and incorruptibility of the soul, those great articles of religion, are they not proved with the clearest and most immediate evidence ? When I say the being of a *God*, I do not mean an obscure general cause of things, whereof we have no conception, but *God*, in the strict and proper sense of the word, a being whose spirituality, omnipresence, providence, omniscience, infinite power and goodness, are as conspicuous as the existence of sensible things, of which (notwithstanding the fallacious pretences and affected scruples of *sceptics*) there is no more reason to doubt, than of our own being. Then with relation to human sciences; in natural philosophy, what intricacies, what obscurities, what contradictions, hath the belief of matter led men into ! To say nothing of the numberless disputes about its extent, continuity, homogeneity, gravity, divisibility, etc., do they not pretend to explain all things by bodies operating on bodies, according to the laws of motion ? And yet, are they able to comprehend how any one body should move another ? Nay, admitting there was no difficulty in reconciling the notion of an inert being with a cause; or in conceiving how an accident might pass from one body to another; yet by all their strained thoughts and extravagant suppositions, have they been able to reach the mechanical production of any one animal or vegetable body ? Can they account by the laws of motion, for sounds, tastes, smells, or colours, or for the regular course of things ? Have they accounted by physical principles for the aptitude and contrivance, even of the most inconsiderable parts of the universe ? But laying aside matter and corporeal causes, and admitting only the efficiency of an all-perfect mind, are not all the effects of Nature easy and intelligible ? If the *phenomena* are nothing else but *ideas;* God is a *spirit*, but matter an unintelligent, unperceiving being. If they demonstrate an unlimited power in their cause; God is active and omnipotent, but matter an inert mass. If the order, regularity and usefulness of them can never be sufficiently admired; God is infinitely wise and provident, but matter destitute of all contrivance and design. These surely are great advantages in *physics*. Not to mention that the apprehension of a distant Deity naturally disposes men to a negligence in their *moral* actions, which they would be more cautious of, in case they thought him immediately present, and acting on their minds without the interposition of matter, or unthinking second causes. Then in *metaphysics*; what difficulties concerning entity in abstract, substantial forms, hylarchic principles, plastic natures, substance and accident, principle of individuation, possibility of matter's thinking, origin of ideas, the manner how two independent substances, so widely different as *spirit* and *matter*, should mutually operate on each other? What difficulties, I say, and endless disquisitions concerning these and innumerable other the like points, do we escape by supposing only spirits and ideas? Even the *mathematics* themselves, if we take away the absolute existence of extended things, become much more clear and easy; the most shocking paradoxes and intricate speculations in those sciences, depending on the infinite divisibility of finite extension,[1] which depends on that supposition. But what need is there to insist on the particular sciences? Is not that opposition to all science whatsoever, that frenzy of the ancient and modern *sceptics*, built on the same foundation? Or can you produce so much as one argument against the reality of corporeal things, or in behalf of that avowed utter ignorance of their natures, which doth not suppose their reality to consist in an external absolute existence? Upon this supposition indeed, the objections from the change of colours in a pigeon's neck, or the appearances of a broken oar in the water, must be allowed to have weight. But those and the like objections vanish, if we do not maintain the being of absolute external originals, but place the reality of things in ideas, fleeting indeed, and changeable; however, not changed at random, but according to the fixed order of Nature. For herein consists that con-

[1] [See *Princ.*, Sects. 123 f.—ED.]

stancy and truth of things, which secures all the concerns of life, and distinguishes that which is *real* from the irregular visions of the fancy . . .

HYLAS. I own myself entirely satisfied for the present in all respects. But what security can I have that I shall still continue the same full assent to your opinion, and that no unthought-of objection or difficulty will occur hereafter ?

PHILONOUS. Pray, Hylas, do you in other cases, when a point is once evidently proved, withhold your assent on account of objections or difficulties it may be liable to ? Are the difficulties that attend the doctrine of incommensurable quantities, of the angle of contact, of the asymptotes to curves or the like, sufficient to make you hold out against mathematical demonstration ? Or will you disbelieve the providence of God, because there may be some particular things which you know not how to reconcile with it ? If there are difficulties attending immaterialism, there are at the same time direct and evident proofs for it. But for the existence of matter, there is not one proof, and far more numerous and insurmountable objections lie against it. But where are those mighty difficulties you insist on ? Alas ! you know not where or what they are ; something which may possibly occur hereafter. If this be a sufficient pretence for withholding your full assent, you should never yield it to any proposition, how free soever from exceptions, how clearly and solidly soever demonstrated.

HYLAS. You have satisfied me, Philonous.

PHILONOUS. But to arm you against all future objections, do but consider, that which bears equally hard on two contradictory opinions, can be a proof against neither. Whenever therefore any difficulty occurs, try if you can find a solution for it on the hypothesis of the *materialists*.

Be not deceived by words; but sound your own thoughts. And in case you cannot conceive it easier by the help of *materialism*, it is plain it can be no objection against *immaterialism*. Had you proceeded all along by this rule, you would probably have spared yourself abundance of trouble in objecting; since of all your difficulties I challenge you to show one that is explained by matter; nay, which is not more unintelligible with, than without that supposition, and consequently makes rather *against* than *for* it. You should consider in each particular, whether the difficulty arises from the *non-existence of matter*. If it doth not, you might as well argue from the infinite divisibility of extension against the divine prescience, as from such a difficulty against *immaterialism*. And yet upon recollection I believe you will find this to have been often, if not always, the case. You should likewise take heed not to argue on a *petitio principii*. One is apt to say, the unknown substances ought to be esteemed real things, rather than the ideas in our minds: and who can tell but the unthinking external substance may concur as a cause or instrument in the production of our ideas? But is not this proceeding on a supposition that there are such external substances? And to suppose this, is it not begging the question? But above all things you should beware of imposing on yourself by that vulgar sophism, which is called *ignoratio elenchi*. You talked often as if you thought I maintained the non-existence of sensible things: whereas in truth no one can be more thoroughly assured of their existence than I am: and it is you who doubt; I should have said, positively deny it. Everything that is seen, felt, heard, or any way perceived by the senses, is, on the principles I embrace, a real being, but not on yours. Remember the matter you contend for is an unknown somewhat (if indeed it may be termed *somewhat*) which

198

is quite stripped of all sensible qualities, and can neither be perceived by sense, nor apprehended by the mind. Remember, I say, that it is not any object which is hard or soft, hot or cold, blue or white, round or square, etc. For all these things I affirm do exist. Though indeed I deny they have an existence distinct from being perceived; or that they exist out of all minds whatsoever. Think on these points; let them be attentively considered and still kept in view. Otherwise you will not comprehend the state of the question; without which your objections will always be wide of the mark, and instead of mine, may possibly be directed (as more than once they have been) against your own notions . . .

CONCERNING MOTION

Or concerning the principle and nature
of motion, and concerning the cause
of the communication of motions

First published 1721   Final Edition 1752

EDITOR'S NOTE

Berkeley wrote this tract in 1720 in Lyons, on his way home from Italy, in competition for a prize offered by the Académie Royale des Sciences (Paris) for an essay on motion.

His main purpose is to insist on the distinction between the scientific and the philosophical study of motion. The former can do no more than precisely describe the phenomena and bring them under general hypotheses mathematical in form. Causes fall outside its province, for none can be found in the phenomena, the only causality empirically known being mental, and consequently the subject-matter of metaphysics. Even within its province mechanics is missing its way, raising false problems by framing subtle definitions of what as given is quite plain, and by trying to reason with abstract terms that have no sensory meaning and therefore no sensory control, terms such as absolute motion, absolute space, infinite and infinitesimal. Berkeley is here viewing motion in the light of his own philosophy; the tract may be read as an expansion of Sects. 103-16 of his *Principles*. Here and there he mentions cursorily other points of his doctrine, e.g. that bodies are analysable wholly into sensa, and that the bodily can be apprehended only in sense or imagination, intellect being a faculty not of abstraction but of apprehension of the mental. Writing in France, he makes a courteous reference to Descartes's service in emphasising the radical heterogeneity of mind and body, the definition of which heterogeneity is the basis of his own philosophy.

The tract, being submitted to a foreign academy, was composed in Latin. I have translated the passages from the final text of 1752 (in Berkeley's *Miscellany*). Dr Luce has translated the entire piece in Vol. IV (1951) of Berkeley's *Works*. There are three parts—the origin of motion, Sects. 1-42; the nature of motion, Sects. 43-66; the communication of motion, Sects. 67-72.

CONCERNING MOTION

2. The consideration of motion has strangely distorted the minds of ancient philosophers, giving rise to varying opinions that are extraordinarily difficult, if not absurd. Since these opinions have virtually died out, there is no need to tarry over them. But even recent and sensible philosophers of the present age, when they treat of motion, use a fair number of terms that are extremely abstract and obscure, *e.g. solicitation of gravity, effort, dead forces, etc.*, which throw darkness over writings otherwise competent, and suggest views that are as repugnant to truth as to common sense. These it is necessary to discuss, and not for love of refutation, but for truth's sake.

3. *Solicitation,* and *striving* or *effort,* really refer only to beings that have life. When they are applied to other things, they must be taken metaphorically. But philosophers should avoid metaphors. That those words have no clear and distinct meaning when not referring to either animal sensibility or the motion of the body will be plain to anyone who considers the subject seriously.

4. While we are supporting heavy bodies we are aware of effort, fatigue and discomfort in ourselves. In falling bodies of some weight we perceive an accelerating motion towards the centre of the earth; and by means of the senses we perceive nothing else. Reason, however, tells us that there is some cause or principle of these phenomena; and this is commonly called *gravity.* Now since the cause of the falling of bodies is blind and unknown, gravity in that sense cannot properly be called a sensible quality. It must, then, be an occult quality. But it is scarcely (if at all) possible to conceive what an occult quality is, or how any

mere quality can act or effect anything. It would be better, therefore, to leave the notion of occult quality out of account, and attend only to the sensible effects; in other words, to exclude from our thinking abstract terms (however useful these may be for discourse) and fix the mind on what is particular and concrete, that is, on the things themselves.

5. *Force* also is attributed to bodies. The term is used, however, as if it meant a quality that is known, yet is not motion, shape or any other sensible object, nor a feature of animal sensibility; which a little inspection will show to be nothing but an occult quality. Animal effort and bodily motion are commonly regarded as concomitants and measures of this occult quality.

6. Obviously, then, gravity or force cannot be laid down as the source or principle of motion, for can that principle be any more clearly known by calling it an occult quality? That which is itself occult explains nothing—not to mention that an unknown acting cause could be more rightly called a substance than a quality. Further, *force*, *gravity* and suchlike terms are more often and more suitably used with a concrete meaning, to stand for the body moved, difficulty in our resisting, etc. When they are used by philosophers to mean something altogether different from that—something that neither falls under the senses, nor can be understood by any power of the mind, nor can be fashioned in the imagination—sooner or later they beget error and confusion.

17. *Force, gravity, attraction* and suchlike terms are useful in reasonings and calculations about motion and moved bodies, but not for the understanding of the simple nature of motion itself, or for the designation of as many distinct qualities. As for *attraction*, it is evidently used by Newton to indicate not a real and physical quality but only a mathematical hypothesis; and Leibniz, while distinguish-

ing elementary effort from impetus, admits that such entities are not actually found in Nature, but have to be constructed by abstraction.

21. No light can be thrown on Nature by adducing anything that is neither accessible to the senses nor intelligible to reason. In every case, therefore, we have to see what evidence is offered by sense, by the course of experience, and by reason so far as it is dependent on these. Now all things fall into two classes, body and mind. Things that are extended, solid, mobile, shaped, and possess any other sensory qualities, we know by means of the senses; and things that are sentient, percipient and understanding, we know by a sort of internal awareness; and that these two groups of things are extremely different in kind is evident to us. I am writing of things that are known; things that are unknown it would be useless to discuss.

22. No known thing that we would call a *body* contains within itself anything that could be the origin or efficient cause of motion. For impenetrability, extension and shape do not include or mean any power of producing motion; on the contrary, not only they, but also all other bodily qualities whatsoever, gone through one by one, will be seen to be in fact passive, having in them nothing active, nothing that can in any way be understood as the fount and origin of motion. As for gravity, we have already shown that that term cannot stand for any known thing that is other than the sensible effect the cause of which is in question: for example, when we say that a body is heavy, we can mean nothing more than it is borne downwards, with no notion whatever concerning the cause of this sensible effect.

23. Of body we may declare quite confidently, then, as an established fact, that it is not the origin of motion; so that if anyone should maintain that the term *body* includes

as a part of its meaning not only solid extension and its modifications but in addition some occult quality, potency, form or essence, it would be idle to dispute with him, there being no ideas to dispute with, and words being wasted when used with no definite meaning. The sane rule of philosophising seems rather to be that we should abstain as far as possible from all abstract and general notions—if, indeed, we can use the term *notion* for what has no meaning for us.

24. The whole content of the idea of body is open to us, and it is certain that what we find in it is not the origin of motion. Anyone who talks of an unknown something in matter, while having no idea of it, and calls that the origin of motion, is really saying nothing more than that the origin of motion is unknown. But it would be tedious to tarry over subtleties of that sort.

25. Besides bodily things there is the other class of thinking things. That these, on the contrary, do have in themselves the power of moving bodies we learn from our experience of ourselves, for the mind can at will rouse and stop the motion of our limbs, however puzzling the fact may be. This much is certain, that bodies are moved at the will of minds, so that mind can rightly be called the source of motion, though a particular and dependent source, since it itself depends on the primary and universal source.

27. Body in fact persists in either of the two states it may be in, as much in motion as in rest. Such inertia can no more be called an action of body than the existence of body can be. Inertia is nothing but continuance in the same manner of existing, and this cannot properly be called an action. Similarly, when we suppose that the resistance which we experience in stopping a body in motion is an action of that body, we are deceived. Such felt resistance is in fact a passion in ourselves, is a proof not

that the body acts but that we are acted upon; and anyhow it is plain that this experience of being acted upon would be the same whether the body were moved by itself or were impelled by something else.

29. If extension, solidity and shape were taken away from the idea of body, what would remain would be nothing. But those qualities are indifferent in respect of motion, having in them nothing that can be called the source of motion. This is perfectly evident in the ideas we have of them. If the term *body* mean, then, what we do apprehend, we obviously cannot look for the principle of motion in it, for no part or attribute of it is an efficient cause productive of motion. Now to utter a word and mean nothing by it is unworthy of a philosopher.

30. Something thinking and active is a fact, and we experience it in ourselves as a source of motion. We call it soul, mind, or spirit. Also a fact is something extended, inert, impenetrable and mobile, which is completely different from the former, constituting a distinct class. How great the difference is between thinking beings and extended beings was first noticed by Anaxagoras, a man of great sagacity, who asserted that mind has nothing in common with bodies, as we learn from Book I of Aristotle's *De Anima*. Among the moderns, Descartes is the one who has done most justice to that distinction. After him, other writers, by their use of obscure terms, have turned a clear point into an obstacle and a difficulty.

31. From what has been said it is plain that those who declare that active force, action, or the source of motion really is in bodies have adopted a view that has no foundation in any experience whatever, and prop up that view with obscure and general terms, and do not themselves understand what they are after. Those, on the other hand, who hold that mind is the source of motion are making a judgment that rests on their experience of

themselves, and is supported by the most competent thinkers of every age.

41. Mechanical principles and the universal laws of motion or of Nature, happily discovered in the last century, and treated of and applied with the help of geometry, have thrown remarkable light on [natural] philosophy. But metaphysical principles, and the real efficient causes of motion and of the existence of bodies and of bodily attributes, fall entirely outside the scope of mechanics and experimental inquiries and can throw no light on these, except so far as, being prior in the order of knowledge, they serve to prescribe the boundaries of Physics, and in that way remove difficulties and problems that are alien to this science.

42. Those who look to spirits for the origin of motion understand by the term *spirit* either something corporeal or something incorporeal. If corporeal, however tenuous it may be supposed to be, the difficulty referred to recurs; and if incorporeal, this view, however true it may be, takes us beyond the proper field of physics. Of course, if we were to extend natural philosophy beyond the limits of experiments and of mechanics, so as to include the study of incorporeal and unextended things, such a wider use of the term would bring under it the consideration of the soul [*anima*], mind or vital principle. But it will be more convenient to distinguish, in accordance with general usage, the branches of knowledge by assigning to each its own boundaries. The natural philosopher would then be confined to experiments, the laws of motion and mechanical principles, and the arguments that can be drawn from these; and whatever he may allege concerning other matters he would regard as falling within the field of some higher science. On the one hand, from the Laws of Nature now known some very elegant theories, and also some mechanical rules of practical value, have re-

sulted. On the other hand, from the knowledge of the very Author of Nature far more important reflexions have sprung, but they belong to metaphysics, theology, and moral philosophy.

43. So far concerning the principles of motion : we must now discuss its nature. Since motion is clearly perceived by the senses, what has made it obscure is not so much its own nature as the opinions of learned philosophers. Motion never appears to sense without bodily mass, space and time. There are some thinkers, however, who try to apprehend motion as if it were a simple and abstract idea, distinct from everything else; but such an idea is too tenuous or subtle for the intellect to grasp—as anyone may see if he will make the attempt. From it spring great difficulties concerning the nature of motion, and definitions far more obscure than the very thing which they ought to illuminate. . . .

44. Not content with that, they go further, distinguishing and dividing parts of motion from one another, and trying to form distinct ideas of them, as if they were really distinct beings. There are as well thinkers who distinguish motion and movement, regarding the former as the instantaneous element of the latter. They will have it besides that velocity, effort, force and impetus are so many things different in essence, of each of which we have before the intellect a peculiar and abstract idea distinct from all other ideas. But there is no point in dwelling on these matters, in view of what has been said above.

45. Many have defined motion in terms of transition, forgetting that transition is unintelligible apart from motion and has to be defined in terms of motion. This is one instance of the truth that definitions, while in some matters bringing light, in others bring darkness. As for the things perceived by the senses, they can scarcely be made clearer

or better known by definition. In the vain hope of making them so, philosophers have made easy matters hard, and have entangled their minds in difficulties which for the most part they have themselves created. Because of this passion for defining and abstracting, many extremely subtle questions, of no use whatever, about motion as about other matters, have perverted the intelligence of men, so much so that Aristotle, for example, has freely confessed in several places that he finds motion to be " something hard to know "; and some of the ancients have gone so far in their trifling as to deny outright the existence of motion.

46. It would be tedious to linger over petty points of that kind. It must suffice to have indicated the grounds on which they can be dissolved; to which we may add that what has been handed down in mathematics concerning the infinite division of space and time has brought, because of a natural affinity, paradoxes and thorny theories (all theories that treat of the infinite are thorny) into the inquiries concerning motion. . . .

47. Just as on the one hand there has been too much abstraction or division of things that are in reality inseparable, so on the other hand there has been a composition, or rather confusion, of things that are very diverse, with the result that the nature of motion has been made to seem intricate. It has become usual, for instance, to confuse motion with the efficient cause of motion, so that motion is thought of as having two aspects, one open to the senses and the other wrapped in gloomy night. Hence obscurity and confusion, and various paradoxes about motion, due to attributing to an effect what really belongs to the cause.

52. . . . Motion cannot be understood without an understanding of place. This is defined by the moderns as the part of space that is occupied by body, and consequently it is divided, with respect to space, into relative

and absolute—for they distinguish space too into absolute or real, and relative or apparent. They maintain that there is a space that is infinite in all directions, immobile, not perceivable by the senses, permeating and containing all bodies; and this they call absolute space. The space that is included in or marked out by bodies, and to that extent open to the senses, is called relative, apparent, or everyday space.

53. Let us imagine, then, all bodies to be utterly destroyed. What is left the moderns call absolute space, every relation that springs from the place and distances of bodies having been removed along with the bodies themselves. Further, that space is infinite, immobile, indivisible, imperceptible, without relation and without internal distinction. All its attributes, that is, are privative or negative; so that it seems to me to be just nothing—except that it gives rise to the difficulty that, since it remains extended, extension is a positive quality. Now what sort of extension can it be that cannot be divided or measured, and whose parts cannot be either perceived by the senses or imagined?—for nothing can be formed in imagination that cannot by its nature be perceived by sense, since imagination is simply the power of representing sensible things actual or possible. Such extension also escapes pure intellect, since this faculty has to do only with spiritual and unextended things, such as minds and their states, passions, virtues and similar objects. If, then, we take away from absolute space nothing but the above terms, nothing will remain in sense, imagination, or intellect, so that those terms do mean no more than privation or negation, that is, just nothing.

54. It must be admitted that about this matter we have the strongest prejudices, to free ourselves from which requires the utmost effort of mind. Many, for example, are so far from regarding absolute space as nothing that they

count it to be the only thing there is (other than God) that cannot be annihilated : they declare that by virtue of its own nature it exists necessarily, is eternal and uncreated, and to that extent shares in the attributes of the Divine. Since, however, it is entirely certain that everything to which we give a name is known because of some quality, relation, or other aspect (for it would be pointless to use words that stood for nothing known, for no notion, idea or concept), let us carefully examine whether it be possible to form any idea of that pure, real and absolute space which is supposed to persist when all bodies have been annihilated. On inspecting such an idea with some exactness, I find it to be the perfectly pure idea of nothing, if indeed, it may be called an idea at all. . . .

55. We tend to be deceived because when in imagination we have abolished all other bodies, each of us nevertheless assumes that his own body remains. On this assumption, we imagine the motion of our limbs to be completely free in every direction. But motion cannot be conceived without space. If we think the matter over carefully, it will become clear to us, first that what we are thinking of is relative space, marked out by reference to the parts of the body, and secondly, that our power to move our limbs is not being hindered by any obstacle. Besides these two aspects there is nothing. We falsely believe, however, that there is a third thing, namely, infinite space, really existing and allowing us the power to move our own body. For this power, however, nothing is required but the absence of other bodies, which absence or privation, we are surely bound to admit, is not a positive thing at all.

58. From what has been said it is evidently not right to define the real place of a body as that part of absolute space which the body occupies, and real or absolute motion as a change of real and absolute place ; for all place is relative, just as all motion is. This will become

clearer if we observe that no motion can be understood without some determination or direction, which cannot itself be understood unless, besides the body moved, we suppose our own body, or some other, to exist at the same time. For upwards, downwards, to the left, to the right, and all areas or regions, are what they are in virtue of some relation, and necessarily include or suppose a body other than the one that is moved. If, then, we suppose, say, a globe as being the only thing that exists, all other bodies being annihilated, we could not conceive any motion in it at all. . . .

63. No motion can be perceived or measured except by means of sensory objects. Since, then, absolute space never appears in any guise to the senses, it follows that it is utterly useless for distinguishing motions. Besides, some determination or direction is an essential feature of motion, and direction is essentially relative. Therefore absolute motion is inconceivable.

64. Further, since the motion of the same body will vary with variation in its relative place, and since, indeed, anything can be said to be moved in one respect and in another to be at rest, for the determination of true motion and true rest in a way that would remove ambiguity and serve the purpose of mechanical philosophers, who view the system of things more broadly, it would be enough to suppose, instead of an absolute space, relative space bounded by the heaven of the fixed stars, this being regarded as at rest. Motion and rest marked out within such a relative space can be conveniently used instead of absolute motion and rest, which latter cannot be distinguished in any empirical way from the former. Let forces be impressed as you please, let there be whatever impelling tendencies you please, and let me concede that motion is distinguished by means of actions applied to bodies, nevertheless it can never follow that there is an absolute

space, and an absolute place, and that change of this is true motion. [1]

66. It is evident from the preceding considerations that for the understanding of the true nature of motion it is of the greatest importance (1) to distinguish between mathematical hypotheses and the actual natures of things; (2) to beware of abstractions; (3) to treat motion as something sensible, or at any rate imaginable, and to be content with relative measurements. If we observe these points, we shall both preserve intact the best theorems of the mechanical philosophy, which open up the secret places of nature and make the system of the world susceptible of mathematical treatment, and free the study of motion from a thousand minutiae, subtleties, and abstract ideas. Let so much suffice concerning the nature of motion.

67. We have now to discuss the question of the cause of the communication of motions. . . .

68. Let it be laid down that a new motion is maintained in the struck body, either by the inherent force in virtue of which every body continues in its state of rest or of uniform motion [2] in a straight line, or by the impressed force received at the time of percussion and remaining in the struck body—for in both these cases the effect apprehended is the same, the difference being one of words only. Similarly, when the striking body loses and the struck body acquires motion, it is idle to dispute whether the motion acquired is numerically the same as the motion lost, for such a dispute would lead us into metaphysical and entirely verbal minutiae about identity. It follows that, whether we say that motion is transmitted from the striking to the

---

[1] [Reading *motum* instead of *locum*.—ED.]

[2] [Reading *vel quietis vel motus uniformis* instead of *vel motus vel quietis uniformis*.—ED.]

struck body, or that it is generated anew in the latter and is destroyed in the former, the fact or effect is the same. In either case all that is understood is that one body has lost motion and the other has acquired it.

69. That the Mind which moves and controls this bodily universe and is the true efficient cause of motion is, strictly speaking, the cause of the communication of motion, I would by no means deny. In physical philosophy, however, the causes and explanations of phenomena have to be derived from mechanical principles. A thing is physically explained, therefore, not by assigning its really operative and incorporeal cause, but by demonstrating the connexion of the thing with mechanical principles— as, for example, the principle that action and reaction are always opposite and equal, from which, as a primary principle and source, spring rules concerning the communication of motions, which to the great benefit of the sciences have already been discovered and demonstrated by our modern investigators.

71. In physics, sensation and experience, which have to do with manifest effects only, have their place. In mechanics, the abstract notions of mathematics are admitted. In First Philosophy or metaphysics we are treating of incorporeal things, of the causes, truth and existence of things. The physicist considers the series or successions of sensible things, noting by what laws they are connected, and in what order, what preceding as if it were a cause, and what following as if it were an effect. From this point of view we say that one moved body is the cause of motion in another, or impresses motion upon it, and also that it draws or impels. In this use of *cause* we are to understand secondary corporeal causes, no account being taken of the real seat of the forces or active powers, or of the real cause in which these reside. Besides body, shape and motion, we may also call causes or mechanical

principles the primary axioms of mechanics, regarded as if they were the causes of what follows from them.

72. The truly active causes can be drawn out of the darkness in which they are wrapped, and to some extent be known, only by means of meditation and reasoning. It is, however, the function of First Philosophy or metaphysics to treat of them. If to every science we allotted its own province and boundaries, and distinguished with precision the principles and objects that belong to it, we should be able to pursue our inquiries with both greater ease and greater clearness.

[FINIS]

ALCIPHRON

or

THE MINUTE PHILOSOPHER [1]

Containing an Apology for the Christian
religion against those who are called
Free-thinkers.

THE SECOND DIALOGUE

First published 1732   Final Edition 1752

---

[1] [*I.e.*, a man who belittles everything—Berkeley's term for the ' free-
thinker '.—ED.]

EDITOR'S NOTE

Alciphron was written in Newport (Rhode Island), which supplies the scenic background. The seven dialogues are so superbly written that they alone would place Berkeley among the most eminent writers of English prose. They form a handsome treatise on Christian apologetics, in which some of his philosophical views are used but are not developed or added to.

The second dialogue, taking up an ethical theme, is a vivacious and withering criticism of the cynical *Fable of the Bees* (1714), in which Mandeville, pushing Hobbes's theory of man's egoism to an outrageous extreme, argues that what are commonly called vices are the condition of social prosperity; e.g. spendthrifts and gamblers promote the quick circulation of money. The first dialogue had concluded that the end of conduct is the general good of mankind. The problem of the second is whether that end requires strictly moral convictions. Two positions are stated and countered: (*a*) that vices alone can produce a happy nation—which is contradicted by fact and principle; (*b*) that only the pleasures of sense are natural and satisfying—which is rejected as false in fact, as ignoring the presence and place of reason in human nature, and as binding us in servitude to our appetites, in short, as the opposite of the rationality and liberty which the "free-thinkers" pretend to champion.

The characters in this dialogue are Lysicles, a brash young "free-thinker"; Crito, the host of the company, whose caustic wit expresses one aspect of Berkeley's judgment; and Euphranor, a well-educated farmer, honest and devout. Alciphron, mentioned in the opening sentence, is the chief interlocutor with Euphranor in the remaining dialogues.

ALCIPHRON : THE SECOND DIALOGUE

1. NEXT morning Alciphron and Lysicles said the weather was so fine they had a mind to spend the day abroad, and take a cold dinner under a shade in some pleasant part of the country. Whereupon, after breakfast, we went down to a beach about half a mile off, where we walked on the smooth sand, with the ocean on one hand, and on the other wild broken rocks, intermixed with shady trees and springs of water, till the sun began to be uneasy. We then withdrew into a hollow glade, between two rocks, where we had no sooner seated ourselves but Lysicles, addressing himself to Euphranor, said :—I am now ready to perform what I undertook last evening, which was to show there is nothing in that necessary connexion which some men imagine between those principles you contend for, and the public good. I freely own that, if this question was to be decided by the authority of legislators or philosophers, it must go against us. For those men generally take it for granted that vice is pernicious to the public ; and that men cannot be kept from vice but by the fear of God, and the sense of a future state : whence they are induced to think the belief of such things necessary to the well-being of human-kind. This false notion hath prevailed for many ages in the world, and done an infinite deal of mischief, being in truth the cause of religious establishments, and gaining the protection and encouragement of laws and magis-trates to the clergy and their superstitions. Even some of the wisest among the ancients, who agreed with our sect in denying a Providence and the immortality of the soul, had nevertheless the weakness to lie under

the common prejudice, that vice was hurtful to societies of men. But England hath of late produced great philosophers who have undeceived the world, and proved to a demonstration that private vices are public benefits. This discovery was reserved to our times, and our sect hath the glory of it.

CRITO. It is possible some men of fine understanding might in former ages have had a glimpse of this important truth; but it may be presumed they lived in ignorant times and bigoted countries, which were not ripe for such a discovery.

LYSICLES. Men of narrow capacities and short sight, being able to see no further than one link in a chain of consequences, are shocked at small evils which attend upon vice. But those who can enlarge their view, and look through a long series of events, may behold happiness resulting from vice, and good springing out of evil, in a thousand instances. To prove my point, I shall not trouble you with authorities, or far-fetched arguments, but bring you to plain matter of fact. Do but take a view of each particular vice, and trace it through its effects and consequences, and then you will clearly perceive the advantage it brings to the public.

2. Drunkenness, for instance, is by your sober moralists thought a pernicious vice; but it is for want of considering the good effects that flow from it. For, in the first place, it increases the malt tax, a principal branch of his Majesty's revenue, and thereby promotes the safety, strength, and glory of the nation. Secondly, it employs a great number of hands, the brewer, the maltster, the ploughman, the dealer in hops, the smith, the carpenter, the brazier, the joiner, with all other artificers necessary to supply those enumerated with their respective instruments and utensils. All which advantages are procured from drunkenness in the vulgar way, by

strong beer. This point is so clear it will admit of no dispute. But, while you are forced to allow thus much, I foresee you are ready to object against drunkenness occasioned by wine and spirits, as exporting wealth into foreign countries. But you do not reflect on the number of hands which even this sets on work at home : the distillers, the vintners, the merchants, the sailors, the shipwrights, with all those who are employed towards victualling and fitting out ships, which upon a nice computation will be found to include an incredible variety of trades and callings. Then, for freighting our ships to answer these foreign importations, all our manufactures throughout the kingdom are employed, the spinners, the weavers, the dyers, the wool-combers, the carriers, the packers. And the same may be said of many other manufactures, as well as the woollen. And if it be further considered how many men are enriched by all the forementioned ways of trade and business, and the expenses of these men and their families, in all the several articles of convenient and fashionable living, whereby all sorts of trades and callings, not only at home but throughout all parts wherever our commerce reaches, are kept in employment ; you will be amazed at the wonderfully extended scene of benefits which arise from the single vice of drunkenness, so much run down and declaimed against by all grave reformers.

With as much judgment your half-witted folk are accustomed to censure gaming. And indeed (such is the ignorance and folly of mankind) a gamester and a drunkard are thought no better than public nuisances, when in truth they do each in their way greatly conduce to the public benefit. If you look only on the surface and first appearance of things, you will no doubt think playing at cards a very idle and fruitless occupation. But dive deeper, and you shall perceive this idle amusement employs the card-maker, and he sets the paper-mills at work, by which the poor rag-man is supported; not to mention the builders and workers in wood and iron that are employed in erecting and furnishing those mills. Look still deeper, and you shall find that candles and chair-hire employ the industrious and the poor, who by these means come to be relieved by sharpers and gentlemen, who would not give one penny in charity. But you will say that many gentlemen and ladies are ruined by play, without considering that what one man loses another gets, and that, consequently, as many are made as ruined: money changeth hands, and in this circulation the life of business and commerce consists. When money is spent, it is all one to the public who spends it. Suppose a fool of quality becomes the dupe of a man of mean birth and circumstance who has more wit. In this case what harm doth the public sustain? Poverty is relieved, ingenuity is rewarded, the money stays at home, and has a lively circulation, the ingenious sharper being enabled to set up an equipage and spend handsomely, which cannot be done without employing a world of people. But you will perhaps object that a man reduced by play may be put upon desperate courses, hurtful to the public. Suppose the worst, and that he turns highwayman; such a man hath a short life and a merry. While he lives, he spends, and for one that he robs makes twenty the better for his expense; and, when his time is come, a poor family may be relieved by fifty or a hundred pounds set upon his head. A vulgar eye looks on many a man as an idle or mischievous fellow, whom a true philosopher, viewing in another light, considers as a man of pleasant occupation, who diverts himself, and benefits the public, and that with so much ease that he employs a multitude of men, and sets an infinite machine in motion without knowing the good he does, or even intending to do any : which is peculiar to that gentleman-like way of doing good by vice. I was considering play, and that insensibly led me to the advantages which attend robbing on the highway. Oh the beautiful and never-enough-admired connexion of vices ! It would take too much time to show how they all hang together, and what an infinite deal of good takes its rise from every one of them. One word for a favourite vice, and I shall leave you to make out the rest yourself, by applying the same way of reasoning to all other vices. A poor girl, who might not have the spending of half-a-crown a week in what you call an honest way, no sooner hath the good fortune to be a kept mistress, but she employs milliners, laundresses, tire-women, mercers, and a number of other trades, to the benefit of her country. It would be endless to trace and pursue every particular vice through its consequences and effects, and show the vast advantage they all are of to the public. The true springs that actuate the great machine of commerce, and make a flourishing state, have been hitherto little understood. Your moralists and divines have for so many ages been corrupting the genuine sense of mankind, and filling their heads with such absurd principles, that it is in the power of few men to contemplate real life with an unprejudiced eye. And fewer still have sufficient parts and sagacity to pursue a long train of consequences, relations, and dependences, which must be done in order to form a just and entire notion of the public weal. But, as I said before, our sect hath produced men capable of these discoveries, who have displayed them in a full light, and made them public for the benefit of their country.

3. Oh! said EUPHRANOR, who heard this discourse with great attention, you, Lysicles, are the very man I

wanted, eloquent and ingenious, knowing in the principles of your sect, and willing to impart them. Pray tell me, do these principles find an easy admission in the world?

LYSICLES. They do among ingenious men and people of fashion, though you will sometimes meet with strong prejudices against them in the middle sort, an effect of ordinary talents and mean breeding.

EUPHRANOR. I should wonder if men were not shocked at notions of such a surprising nature, so contrary to all laws, education, and religion.

LYSICLES. They would be shocked much more if it had not been for the skilful address of our philosophers, who, considering that most men are influenced by names rather than things, have introduced a certain polite way of speaking, which lessens much of the abhorrence and prejudice against vice.

EUPHRANOR. Explain me this.

LYSICLES. Thus, in our dialect, a vicious man is a man of pleasure, a sharper is one that plays the whole game, a lady is said to have an affair, a gentleman to be gallant, a rogue in business to be one that knows the world. By this means we have no such things as sots, debauchees, whores or rogues in the *beau monde*, who may enjoy their vices without incurring disagreeable appellations.

EUPHRANOR. Vice then is, it seems, a fine thing with an ugly name.

LYSICLES. Be assured it is.

EUPHRANOR. It should seem then that Plato's fearing lest youth might be corrupted by those fables which represented the gods vicious was an effect of his weakness and ignorance.

LYSICLES. It was, take my word for it.

EUPHRANOR. And yet Plato had kept good company, and

lived in a court. And Cicero, who knew the world well, had a profound esteem for him.

CRITO. I tell you, Euphranor, that Plato and Tully might perhaps make a figure in Athens or Rome : but, were they to revive here in our days, they would pass but for underbred pedants, there being at most coffee-houses in London several able men who could convince them they knew nothing in what they are valued so much for, morals and politics.

LYSICLES. How many long-headed men do I know, both in the court-end and the city, with five times Plato's sense, who care not one straw what notion their sons have of God or virtue.

4. CRITO. I can illustrate this doctrine of Lysicles by examples that will make you perceive its force. Cleophon, a minute philosopher, took strict care of his son's education, and entered him betimes in the principles of his sect. Callicles (that was his son's name), being a youth of parts, made a notable progress ; insomuch that before he became of age he killed his old covetous father with vexation, and soon after ruined the estate he left behind him ; or, in other words, made a present of it to the public, spreading the dunghill collected by his ancestors over the face of the nation, and making out of one overgrown estate several pretty fortunes for ingenious men who live by the vices of the great. Telesilla, though a woman of quality and spirit, made no figure in the world, till she was instructed by her husband in the tenets of the minute philosophy, which he wisely thought would prevent her giving anything in charity. From that time, she took a turn towards expensive diversions, particularly deep play, by which means she soon transferred a considerable share of his fortune to several acute men skilled in that mystery, who wanted it more, and circulate it quicker, than her

husband would have done, who in return hath got an heir to his estate, having never had a child before. That same Telesilla, who was good for nothing so long as she believed her catechism, now shines in all public places, is a lady of gallantry and fashion, and has, by her extravagant parade in lace and fine clothes, raised a spirit of expense in other ladies, very much to the public benefit, though, it must be owned, to the mortification of many frugal husbands.

While Crito related these facts with a grave face, I could not forbear smiling, which LYSICLES observing— Superficial minds, said he, may perhaps find something to ridicule in these accounts; but all who are masters of a just way of thinking must needs see that those maxims the benefit whereof is universal, and the damage only particular to private persons or families, ought to be encouraged in a wise commonwealth.

For my part, said EUPHRANOR, I profess myself to be rather dazzled and confounded than convinced by your reasoning; which, as you observed yourself, taking in the connexion of many distant points, requires great extent of thought to comprehend it. I must therefore entreat you to bear with my defects; suffer me to take to pieces what is too big to be received at once; and, where I cannot keep pace with you, permit me to follow you step by step, as fast as I can.

LYSICLES. There is reason in what you say. Everyone cannot suddenly take a long concatenation of argument.

5. EUPHRANOR. Your several arguments seem to centre in this: that vice circulates money and promotes industry, which causeth a people to flourish. Is it not so?

LYSICLES. It is.

EUPHRANOR. And the reason that vice produceth this effect is, because it causeth an extravagant consumption, which is the most beneficial to the manufacturers, their encouragement consisting in a quick demand and high price.

LYSICLES. True.

EUPHRANOR. Hence you think a drunkard most beneficial to the brewer and the vintner, as causing a quick consumption of liquor, inasmuch as he drinks more than other men?

LYSICLES. Without doubt.

EUPHRANOR. Say, Lysicles, who drinks most, a sick man or a healthy?

LYSICLES. A healthy.

EUPHRANOR. And which is healthiest, a sober man or a drunkard?

LYSICLES. A sober man.

EUPHRANOR. A sober man, therefore, in health may drink more than a drunkard when he is sick?

LYSICLES. He may.

EUPHRANOR. What think you, will a man consume more meat and drink in a long life or a short one?

LYSICLES. In a long.

EUPHRANOR. A sober, healthy man, therefore, in a long life, may circulate more money by eating and drinking, than a glutton or drunkard in a short one?

LYSICLES. What then?

EUPHRANOR. Why then it should seem that he may be more beneficial to the public, even in this way of eating and drinking.

LYSICLES. I shall never own that temperance is the way to promote drinking.

EUPHRANOR. But you will own sickness lessens, and death puts an end to all drinking? The same argument will hold, for aught I can see, with respect to all other vices that impair men's health and shorten their lives. And, if we admit this, it will not be so clear a point that vice hath merit towards the public.

LYSICLES. But, admitting that some artificers or traders might be as well encouraged by the sober men as the vicious ; what shall we say of those who subsist altogether by vice and vanity ?

EUPHRANOR. If such there are, may they not be otherwise employed without loss to the public ? Tell me, Lysicles, is there anything in the nature of vice, as such, that renders it a public blessing, or is it only the consumption it occasions ?

LYSICLES. I have already shown how it benefits the nation by the consumption of its manufactures.

EUPHRANOR. And you have granted that a long and healthy life consumes more than a short and sickly one ; and you will not deny that many consume more than one. Upon the whole then, compute and say, which is most likely to promote the industry of his countrymen, a virtuous married man with a healthy numerous offspring, and who feeds and clothes the orphans in his neighbourhood, or a fashionable rake about town ? I would fain know whether money spent innocently doth not circulate as well as that spent upon vice ? And, if so, whether by your own rule it doth not benefit the public as much ?

LYSICLES. What I have proved, I proved plainly, and there is no need of more words about it.

EUPHRANOR. You seem to me to have proved nothing, unless you can make it out that it is impossible to spend a fortune innocently. I should think the public weal of a nation consists in the number and good condition of its inhabitants ; have you anything to object to in this ?

LYSICLES. I think not.

EUPHRANOR. To this end which would most conduce, the employing men in open air and manly exercise, or in sedentary business within doors ?

LYSICLES. The former, I suppose.

EUPHRANOR. Should it not seem, therefore, that building, gardening, and agriculture would employ men more usefully to the public than if tailors, barbers, perfumers, distillers, and such arts were multiplied?

LYSICLES. All this I grant; but it makes against you. For what moves men to build and plant but vanity, and what is vanity but vice?

EUPHRANOR. But if a man should do those things for his convenience or pleasure, and in proportion to his fortune, without a foolish ostentation, or overrating them beyond their due value, they would not then be the effect of vice; and how do you know but this may be the case?

CRITO. One thing I know, that the readiest way to quicken that sort of industry, and employ carpenters, masons, smiths, and all such trades, would be to put in practice the happy hint of a celebrated minute philosopher, who, by profound thinking, has discovered that burning the city of London would be no such bad action as silly prejudiced people might possibly imagine; inasmuch as it would produce a quick circulation of property, transferring it from the rich to the poor, and employing a great number of artificers of all kinds. This, at least, cannot be denied, that it hath opened a new way of thinking to our incendiaries, of which the public hath of late begun to reap the benefit.

EUPHRANOR. I cannot sufficiently admire this ingenious thought.

6. But methinks it would be dangerous to make such notions public.

CRITO. Dangerous! To whom?

EUPHRANOR. In the first place to the publisher.

CRITO. That is a mistake; for such notions have been published and met with due applause, in this most wise and happy age of free-thinking, free-speaking, free-writing, and free-acting.

EUPHRANOR. How! May a man then publish and practise such things with impunity?

CRITO. To speak the truth, I am not so clear as to the practic part. An unlucky accident now and then befalls an ingenious man. The minute philosopher Magirus, being desirous to benefit the public by circulating an estate possessed by a near relation who had not the heart to spend it, soon convinced himself, upon these principles, that it would be a very worthy action to dispatch out of the way such a useless fellow, to whom he was next heir. But, for this laudable attempt, he had the misfortune to be hanged by an underbred judge and jury. Could anything be more unjust?

EUPHRANOR. Why unjust?

CRITO. Is it not unjust to punish actions, when the principles from which they directly follow are tolerated and applauded by the public? Can anything be more inconsistent than to condemn in practice what is approved in speculation? Truth is one and the same; it being impossible a thing should be practically wrong and speculatively right. Thus much is certain, Magirus was perfect master of all this theory, and argued most acutely about it with a friend of mine, a little before he did the fact for which he died.

LYSICLES. The best on't is, the world every day grows wiser; though it must be owned, the writers of our sect have not yet shaken off all respect for human laws, whatever they may do as to divine. It seems they venture no further than to recommend an inward principle of vice, operating under an outward restraint of human laws.

CRITO. That writer who considers man only as an instrument of passion, who absolves him from all ties of conscience and religion, and leaves him no law to respect or to fear but the law of the land, is to be sure a public benefit. You mistake, Euphranor, if you think the minute philosophers idle theorists; they are men of practical views.

EUPHRANOR. As much as I love liberty, I should be afraid to live among such people; it would be, as Seneca somewhere expresseth it, *in libertate bellis ac tyrannis sæviore.*

LYSICLES. What do you mean by quoting Plato and Seneca? Can you imagine a free-thinker is to be influenced by the authority of such old-fashioned writers?

EUPHRANOR. You, Lysicles, and your friend, have quoted to me ingenious moderns, profound fine gentlemen, with new names of authors in the minute philosophy, to whose merits I am a perfect stranger. Suffer me in my turn to cite such authorities as I know, and have passed for many ages upon the world. . . .

8. EUPHRANOR. Though much may be hoped from the unprejudiced education of young gentlemen, yet it seems we are not to expect a settled and entire happiness before vice reigns pure and unmixed: till then, much is to be feared from the dangerous struggle between vice and virtue, which may perchance overturn and dissolve this government, as it hath done others.

LYSICLES. No matter for that, if a better comes in its place. We have cleared the land of all prejudices towards government or constitution, and made them fly like other phantasms before the light of reason and good sense. Men who think deeply cannot see any reason why power should not change hands as well as property; or why the fashion of a government should not be changed as easily as that of a garment. The perpetual circulating and revolving of wealth and power, no matter through what or whose hands, is that which keeps up life and spirit in a state. Those who are even slightly read in our philosophy know that of all prejudices the silliest is an attachment to forms.

CRITO. To say no more upon so clear a point, the over-turning a government may be justified upon the same principles as the burning a town would produce parallel effects, and equally contribute to the public good. In both cases, the natural springs of action are forcibly exerted; and, in this general industry, what one loses another gets, a quick circulation of wealth and power making the sum total to flourish.

EUPHRANOR. And do the minute philosophers publish these things to the world?

LYSICLES. It must be confessed our writers proceed in politics with greater caution than they think necessary with regard to religion.

CRITO. But those things plainly follow from their prin-ciples, and are to be admitted for the genuine doctrine of the sect, expressed perhaps with more freedom and perspicuity than might be thought prudent by those who would manage the public, or not offend weak brethren.

EUPHRANOR. And pray, is there not need of caution, a rebel or incendiary being characters that many men have a prejudice against?

LYSICLES. Weak people of all ranks have a world of absurd prejudices.

EUPHRANOR. But the better sort, such as statesmen and legislators; do you think they have not the same in-disposition towards admitting your principles?

LYSICLES. Perhaps they may; but the reason is plain.

CRITO. This puts me in mind of that ingenious philosopher, the gamester Glaucus, who used to say that statesmen and lawgivers may keep a stir about right and wrong, just

and unjust, but that, in truth, property of every kind
had so often passed from the right owners by fraud and
violence that it was now to be considered as lying on the
common, and with equal right belonged to everyone
that could seize it.

EUPHRANOR. What are we to think then of laws and
regulations relating to right and wrong, crimes and
duties?

LYSICLES. They serve to bind weak minds, and keep the
vulgar in awe: but no sooner doth a true genius arise,
but he breaks his way to greatness through all the
trammels of duty, conscience, religion, law; to all
which he showeth himself infinitely superior. . . .

10. EUPHRANOR. But you, Lysicles, who are master of this
subject, will be pleased to inform me whether the
public good of a nation doth not imply the particular
good of its individuals?

LYSICLES. It doth.

EUPHRANOR. And doth not the good or happiness of a
man consist in having both soul and body sound and
in good condition, enjoying those things which their
respective natures require, and free from those things
which are odious or hurtful to them?

LYSICLES. I do not deny all this to be true.

EUPHRANOR. Now, it would seem worth while to consider whether the regular decent life of a virtuous man
may not as much conduce to this end as the mad sallies
of intemperance and debauchery.

LYSICLES. I will acknowledge that a nation may merely
subsist, or be kept alive, but it is impossible it should
flourish, without the aid of vice. To produce a quick
circulation of traffic and wealth in a state, there must
be exorbitant and irregular motions in the appetites
and passions.

EUPHRANOR. The more people a nation contains, and the happier those people are, the more that nation may be said to flourish. I think we are agreed in this point.

LYSICLES. We are.

EUPHRANOR. You allow then that riches are not an ultimate end, but should only be considered as the means to procure happiness?

LYSICLES. I do.

EUPHRANOR. It seems that means cannot be of use without our knowing the end, and how to apply them to it?

LYSICLES. It seems so.

EUPHRANOR. Will it not follow that in order to make a nation flourish it is not sufficient to make it wealthy, without knowing the true end and happiness of mankind, and how to apply wealth towards attaining that end? In proportion as these points are known and practised, I think the nation should be likely to flourish. But, for a people who neither know nor practise them, to gain riches seems to me the same advantage that it would be for a sick man to come at plenty of meat and drink, which he could not use but to his hurt.

LYSICLES. This is mere sophistry; it is arguing without persuading. Look into common life; examine the pursuits of men; have a due respect for the consent of the world; and you will soon be convinced that riches alone are sufficient to make a nation flourishing and happy. Give them riches and they will make themselves happy, without that political invention, that trick of statesmen and philosophers, called virtue.

11. EUPHRANOR. Virtue then, in your account, is a trick of statesmen?

LYSICLES. It is.

EUPHRANOR. Why then do your sagacious sect betray and divulge that trick or secret of state, which wise men have judged necessary for the good government of the world ?

Lysicles hesitating, CRITO made answer, that he presumed it was because their sect, being wiser than all other wise men, disdained to see the world governed by wrong maxims, and would set all things on a right bottom.

EUPHRANOR. Thus much is certain : if we look into all institutions of government, and the political writings of such as have heretofore passed for wise men, we shall find a great regard for virtue.

LYSICLES. You shall find a strong tincture of prejudice ; but, as I said before, consult the multitude if you would find nature and truth.

EUPHRANOR. But, among country gentlemen, and farmers, and the better sort of tradesmen, is not virtue a reputable thing ?

LYSICLES. You pick up authorities among men of low life and vile education.

EUPHRANOR. Perhaps we ought to pay a decent respect to the authority of minute philosophers.

LYSICLES. And I would fain know whose authority should be more considered than that of those gentlemen who are alone above prejudice, and think for themselves.

EUPHRANOR. How doth it appear that you are the only unprejudiced part of mankind ? May not a minute philosopher, as well as another man, be prejudiced in favour of the leaders of his sect ? May not an atheistical education prejudice towards atheism ? What should hinder a man's being prejudiced against religion, as well as for it ? Or can you assign any reason why an attachment to pleasure, interest, vice, or vanity, may not be supposed to prejudice men against virtue ?

LYSICLES. This is pleasant. What ! Suppose those very

men influenced by prejudice who are always disputing against it, whose constant aim it is to detect and demolish prejudices of all kinds !

Except their own, replied CRITO ; for, you must pardon me if I cannot help thinking they have some small prejudice, though not in favour of virtue.

12. I observe, Lysicles, that you allowed to Euphranor, the greater number of happy people are in a State, the more that State may be said to flourish : it follows, therefore, that such methods as multiply inhabitants are good, and such as diminish them are bad for the public. And one would think nobody need be told that the strength of a State consists more in the number and sort of people than in anything else. But, in proportion as vice and luxury, those public blessings encouraged by this minute philosophy, prevail among us, fewer are disposed to marry, too many being diverted by pleasure, disabled by disease, or frightened by expense. Nor doth vice only thin a nation, but also debaseth it by a puny degenerate race. I might add that it is ruinous to our manufactures ; both as it makes labour dear, and thereby enables our more frugal neighbours to undersell us ; and also as it diverts the lower sort of people from honest callings to wicked projects. If these and such considerations were taken into the account, I believe it would be evident to any man in his senses that the imaginary benefits of vice bear no proportion to the solid real woes that attend it.

LYSICLES, upon this, shook his head, and smiled at Crito, without vouchsafing any other answer. After which, addressing himself to Euphranor, There cannot, said he, be a stronger instance of prejudice than that a man should at this time of day preserve a reverence for that idol Virtue, a thing so effectually exposed and exploded by the most knowing men of the age, who have shown that a man is a mere engine, played upon and driven about by sensible objects; and that moral virtue is only a name, a notion, a chimera, an enthusiasm, or at best a fashion, uncertain and changeable, like all other fashions. [1]

EUPHRANOR. What do you think, Lysicles, of health; doth it depend on fancy and caprice, or is it something real in the bodily composition of a man?

LYSICLES. Health is something real, which results from the right constitution and temperature of the organs and the fluids circulating through them.

EUPHRANOR. This you say is health of body?

LYSICLES. It is.

EUPHRANOR. And may we not suppose a healthy constitution of soul, when the notions are right, the judgments true, the will regular, the passions and appetites directed to their proper objects, and confined within due bounds? This, in regard to the soul, seems what health is to the body. And the man whose mind is so constituted, is he not properly called virtuous? And to produce this healthy disposition in the minds of his countrymen, should not every good man employ his endeavours? If these things have any appearance of truth, as to me they seem to have, it will not then be so clear a point that virtue is a mere whim or fashion, as you are pleased to represent it—I must own something unexpectedly, after what had been discoursed in last evening's conference, which if you would call to mind, might perhaps save both of us some trouble.

LYSICLES. Would you know the truth, Euphranor? I must own I have quite forgot all your discourse about virtue, duty, and all such points, which, being of an airy notional nature, are apt to vanish, and leave no

---

[1] " In morals there is no greater certainty than in fashions." *Fable of the Bees*, Part I, p. 379.

trace on a mind accustomed only to receive impression from realities.

13. Having heard these words, EUPHRANOR looked at Crito and me, and said, smiling, I have mistaken my part: it was mine to learn and his to instruct. Then, addressing himself to Lysicles, Deal faithfully, said he, and let me know whether the public benefit or vice be in truth that which makes you plead for it?

LYSICLES. I love to speak frankly what I think. Know then that private interest is the first and principal consideration with philosophers of our sect. Now of all interests pleasure is that which hath the strongest charms, and no pleasures like those which are heightened and enlivened by licence. Herein consists the peculiar excellency of our principles, that they show people how to serve their country by diverting themselves, causing the two streams of public spirit and self-love to unite and run in the same channel. I have told you already that I admit a nation might subsist by the rules of virtue. But, give me leave to say, it will barely subsist in a dull joyless insipid State; whereas the sprightly excesses of vice inspire men with joy. And where particulars rejoice, the public, which is made up of particulars, must do so too: that is, the public must be happy. This I take to be an irrefragable argument. But, to give you its full force, and make it as plain as possible, I will trace things from their original. Happiness is the end to which created things naturally tend; but we find that all animals, whether men or brutes, do naturally and principally pursue real pleasure of sense; which is therefore to be thought their supreme good, their true end and happiness. It is for this men live; and who-ever understands life must allow that man to enjoy the top and flower of it who hath a quick sense of pleasure, and withal spirit, skill, and fortune sufficient to gratify every appetite and every taste. Niggards and fools will envy or traduce such a one because they cannot equal him. Hence all that sober trifling in disparagement of what every one would be master of if he could, a full freedom and unlimited scope of pleasure.

EUPHRANOR. Let me see whether I understand you. Pleasure of sense, you say, is the chief pleasure?

LYSICLES. I do.

EUPHRANOR. And this would be cramped and diminished by virtue?

LYSICLES. It would.

EUPHRANOR. Tell me, Lysicles, is pleasure then at the height when the appetites are satisfied?

LYSICLES. There is then only an indolence, the lively sense of pleasure being past.

EUPHRANOR. It should seem therefore that the appetites must be always craving, to preserve pleasure alive?

LYSICLES. That is our sense of the matter.

EUPHRANOR. The Greek philosopher, therefore, was in the right, who considered the body of a man of pleasure as a leaky vessel, always filling and never full.

LYSICLES. You may divert yourself with allegories, if you please. But all the while ours is literally the true taste of nature. Look throughout the universe, and you shall find birds and fishes, beasts and insects, all kinds of animals, with which the creation swarms, constantly engaged by instinct in the pursuit of sensible pleasure. And shall man alone be the grave fool who thwarts, and crosses, and subdues his appetites, while his fellow-creatures do all most joyfully and freely indulge them?

EUPHRANOR. How, Lysicles! I thought that being governed by the senses, appetites, and passions was the most grievous slavery; and that the proper business of free-thinkers, or philosophers, had been to set men free from the power of ambition, avarice and sensuality!

LYSICLES. You mistake the point. We make men relish the world, attentive to their interests, lively and luxurious in their pleasures, without fear or restraint either from God or man. We despise those preaching writers who used to disturb or cramp the pleasures and amusements of human life. We hold that a wise man who meddles with business doth it altogether for his interest, and refers his interest to his pleasure. With us it is a maxim, that a man should seize the moments as they fly. Without love, and wine, and play, and late hours we hold life not to be worth living. I grant indeed, that there is something gross and ill-bred in the vices of mean men, which the genteel philosopher abhors.

CRITO. But to cheat, whore, betray, get drunk, do all these things decently, this is true wisdom, and elegance of taste.

14. EUPHRANOR. To me, who have been used to another way of thinking, this new philosophy seems difficult to digest. I must, therefore, beg leave to examine its principles with the same freedom that you do those of other sects.

LYSICLES. Agreed.

EUPHRANOR. You say, if I mistake not, that a wise man pursues only his private interest, and that this consists in sensual pleasure; for proof whereof you appeal to nature. Is not this what you advance?

LYSICLES. It is.

EUPHRANOR. You conclude, therefore, that as other animals are guided by natural instinct, man too ought to follow the dictates of sense and appetite?

LYSICLES. I do.

EUPHRANOR. But in this do you not argue as if man had only sense and appetite for his guides, on which supposition there might be truth in what you say? But what if he hath intellect, reason, a higher instinct and a nobler life? If this be the case, and you, being man, live like a brute, is it not the way to be defrauded of your true happiness, to be mortified and disappointed? Consider most sorts of brutes: you shall perhaps find they have a greater share of sensual happiness than man.

LYSICLES. To our sorrow we do. This hath made several gentlemen of our sect envy brutes, and lament the lot of human-kind.

CRITO. It was a consideration of this sort which inspired Erotylus with the laudable ambition of wishing himself a snail, upon hearing of certain particularities discovered in that animal by a modern virtuoso.

EUPHRANOR. Tell me, Lysicles, if you had an inexhaustible fund of gold and silver, should you envy another for having a little more copper than you?

LYSICLES. I should not.

EUPHRANOR. Are not reason, imagination, and sense, faculties differing in kind, and in rank higher one than another?

LYSICLES. I do not deny it.

EUPHRANOR. Their acts, therefore, differ in kind?

LYSICLES. They do.

EUPHRANOR. Consequently the pleasures perfective of those acts are also different.

LYSICLES. They are.

EUPHRANOR. You admit, therefore, three sorts of pleasure: pleasure of reason, pleasure of imagination, and pleasure of sense.

LYSICLES. I do.

EUPHRANOR. And, as it is reasonable to think the operation of the highest and noblest faculty to be attended with the highest pleasure, may we not suppose the two former to be as gold or silver, and the latter only as copper? Whence it should seem to follow that man need not envy or imitate a brute.

LYSICLES. And, nevertheless, there are very ingenious men who do. And surely every one may be allowed to know what he wants, and wherein his true happiness consists.

EUPHRANOR. Is it not plain that different animals have different pleasures? Take a hog from his ditch or dung-hill, lay him on a rich bed, treat him with sweetmeats, and music, and perfumes. All these things will be no entertainment to him. Do not a bird, a beast, a fish amuse themselves in various manners, insomuch that what is pleasing to one may be death to another? Is it ever seen that one of these animals quits its own element or way of living, to adopt that of another? And shall man quit his own nature to imitate a brute?

LYSICLES. But sense is not only natural to brutes; is it not also natural to man?

EUPHRANOR. It is, but with this difference: it maketh the whole of a brute's, but is the lowest part or faculty of a human soul. The nature of anything is peculiarly that which doth distinguish it from other things, not what it hath in common with them. Do you allow this to be true?

LYSICLES. I do.

EUPHRANOR. And is not reason that which makes the principal difference between man and other animals?

LYSICLES. It is.

EUPHRANOR. Reason, therefore, being the principal part of our nature, whatever is most reasonable should seem most natural to man. Must we not therefore think rational pleasures more agreeable to human-kind than those of sense? Man and beast, having different natures, seem to have different faculties, different enjoyments, and different sorts of happiness. You can easily conceive, that the sort of life which makes the happiness of a mole or a bat would be a very wretched one for an eagle. And may you not as well conceive that the happiness of a brute can never constitute the true happiness of a man? A beast, without reflexion or remorse, without foresight or appetite of immortality, without notion of vice or virtue, or order, or reason, or knowledge! What motives, what grounds, can there be for bringing down man, in whom are all these things, to a level with such a creature? What merit, what ambition, in the minute philosopher to make such an animal a guide or rule for human life?

15. LYSICLES. It is strange, Euphranor, that one who admits freedom of thought, as you do, should yet be such a slave to prejudice. You still talk of order and virtue, as of real things, as if our philosophers had never demonstrated that they have no foundation in nature, and are only the effects of education.

I know, said CRITO, how the minute philosophers are accustomed to demonstrate this point. They consider the animal nature of man, or man so far forth as he is animal; and it must be owned that, considered in that light, he hath no sense of duty, no notion of virtue. He, therefore, who should look for virtue among mere animals, or human-kind as such, would look in the wrong place. But that philosopher who is attentive only to the animal part of his being, and raiseth his theories from the very dregs of our species, may probably, upon second thoughts, find himself mistaken.

Look you, Crito, said LYSICLES, my argument is with Euphranor; to whom addressing his discourse:—I observe, said he, that you stand much upon the dignity of human nature. This thing of dignity is an old worn-out notion, which depends on other notions, old and stale, and worn-out, such as an immaterial spirit, and a ray derived from the Divinity. But in these days men of sense make a jest of all this grandeur and dignity; and many there are would gladly exchange their share of it for the repose, and freedom, and sensuality of a brute. But comparisons are odious; waiving therefore all inquiry concerning the respective excellencies of man and beast, and whether it is beneath a man to follow or imitate brute animals in judging of the chief good and conduct of life and manners, I shall be content to appeal to the authority of men themselves for the truth of my notions. Do but look abroad into the world, and ask the common run of men whether pleasure of sense be not the only true, solid, substantial good of their kind.

EUPHRANOR. But might not the same vulgar sort of men prefer a piece of sign-post painting to one of Raphael's or a Grub-street ballad to an ode of Horace ? Is there not a real difference between good and bad writing ?

LYSICLES. There is.

EUPHRANOR. And yet you will allow there must be a maturity and improvement of understanding to discern this difference, which doth not make it therefore less real ?

LYSICLES. I will.

EUPHRANOR. In the same manner, what should hinder but there may be in nature a true difference between vice and virtue, although it require some degree of reflexion and judgment to observe it ? In order to know whether a thing be agreeable to the rational nature of man, it seems one should rather observe and consult those who have most employed or improved their reason.

LYSICLES. Well, I shall not insist on consulting the common herd of mankind. From the ignorant and gross vulgar, I might myself appeal in many cases to men of rank and fashion.

EUPHRANOR. They are a sort of men I have not the honour to know much of by my own observation. But I remember a remark of Aristotle, who was himself a courtier, and knew them well. ' Virtue ', saith he,[1] " and good sense are not the property of high birth or a great estate. Nor if they who possess these advantages, wanting a taste for rational pleasures, betake themselves to those of sense, ought we therefore to esteem them eligible, any more than we should the toys and pastimes of children, because they seem so to them?' And indeed one may be allowed to question whether the truest estimate of things was to be expected from a mind intoxicated with luxury, and dazzled with the splendour of high living. . . .

16. LYSICLES. But why need we have recourse to the judgment of other men in so plain a case? I appeal to your own breast: consult that, and then say if sensual pleasure be not the chief good of man.

EUPHRANOR. I, for my part, have often thought those pleasures which are highest in the esteem of sensualists so far from being the chiefest good, that it seemed doubtful, upon the whole, whether they were any good at all, any more than the mere removal of pain. Are not our wants and appetites uneasy?

LYSICLES. They are.

EUPHRANOR. Doth not sensual pleasure consist in satisfying them?

LYSICLES. It doth.

EUPHRANOR. But the cravings are tedious, the satisfaction momentary. Is it not so?

LYSICLES. It is; but what then?

EUPHRANOR. Why, then it should seem that sensual pleasure is but a short deliverance from long pain. A long avenue of uneasiness leads to a point of pleasure, which ends in disgust or remorse.

CRITO. And he who pursues this *ignis fatuus* imagines himself a philosopher and free-thinker.

---

[1] *Ethic. ad Nicom.*, lib. x, cap. vi.

LYSICLES. Pedants are governed by words and notions, while the wiser men of pleasure follow fact, nature, and sense.

CRITO. But what if notional pleasures should in fact prove the most real and lasting? Pure pleasures of reason and imagination neither hurt the health, nor waste the fortune, nor gall the conscience. By them the mind is long entertained without loathing or satiety. On the other hand, a notion (which with you it seems passeth for nothing) often embitters the most lively sensual pleasures, which at bottom will be found also to depend upon notion more than perhaps you imagine: it being a vulgar remark, that those things are more enjoyed by hope and foretaste of the soul than by possession. Thus much is yielded, that actual enjoyment is very short, and the alternative of appetite and disgust long as well as uneasy. So that, upon the whole, it should seem those gentlemen who are called men of pleasure, from their eager pursuit of it, do in reality, with great expense of fortune, ease, and health, purchase pain.

LYSICLES. You may spin out plausible arguments, but will after all find it a difficult matter to convince me that so many ingenious men should not be able to distinguish between things so directly opposite as pain and pleasure. How is it possible to account for this?

CRITO. I believe a reason may be assigned for it, but to men of pleasure no truth is so palatable as a fable. Jove once upon a time having ordered that pleasure and pain should be mixed in equal proportions in every dose of human life, upon a complaint that some men endeavoured to separate what he had joined, and taking more than their share of the sweet, would leave all the sour for others, commanded Mercury to put a stop to this evil, by fixing on each delinquent a pair of invisible spectacles, which should change the appearance of things, making pain look like pleasure, and pleasure like pain, labour like recreation, and recreation like labour. From that time the men of pleasure are eternally mistaking and repenting.

LYSICLES. If your doctrine takes place, I would fain know what can be the advantage of a great fortune, which all mankind so eagerly pursue.

CRITO. It is a common saying with Eucrates, that *a great fortune is an edged tool, which a hundred may come at for one who knows how to use it,* so much easier is the art of getting than that of spending. What its advantage is I will not say, but I will venture to declare what it is not. I am sure that where abundance excludes want, and enjoyment prevents appetite, there is not the quickest sense of those pleasures we have been speaking of, in which the footman hath often a greater share than his lord, who cannot enlarge his stomach in proportion to his estate.

17. Reasonable and well-educated men of all ranks have, I believe, pretty much the same amusements, notwithstanding the difference of their fortunes : but those who are particularly distinguished as men of pleasure seem to possess it in a very small degree.

EUPHRANOR. I have heard that among persons of that character a game of cards is esteemed a chief diversion.

LYSICLES. Without cards there could be no living for people of fashion. It is the most delightful way of passing an evening when gentlemen and ladies are got together, who would otherwise be at a loss what to say or do with themselves. But a pack of cards is so engaging that it doth not only employ them when they are met, but serves to draw them together. Quadrille gives them pleasure in prospect during the dull hours of the day, they reflect on it with delight, and it furnishes discourse when it is over.

CRITO. One would be apt to suspect these people of condition pass their time but heavily, and are but little the better for their fortunes, whose chief amusement is a thing in the power of every footman, who is as well qualified to receive pleasure from cards as a peer. I can easily conceive that, when people of a certain turn are got together, they should prefer doing anything to the ennui of their own conversation; but it is not easy to conceive that there is any great pleasure in this. What a card-table can afford requires neither parts nor fortune to judge of.

LYSICLES. Play is a serious amusement, that comes to the relief of a man of pleasure, after the more lively and affecting enjoyments of sense. It kills time beyond anything; and is a most admirable anodyne to divert or prevent thought, which might otherwise prey upon the mind.

CRITO. I readily comprehend that no man upon earth ought to prize anodynes for the spleen more than a man of fashion and pleasure. An ancient sage, speaking of one of that character, saith he is made wretched by disappointments and appetites. And if this was true of the Greeks, who lived in the sun, and had so much spirit, I am apt to think it is still more so of our modern English. Something there is in our climate and complexion that makes idleness nowhere so much its own punishment as in England, where an uneducated fine gentleman pays for his momentary pleasures with long and cruel intervals of spleen; for relief of which he is driven into sensual excesses that produce a proportionable depression of spirits, which, as it createth a greater want of pleasures, so it lessens the ability to enjoy them. There is a cast of thought in the complexion of an Englishman which renders him the most unsuccessful rake in the world. He is (as Aristotle expresseth it) at variance with himself. He is neither brute enough to enjoy his appetites, nor man enough to govern them. He knows and feels that

what he pursues is not his true good; his reflexion
serving only to show him that misery which his habitual
sloth and indolence will not suffer him to remedy.
At length, being grown odious to himself, and abhorring
his own company, he runs into every idle assembly,
not from the hopes of pleasure, but merely to respite the
pain of his own mind. Listless and uneasy at the present,
he hath no delight in reflecting on what is past, or in
the prospect of anything to come. This man of pleasure,
when, after a wretched scene of vanity and woe, his
animal nature is worn to the stumps, wishes and dreads
death by turns, and is sick of living, without having ever
tried or known the true life of man.

EUPHRANOR. It is well this sort of life, which is of so little
benefit to the owner, conduceth so much to that of the
public. But pray tell me, do these gentlemen set up
for minute philosophers?

CRITO. That sect, you must know, contains two sorts of
philosophers, the wet and the dry. Those I have been
describing are of the former kind. They differ rather in
practice than in theory, as an older, graver, or duller
man from one that is younger and more capable or fond
of pleasure. The dry philosopher passeth his time but
dryly. He has the honour of pimping for the vices of more
sprightly men, who in return offer some small incense to
his vanity. Upon this encouragement, and to make his
own mind easy when it is past being pleased, he employs
himself in justifying those excesses he cannot partake in.
But, to return to your question, those miserable folk
are mighty men for the minute philosophy.

EUPHRANOR. What hinders them then from putting an
end to their lives?

CRITO. Their not being persuaded of the truth of what they
profess. Some, indeed, in a fit of despair, do now and
then lay violent hands on themselves. And as the

249

minute philosophy prevails, we daily see more examples
of suicide. But they bear no proportion to those who
would put an end to their lives if they durst. My
friend Clinias, who had been one of them, and a philosopher of rank, let me into the secret history of their
doubts and fears, and irresolute resolutions of making
away with themselves, which last he assures me is a
frequent topic with men of pleasure, when they have
drunk themselves into a little spirit. It was by virtue
of this mechanical valour the renowned philosopher
Hermocrates shot himself through the head. The same
thing hath since been practised by several others, to
the great relief of their friends. Splenetic, worried, and
frightened out of their wits, they run upon their doom
with the same courage as a bird runs into the mouth
of a rattle-snake, not because they are bold to die, but
because they are afraid to live. Clinias endeavoured
to fortify his irreligion by the discourse and opinion of
other minute philosophers, who were mutually strength-
ened in their own belief by his. After this manner,
authority working in a circle, they endeavoured to
atheise one another. But though he pretended even to
a demonstration against the being of a God, yet he
could not inwardly conquer his own belief. He fell
sick, and acknowledged this truth, is now a sober
man and a Christian; owns he was never so happy
as since he became such, nor so wretched as while
he was a minute philosopher. And he who has
tried both conditions may be allowed a proper judge
of both.

LYSICLES. Truly a fine account of the brightest and bravest
men of the age !

CRITO. Bright and brave are fine attributes. But our
curate is of opinion that all your free-thinking rakes are
either fools or cowards. Thus he argues : if such a man

doth not see his true interest, he wants sense ; if he doth, but dare not pursue it, he wants courage. In this manner, from the defect of sense and courage, he deduceth that whole species of men who are so apt to value themselves upon both those qualities.

LYSICLES. As for their courage, they are at all times ready to give proof of it ; and for their understanding, thanks to nature, it is of a size not to be measured by country parsons.

18. EUPHRANOR. But Socrates, who was no country parson, suspected your men of pleasure were such through ignorance.

LYSICLES. Ignorance ! Of what ?

EUPHRANOR. Of the art of computing. It was his opinion that rakes cannot reckon,[1] and that for want of this skill they make wrong judgments about pleasure, on the right choice of which their happiness depends.

LYSICLES. I do not understand you.

EUPHRANOR. Do you grant that sense perceiveth only sensible things ?

LYSICLES. I do.

EUPHRANOR. Sense perceiveth only things present ?

LYSICLES. This too I grant.

EUPHRANOR. Future pleasures, therefore, and pleasures of the understanding are not to be judged of by sense ?

LYSICLES. They are not.

EUPHRANOR. Those therefore who judge of pleasures by sense may find themselves mistaken at the foot of the account. . . .

To make a right computation, should you not consider all the faculties, and all the kinds of pleasure, taking into your account the future as well as the present, and rating them all according to their true value ?

[1] Plato in *Protagoras*.

CRITO. The Epicureans themselves allowed that pleasure which procures a greater pain, or hinders a greater pleasure, should be regarded as a pain ; and that pain which procures a greater pleasure, or prevents a greater pain, is to be accounted a pleasure. In order therefore to make a true estimate of pleasure, the great spring of action, and that from whence the conduct of life takes its bias, we ought to compute intellectual pleasures and future pleasures, as well as present and sensible ; we ought to make allowance, in the valuation of each partic- ular pleasure, for all the pains and evils, for all the disgust, remorse, and shame, that attend it ; we ought to regard both kind and quantity, the sincerity, the intenseness, and the duration of pleasures. Let a free-thinker but bethink himself, how little of human pleasure consists in actual sensation, and how much in prospect ! Let him then compare the prospect of a virtuous believer with that of an unbelieving rake.

EUPHRANOR. And, all these points duly considered, will not Socrates seem to have had reason on his side when he thought ignorance made rakes, and particularly their being ignorant of what he calls the science of more and less, greater and smaller, equality and comparison, that is to say, of the art of computing ?

LYSICLES. All this discourse seems notional. For real abilities of every kind, it is well known we have the brightest men of the age among us. But all those who know the world do calculate that what you call a good Christian, who hath neither a large conscience nor unprejudiced mind, must be unfit for the affairs of it. Thus you see, while you compute yourselves out of pleasure, others compute you out of business. What then are you good for with all your computation ?

EUPHRANOR. I have all imaginable respect for the abilities of free-thinkers. My only fear was, their parts might be too lively for such slow talents as forecast and computation, the gifts of ordinary men.

19. CRITO. I cannot make them the same compliment that Euphranor does. For, though I shall not pretend to characterise the whole sect, yet thus much I may truly affirm : that those who have fallen in my way have been mostly raw men of pleasure, old sharpers in business, or a third sort of lazy sciolists, who are neither men of business, nor men of speculation, but set up for judges or critics in all kinds, without having made a progress in any. These, among men of the world, pass for profound theorists, and among speculative men would seem to know the world: a conceited race, equally useless to the affairs and studies of mankind. Such as these, for the most part, seem to be sectaries of the minute philosophy. I will not deny that now and then you may meet with a man of easy manners, that, without those faults and affectations, is carried into the party by the mere stream of education, fashion, or company; all which do in this age prejudice men against religion, even those who mechanically rail at prejudice. I must not forget that the minute philosophers have also a strong party among the beaux and fine ladies; and, as affectations out of character are often the strongest, there is nothing so dogmatical and inconvincible as one of these fine things, when it sets up for free-thinking. But, be these professors of the sect never so dogmatical, their authority must needs be small with men of sense. Who would choose for his guide, in the search of truth, one whose thoughts and time are taken up with dress, visits, and diversions ? Or whose education hath been behind a counter, or in an office ? Or whose speculations have been employed on the forms of business, who is only well read in the ways and commerce of mankind, in stockjobbing, purloining, supplanting, bribing ?

253

Or would any man in his senses give a fig for meditations and discoveries made over a bottle ? And yet it is certain that, instead of thought, books, and study, most free-thinkers are the proselytes of a drinking club. Their principles are often settled, and decisions on the deepest points made, when they are not fit to make a bargain.

LYSICLES. You forget our writers, Crito. They make a world of proselytes.

CRITO. So would worse writers in such a cause. Alas ! how few read ! and of these, how few are able to judge ! How many wish your notions true ! How many had rather be diverted than instructed ! How many are convinced by a title ! [1] I may allow your reasons to be effectual, without allowing them to be good. Arguments, in themselves of small weight, have great effect when they are recommended by a mistaken interest, when they are pleaded for by passion, when they are countenanced by the humour of the age ; and above all, with some sort of men, when they are against law, government, and established opinions, things which, as a wise or good man would not depart from without clear evidence, a weak or a bad man will affect to disparage on the slightest grounds.

LYSICLES. And yet the arguments of our philosophers alarm.

CRITO. The force of their reasoning is not what alarms : their contempt of laws and government is alarming : their application to the young and ignorant is dangerous.

EUPHRANOR. But without disputing or disparaging their talent at ratiocination, it seems very possible their success might not be owing to that alone. May it not in some measure be ascribed to the defects of others, as

---

[1] [Apparently a reference to the third Earl of Shaftesbury, whose *Characteristics* (1711) was valued by some of the 'free-thinkers'. This work is examined in the third dialogue.—ED.]

well as to their own perfections? My friend Eucrates used to say that the church would thrive and flourish beyond all opposition, if some certain persons minded piety more than politics, practics than polemics, fundamentals than consectaries, substance than circumstance, things than notions, and notions than words.

LYSICLES. Whatever may be the cause, the effects are too plain to be denied. And when a considering man observes that our notions do, in this most learned and knowing age, spread and multiply, in opposition to established laws, and every day gain ground against a body so numerous, so learned, so well supported, protected, encouraged, for the service and defence of religion: I say, when a man observes and considers all this, he will be apt to ascribe it to the force of truth, and the merits of our cause, which, had it been supported with the revenues and establishments of the church and universities, you may guess what a figure it would make, by the figure that it makes without them.

EUPHRANOR. It is much to be pitied that the learned professors of your sect do not meet with the encouragement they deserve.

LYSICLES. All in due time. People begin to open their eyes. It is not impossible those revenues that in ignorant times were applied to a wrong use may, in a more enlightened age, be applied to a better.

CRITO. But why professors and encouragement for what needs no teaching? An acquaintance of mine has a most ingenious footman that can neither write nor read, who learned your whole system in half an hour: he knows when and how to nod, shake his head, smile, and give a hint, as well as the ablest sceptic, and is in fact a very minute philosopher.

LYSICLES. Pardon me, it takes time to unlearn religious prejudices, and requires a strong head.

CRITO. I do not know how it might have been once upon a time. But in the present laudable education, I know several who have been imbued with no religious notions at all; and others who have had them so very slight, that they rubbed off without the least pains. . . .

25. CRITO. . . . The point at present is the usefulness of your principles. And to decide this point we need only take a short view of them fairly proposed and laid together:—that there is no God or providence: that man is as the beasts that perish: that his happiness as theirs consists in obeying animal instincts, appetites, and passions: that all stings of conscience and sense of guilt are prejudices and errors of education: that religion is a State trick: that vice is beneficial to the public: that the soul of man is corporeal and dissolveth like a flame or vapour: that man is a machine actuated according to the laws of motion: that consequently he is no agent, or subject of guilt: that a wise man will make his own particular individual interest in this present life the rule and measure of all his actions: these, and such opinions, are, it seems, the tenets of a minute philosopher, who is himself, according to his own principles, an organ played on by sensible objects, a ball bandied about by appetites and passions. So subtle is he as to be able to maintain all this by artful reasonings, so sharp-sighted and penetrating to the very bottom of things as to find out that the most interested occult cunning is the only true wisdom. To complete his character, this curious piece of clock-work, having no principle of action within itself, and denying that it hath or can have any one free thought or motion, sets up for the patron of liberty, and earnestly contends for *free-thinking*. . . .

ALCIPHRON

SIRIS

A chain of philosophical reflexions
and inquiries concerning the virtues
of tar water and divers other
subjects

First published 1744   Final Edition 1747

EDITOR'S NOTE

The immediate popularity of *Siris* was due to its recommendation of tar water as almost a panacea. From this practical starting-point Berkeley pursues his way through the science of his day (with its many lingering Renaissance elements) to a cosmology in which a subtle kind of fire is posited as the corporeal instrument of all corporeal change, and thence passes to metaphysics, to the real source of life and change in the divine mind. The metaphysical part, from which the sections here printed are taken, repeats Berkeley's early doctrines. There is, indeed, a wider context, a mellow sense of mystery, a frequent reference to the lore of ancient sages, a Neoplatonic interest and a Neoplatonising tendency, but no departure from his first positions. He still affirms that the *esse* of the corporeal is *percipi*, that of the corporeal there can be no abstract ideas, that mechanistic science establishes no more than empirical uniformities, and that mind is the only cause. The old vigorous and incisive arguing gives place to discursive trans-itions of thought, but the style is as concise as ever, and as graceful, and at times, responding to contained feeling, has a haunting beauty.

The passages deal with the following topics. (1) *The limited value of mechanistic science.* No forces in bodies, but only regular connexions—from Sects. 231-51. The language of Nature—Sects. 252-6. (2) *The knowledge of causes is non-sensory*—Sects. 260-4. (3) *No absolute space or motion, or blind Fate*—from Sects. 270-90. (4) *The ascent from phenomena to causes*: the chain of being—Sects. 292-7; the chain of knowing—Sects. 303-31. (5) *Mind alone substantial and one, a person*—from Sects. 346-57. (6) *The pursuit of truth*—Sects. 367 f.

231. The laws of attraction and repulsion are to be regarded as laws of motion; and these only as rules or methods observed in the productions of natural effects, the efficient and final causes whereof are not of mechanical consideration. Certainly, if the explaining a phenomenon be to assign its proper efficient and final cause, it should seem the mechanical philosophers never explained anything; their province being only to discover the laws of nature, that is, the general rules and methods of motion, and to account for particular phenomena by reducing them under, or showing their conformity to, such general rules.

232. Some corpuscularian philosophers of the last age have indeed attempted to explain the formation of this world and its phenomena by a few simple laws of mechanism. But if we consider the various productions of nature, in the mineral, vegetable, and animal parts of the creation, I believe we shall see cause to affirm that not any one of them has hitherto been, or can be, accounted for on principles merely mechanical; and that nothing could be more vain and imaginary than to suppose with Descartes that merely from a circular motion's being impressed by the supreme Agent on the particles of extended substance, the whole world, with all its several parts, appurtenances, and phenomena, might be produced, by a necessary consequence, from the laws of motion.

234. Mechanical laws of nature or motion direct us how to act, and teach us what to expect. Where intellect presides there will be method and order, and therefore rules, which if not stated and constant would cease to be rules.

There is therefore a constancy in things, which is styled the Course of Nature. All the phenomena in nature are produced by motion. There appears a uniform working in things great and small, by attracting and repelling forces. But the particular laws of attraction and repulsion are various. Nor are we concerned at all about the forces, neither can we know or measure them otherwise than by their effects, that is to say, the motions; which motions only, and not the forces, are indeed in the bodies. Bodies are moved to or from each other, and this is performed according to different laws. The natural or mechanic philosopher endeavours to discover those laws by experiment and reasoning. But what is said of forces residing in bodies, whether attracting or repelling, is to be regarded only as a mathematical hypothesis, and not as anything really existing in nature.[1]

243. Attraction cannot produce, and in that sense account for, the phenomena, being itself one of the phenomena produced and to be accounted for. Attraction is performed by different laws, and cannot therefore in all cases be the effect of the elasticity of one uniform medium. The phenomena of electrical bodies, the laws and variations of magnetism, and, not to mention other kinds, even gravity, are not explained by elasticity, a phenomenon not less obscure than itself. But then, although it show not the agent, yet it showeth a rule and analogy in nature to say that the solid parts of animals are endued with attractive powers whereby from contiguous fluids they draw like to like; and that glands have peculiar powers attractive of peculiar juices. Nature seems better known and explained by attractions and repulsions than by those other mechanical principles of size, figure, and the like; that is, by Sir Isaac Newton, than Descartes. And natural philosophers excel, as they are more or less ac-

[1] [See *De Motu*, Sects. 5 ff.—Ed.]

quainted with the laws and methods observed by the Author of Nature.

245. The ancients had some general conception of attracting and repelling powers as natural principles. Galileo had particularly considered the attraction of gravity, and made some discovery of the laws thereof. But Sir Isaac Newton, by his singular penetration, profound knowledge in geometry and mechanics, and great exactness in experiments, hath cast a new light on natural science. The laws of attraction and repulsion were in many instances discovered, and first discovered, by him. He showed their general extent, and therewith, as with a key, opened several deep secrets of nature, in the knowledge whereof he seems to have made a greater progress than all the sects of corpuscularians together had done before him. Nevertheless, the principle of attraction itself is not to be explained by physical or corporeal causes.

247. Though it be supposed the chief business of a natural philosopher to trace out causes from the effects, yet this is to be understood not of agents but of principles, that is, of component parts, in one sense, or of laws or rules, in another. In strict truth, all agents are incorporeal, and as such are not properly of physical consideration. The astronomer, therefore, the mechanic, or the chemist, not as such, but by accident only, treat of real causes, agents or efficients. Neither doth it seem, as is supposed by the greatest of mechanical philosophers, that the true way of proceeding in their science is, from known motions in nature to investigate the moving forces; forasmuch as force is neither corporeal nor belongs to any corporeal thing, nor yet to be discovered by experiments or mathematical reasonings, which reach no farther than discernible effects, and motions in things passive and moved.

249. The mechanical philosopher, as hath been already observed, inquires properly concerning the rules and modes

of operation alone, and not concerning the cause; forasmuch as nothing mechanical is or really can be a cause (Sect. 247). And although a mechanical or mathematical philosopher may speak of absolute space, absolute motion, and of force as existing in bodies, causing such motion and proportional thereto; yet what these forces are which are supposed to be lodged in bodies, to be impressed on bodies, to be multiplied, divided, and communicated from one body to another, and which seem to animate bodies like abstract spirits or souls, hath been found very difficult, not to say impossible, for thinking men to conceive and explain; as may be seen by consulting Borellus *De Vi Percussionis*, and Torricelli in his *Lezioni Academiche*, among other authors.

250. Nor, if we consider the proclivity of mankind to realise their notions, will it seem strange that mechanic philosophers and geometricians should, like other men, be misled by prejudice, and take mathematical hypotheses for real beings existing in bodies, so far as even to make it the very aim and end of their science to compute or measure those phantoms; whereas it is very certain that nothing in truth can be measured or computed beside the very effects or motions themselves. Sir Isaac Newton asks, Have not the minute particles of bodies certain forces or powers by which they act on one another, as well as on the particles of light, for producing most of the phenomena in nature? But, in reality, those minute particles are only agitated according to certain laws of nature, by some other agent, wherein the force exists and not in them, which have only the motion; which motion in the body moved, the Peripatetics rightly judge to be a mere passion, but in the mover to be ἐνέργεια or act.

251. It passeth with many, I know not how, that mechanical principles give a clear solution of the phenomena. The Democritic hypothesis, saith Dr. Cudworth,

doth much more handsomely and intelligibly solve the phenomena than that of Aristotle and Plato. But, things rightly considered, perhaps it will be found not to solve any phenomenon at all : for all phenomena are, to speak truly, appearances in the soul or mind ; and it hath never been explained, nor can it be explained, how external bodies, figures, and motions, should produce an appearance in the mind. These principles, therefore, do not solve, if by solving is meant assigning the real, either efficient or final, cause of appearances, but only reduce them to general rules.

252. There is a certain analogy, constancy, and uniformity in the phenomena or appearances of nature, which are a foundation for general rules : and these are a grammar for the understanding of nature,[1] or that series of effects in the visible world whereby we are enabled to foresee what will come to pass in the natural course of things. Plotinus observes, in his third *Ennead*, that the art of presaging is in some sort the reading of natural letters denoting order, and that so far forth as analogy obtains in the universe, there may be vaticination. And in reality he that foretells the motions of the planets, or the effects of medicines, or the result of chemical or mechanical experiments, may be said to do it by natural vaticination.

253. We know a thing when we understand it ; and we understand it when we can interpret or tell what it signifies. Strictly, the sense knows nothing.[2] We perceive indeed

[1] [On Nature as a divine language, and natural science as the grammar of it, see *Essay on Vision*, Sect. 147 and *Princ.*, Sect. 44.—ED.]

[2] [Not a repudiation of Berkeley's early defence of sense as a direct apprehension of its objects, but simply a terminological restriction of ' know ' to apprehension of the *connexions* of sensory objects, which is the work of natural science, and to apprehension of *causes*, which is the work of metaphysics (Sects. 264, 305).—ED.]

sounds by hearing, and characters by sight; but we are not therefore said to understand them. After the same manner, the phenomena of nature are alike visible to all; but all have not alike learned the connexion of natural things, or understand what they signify, or know how to vaticinate by them. There is no question, saith Socrates *in Theæteto*, concerning that which is agreeable to each person; but concerning what will in time to come be agreeable, of which all men are not equally judges. He who foreknoweth what will be in every kind is the wisest. According to Socrates, you and the cook may judge of a dish on the table equally well, but while the dish is making, the cook can better foretell what will ensue from this or that manner of composing it. Nor is this manner of reasoning confined only to morals or politics, but extends also to natural science.

254. As the natural connexion of signs with the things signified is regular and constant, it forms a sort of rational discourse, and is therefore the immediate effect of an intelligent cause. This is agreeable to the philosophy of Plato, and other ancients. Plotinus indeed saith, that which acts naturally is not intellection, but a certain power of moving matter, which doth not know but only do. And it must be owned that, as faculties are multiplied by philosophers according to their operations, the will may be distinguished from the intellect. But it will not therefore follow that the Will which operates in the Course of Nature is not conducted and applied by intellect, although it be granted that neither will understands, nor intellect wills. Therefore, the phenomena of nature, which strike on the senses and are understood by the mind, form not only a magnificent spectacle, but also a most coherent, entertaining, and instructive Discourse; and to effect this, they are conducted, adjusted, and ranged by the greatest wisdom. This Language or Discourse is studied with different atten-

tion, and interpreted with different degrees of skill. But so
far as men have studied and remarked its rules, and can
interpret right, so far they may be said to be knowing in
nature. A beast is like a man who hears a strange tongue
but understands nothing.

255. Nature, saith the learned Doctor Cudworth, is not
master of art or wisdom : nature is *ratio mersa et confusa*,
reason immersed and plunged into matter, and as it were
fuddled in it and confounded with it. But the formation of
plants and animals, the motions of natural bodies, their
various properties, appearances, and vicissitudes, in a word,
the whole series of things in this visible world, which we
call the Course of Nature, is so wisely managed and carried
on that the most improved human reason cannot thoroughly
comprehend even the least particle thereof; so far is it
from seeming to be produced by fuddled or confounded
reason.

256. Natural productions, it is true, are not all equally
perfect. But neither doth it suit with the order of things,
the structure of the universe, or the ends of Providence,
that they should be so. General rules, we have seen (Sects.
249, 252), are necessary to make the world intelligible ; and
from the constant observation of such rules, natural evils
will sometimes unavoidably ensue : things will be produced
in a slow length of time, and arrive at different degrees of
perfection.

260. All things are made for the supreme good, all things
tend to that end: and we may be said to account for a thing
when we show that it is so best. In the *Phædon*, Socrates
declares it to be his opinion that he who supposed all
things to have been disposed and ordered by a Mind
should not pretend to assign any other cause of them.
He blames physiologers for attempting to account for
phenomena, particularly for gravity and cohesion, by

vortexes and aether, overlooking the τὸ ἀγαθὸν and τὸ δέον, the strongest bond and cement which holds together all the parts of the universe, and not discerning the cause itself from those things which only attend it.

263. It cannot be denied that, with respect to the universe of things, we in this mortal state are like men educated in Plato's cave, looking on shadows with our backs turned to the light. But though our light be dim, and our situation bad, yet if the best use be made of both, perhaps something may be seen. Proclus, in his *Commentary on the Theology of Plato*, observes there are two sorts of philosophers. The one placed Body first in the order of beings, and made the faculty of thinking depend thereupon, supposing that the principles of all things are corporeal; that Body most really or principally exists, and all other things in a secondary sense, and by virtue of that. Others, making all corporeal things to be dependent upon Soul or Mind, think this to exist in the first place and primary sense, and the being of bodies to be altogether derived from and presuppose that of the Mind.

264. Sense and experience acquaint us with the course and analogy of appearances or natural effects. Thought, reason, intellect introduce us into the knowledge of their causes. Sensible appearances, though of a flowing, unstable, and uncertain nature, yet having first occupied the mind, they do by an early prevention render the aftertask of thought more difficult; and, as they amuse the eyes and ears, and are more suited to vulgar uses and the mechanic arts of life, they easily obtain a preference, in the opinion of most men, to those superior principles which are the later growth of the human mind arrived to maturity and perfection, but, not affecting the corporeal sense, are thought to be so far deficient in point of solidity and reality —sensible and real, to common apprehensions, being the same thing; although it be certain that the principles of

science are neither objects of sense nor imagination, and that intellect and reason are alone the sure guides to truth.

270. The doctrine of real, absolute, external space induced some modern philosophers to conclude it was a part or attribute of God, or that God himself was space; inasmuch as incommunicable attributes of the Deity appeared to agree thereto, such as infinity, immutability, indivisibility, incorporeity, being uncreated, impassive, without beginning or ending—not considering that all these negative properties may belong to nothing. . .

271. Concerning absolute space,[1] the phantom of the mechanic and geometrical philosophers (Sect. 250), it may suffice to observe that it is neither perceived by any sense, nor proved by any reason, and was accordingly treated by the greatest of the ancients as a thing merely visionary. From the notion of absolute space springs that of absolute motion; and in these are ultimately founded the notions of external existence, independence, necessity, and fate. Which fate, the idol of many moderns, was by old philosophers differently understood, and in such a sense as not to destroy the αὐτεξούσιον of God or man. Parmenides, who thought all things to be made by necessity or fate, understood justice and Providence to be the same with fate; which, how fixed and cogent soever with respect to man, may yet be voluntary with respect to God. Empedocles declared fate to be a cause using principles and elements. Heraclitus taught that fate was the general reason that runs through the whole nature of the universe; which nature he supposed to be an aethereal body, the seed of the generation of all things. Plato held fate to be the eternal reason or law of nature. Chrysippus supposed that fate was a spiritual power which disposed the world in order; that it

[1] [See *Princ.*, Sects. 111 f., *Three Dialogues* (above, pp. 143 f.), and *De Motu*, Sects. 52 ff.—ED.]

was the reason and law of those things which are administered by Providence.

272. All the foregoing notions of fate, as represented by Plutarch, plainly show that those ancient philosophers did not mean by fate, a blind, headlong, unintelligent principle, but an orderly settled course of things, conducted by a wise and provident Mind. And as for the Egyptian doctrine, it is indeed asserted in the *Pimander* that all things are produced by fate. But Jamblichus, who drew his notions from Egypt, affirms that the whole of things is not bound up in fate, but that there is a principle of the soul higher than nature, whereby we may be raised to a union with the gods, and exempt ourselves from fate. And in the *Asclepian Dialogue* it is expressly said that fate follows the decrees of God. And indeed, as all the motions in nature are evidently the product of reason, it should seem there is no room for necessity in any other sense than that of a steady regular course.

273. Blind fate and blind chance are at bottom much the same thing, and one no more intelligible than the other. Such is the mutual relation, connexion, motion, and sympathy of the parts of this world, that they seem as it were animated and held together by one soul : and such is their harmony, order, and regular course, as showeth the soul to be governed and directed by a Mind. It was an opinion of remote antiquity that the world was an animal. If we may trust the Hermaic writings, the Egyptians thought all things did partake of life. This opinion was also so general and current among the Greeks that Plutarch asserts all others held the world to be an animal, and governed by Providence, except Leucippus, Democritus, and Epicurus. And although an animal containing all bodies within itself could not be touched or sensibly affected from without, yet it is plain they attributed to it an inward sense and feeling, as well as appetites and aversions; and that

from all the various tones, actions, and passions of the universe, they suppose one symphony, one animal act and life to result.

274. Jamblichus declares the world to be one animal, in which the parts, however distant each from other, are nevertheless related and connected by one common nature. And he teacheth, what is also a received notion of the Pythagoreans and Platonics, that there is no chasm in nature, but a Chain or Scale of beings rising by gentle uninterrupted gradations from the lowest to the highest, each nature being informed and perfected by the participation of a higher. As air becomes igneous, so the purest fire becomes animal, and the animal soul becomes intellectual : which is to be understood not of the change of one nature into another, but of the connexion of different natures, each lower nature being, according to those philosophers, as it were a receptacle or subject for the next above it to reside and act in.

275. It is also the doctrine of the Platonic philosophers that Intellect is the very life of living things, the first principle and exemplar of all, from whence by different degrees are derived the inferior classes of life : first the rational, then the sensitive, after that the vegetal ; but so as in the rational animal there is still somewhat intellectual, again in the sensitive there is somewhat rational, and in the vegetal somewhat sensitive, and lastly, in mixed bodies, as metals and minerals, somewhat of vegetation. By which means the whole is thought to be more perfectly connected. Which doctrine implies that all the faculties, instincts, and notions of inferior beings, in their several respective subordinations, are derived from and depend upon Mind and Intellect.

289. All those who conceived the universe to be an animal must, in consequence of that notion, suppose all things to be one. But to conceive God to be the sentient soul of an animal is altogether unworthy and absurd.

There is no sense nor sensory, nor anything like a sense or sensory, in God. Sense implies an impression from some other being, and denotes a dependence in the soul which hath it. Sense is a passion ; and passions imply imperfection. God knoweth all things as pure mind or intellect; but nothing by sense, nor in nor through a sensory. Therefore to suppose a sensory of any kind—whether space or any other—in God, would be very wrong, and lead us into false conceptions of his nature. The presuming there was such a thing as real, absolute, uncreated space seems to have occasioned that modern mistake. But this presumption was without grounds.

290. Body is opposite to spirit or mind. We have a notion of spirit from thought and action. We have a notion of body from resistance. So far forth as there is real power, there is spirit. So far forth as there is resistance, there is inability or want of power ; that is, there is a negation of spirit. We are embodied, that is, we are clogged by weight, and hindered by resistance. But in respect of a perfect spirit, there is nothing hard or impenetrable : there is no resistance to the Deity : nor hath he any body : nor is the supreme Being united to the world as the soul of an animal is to its body, which necessarily implieth defect, both as an instrument, and as a constant weight and impediment.

292. Natural phenomena are only natural appearances. They are, therefore, such as we see and perceive them. Their real and objective natures are, therefore, the same ; passive without anything active, fluent and changing without anything permanent in them. However, as these make the first impressions, and the mind takes her first flight and spring, as it were, by resting her foot on these objects, they are not only first considered by all men, but most considered by most men. They and the phantoms that result from those appearances, the children of imagination grafted

upon sense—such for example as pure space (Sect. 270)—are thought by many the very first in existence and stability, and to embrace and comprehend all other beings.

293. Now, although such phantoms as corporeal forces, absolute motions, and real spaces do pass in physics for causes and principles (Sects. 249, 250), yet are they in truth but hypotheses, nor can they be the objects of real science. They pass nevertheless in physics, conversant about things of sense, and confined to experiments and mechanics. But when we enter the province of the *philosophia prima*, we discover another order of beings, mind and its acts, permanent being, not dependent on corporeal things, nor resulting, nor connected, nor contained; but containing, connecting, enlivening the whole frame, and imparting those motions, forms, qualities, and that order and symmetry, to all those transient phenomena which we term the Course of Nature.

294. It is with our faculties as with our affections : what first seizes holds fast (Sect. 264). It is a vulgar theme, that man is a compound of contrarieties, which breed a restless struggle in his nature between flesh and spirit, the beast and the angel, earth and heaven, ever weighed down and ever bearing up. During which conflict the character fluctuates : when either side prevails, it is then fixed for vice or virtue. And life from different principles takes a different issue. It is the same in regard to our faculties. Sense at first besets and overbears the mind. The sensible appearances are all in all : our reasonings are employed about them ; our desires terminate in them ; we look no farther for realities or causes ; till intellect begins to dawn, and cast a ray on this shadowy scene. We then perceive the true principle of unity, identity, and existence. Those things that before seemed to constitute the whole of Being, upon taking an intellectual view of things, prove to be but fleeting phantoms.

295. From the outward form of gross masses which occupy the vulgar, a curious inquirer proceeds to examine the inward structure and minute parts, and, from observing the motions in nature, to discover the laws of those motions. By the way, he frames his hypothesis and suits his language to this natural philosophy. And these fit the occasion and answer the end of a maker of experiments or mechanic, who means only to apply the powers of nature, and reduce the phenomena to rules. But if proceeding still in his analysis and inquiry, he ascends from the sensible into the intellectual world, and beholds things in a new light and a new order, he will then change his system, and perceive that what he took for substances and causes are but fleeting shadows; that the mind contains all, and acts all, and is to all created beings the source of unity and identity, harmony and order, existence and stability.

296. It is neither acid, nor salt, nor sulphur, nor air, nor aether, nor visible corporeal fire [1]—much less the phantom fate or necessity—that is the real agent, but, by a certain analysis, a regular connexion and climax, we ascend through all those mediums to a glimpse of the First Mover, invisible, incorporeal, unextended, intellectual source of life and being. There is, it must be owned, a mixture of obscurity and prejudice in human speech and reasonings. This is unavoidable, since the veils of prejudice and error are slowly and singly taken off one by one. But, if there are many links in the chain which connects the two extremes of what is grossly sensible and purely intelligible, and it seem a tedious work, by the slow helps of memory, imagination, and reason—oppressed and overwhelmed, as we are, by the senses, through erroneous principles, and long ambages of words and notions—to struggle upwards into the light of

[1] [These alleged chemical and physical principles had been reviewed in the earlier part of *Siris*.—ED.]

truth, yet, as this gradually dawns, further discoveries still correct the style and clear up the notions.

297. The mind, her acts and faculties, furnish a new and distinct class of objects, from the contemplation whereof arise certain other notions, principles, and verities, so remote from, and even so repugnant to, the first prejudices which surprise the sense of mankind that they may well be excluded from vulgar speech and books, as abstract from sensible matters, and more fit for the speculation of truth, the labour and aim of a few, than for the practice of the world, or the subjects of experimental or mechanical inquiry. Nevertheless, though, perhaps, it may not be relished by some modern readers, yet the treating in physical books concerning metaphysical and divine matters can be justified by great authorities among the ancients : not to mention that he who professedly delivers the elements of a science is more obliged to method and system, and tied down to more rigorous laws, than a mere essay writer. It may, therefore, be pardoned if this rude Essay doth, by insensible transitions, draw the reader into remote inquiries and speculations, that were not thought of either by him or by the author at first setting out.

303. The perceptions of sense are gross : but even in the senses there is a difference. Though harmony and proportion are not objects of sense, yet the eye and the ear are organs which offer to the mind such materials by means whereof she may apprehend both the one and the other. By experiments of sense we become acquainted with the lower faculties of the soul ; and from them, whether by a gradual (Sect. 275) evolution or ascent, we arrive at the highest. Sense supplies images to memory. These become subjects for fancy to work upon. Reason considers and judges of the imaginations. And these acts of reason become new objects to the understanding. In this scale, each lower faculty is a step that leads to one above it. And the

uppermost naturally leads to the Deity ; which is rather the object of intellectual knowledge than even of the discursive faculty, not to mention the sensitive. There runs a chain throughout the whole system of beings. In this chain one link drags another. The meanest things are connected with the highest. The calamity therefore is neither strange nor much to be complained of, if a low sensual reader shall, from mere love of the animal life, find himself drawn on, surprised and betrayed, into some curiosity concerning the intellectual.

305. As understanding perceiveth not, that is, doth not hear, or see, or feel, so sense knoweth not : and although the mind may use both sense and fancy, as means whereby to arrive at knowledge, yet sense or soul, so far forth as sensitive, knoweth nothing. For, as it is rightly observed in the *Theaetetus* of Plato, science consists not in the passive perceptions, but in the reasoning upon them.

308. That philosopher [Aristotle] held that the mind of man was a *tabula rasa*, and that there were no innate ideas. Plato, on the contrary, held original ideas in the mind, that is, notions which never were or can be in the sense, such as being, beauty, goodness, likeness, parity. Some, perhaps, may think the truth to be this—that there are properly no *ideas*, or passive objects, in the mind but what were derived from sense : but that there are also besides these her own acts or operations ; such are *notions*.[1]

330. These disquisitions will probably seem dry and use-less to such readers as are accustomed to consider only sensible objects. The employment of the mind on things purely intellectual is to most men irksome, whereas the sensitive powers, by constant use, acquire strength. Hence, the objects of sense more forcibly affect us (Sects. 264, 294), and are too often counted the chief good. For these things men fight, cheat, and scramble. Therefore, in order to tame

[1] [See note on *Princ.*, Sect. 27.—ED.]

274

mankind, and introduce a sense of virtue, the best human means is to exercise their understanding, to give them a glimpse of another world, superior to the sensible, and, while they take pains to cherish and maintain the animal life, to teach them not to neglect the intellectual.

331. Prevailing studies are of no small consequence to a State, the religion, manners, and civil government of a country ever taking some bias from its philosophy, which affects not only the minds of its professors and students, but also the opinions of all the better sort, and the practice of the whole people, remotely and consequentially indeed, though not inconsiderably. Have not the polemic and scholastic philosophy been observed to produce controversies in law and religion? And have not fatalism and Sadducism gained ground during the general passion for the corpuscularian and mechanical philosophy, which hath prevailed for about a century? This, indeed, might usefully enough have employed some share of the leisure and curiosity of inquisitive persons. But when it entered the seminaries of learning as a necessary accomplishment, and most important part of education, by engrossing men's thoughts, and fixing their minds so much on corporeal objects and the laws of motion, it hath, however undesignedly, indirectly and by accident, yet not a little indisposed them for spiritual, moral, and intellectual matters. Certainly, had the philosophy of Socrates and Pythagoras prevailed in this age among those who think themselves too wise to receive the dictates of the Gospel, we should not have seen interest take so general and fast hold on the minds of men, nor public spirit reputed to be $\gamma\epsilon\nu\nu\alpha\hat{\iota}\alpha\nu$ $\epsilon\dot{\upsilon}\acute{\eta}\theta\epsilon\iota\alpha\nu$, a generous folly, among those who are reckoned to be the most knowing as well as the most getting part of mankind.

346. According to the Platonic philosophy, *ens* and *unum* are the same. And consequently our minds participate so

far of existence as they do of unity.   But it should seem that
personality is the indivisible centre of the soul or mind, which
is a monad so far forth as she is a person.   Therefore Person
is really that which exists, inasmuch as it participates of the
divine unity.   In man the monad or indivisible is the αὐτὸ
τὸ αὐτό, the self-same self or very self, a thing in the opinion
of Socrates much and narrowly to be inquired into and
discussed, to the end that, knowing ourselves, we may
know what belongs to us and our happiness.

347. Upon mature reflection, the person or mind of all
created beings seemeth alone indivisible, and to partake
most of unity.   But sensible things are rather considered as
one than truly so, they being in a perpetual flux or succession, ever differing and various. . .[1]

355. Plato teacheth that the doctrine concerning the One
or Unit is a means to lead and raise the mind to the knowledge of him who truly is (Sects. 294, 295).   And it is a
tenet both of Aristotle and Plato, that identity is a certain
unity.   The Pythagoreans also, as well as the Platonic
philosophers, held *unum* and *ens* to be the same.   Consistently with which, that only can be said to exist which is
one and the same.   In things sensible and imaginable, as
such, there seems to be no unity, nothing that can be called
one, prior to all act of the mind ; since they, being in
themselves aggregates, consisting of parts or compounded
of elements, are in effect many.   Accordingly, it is remarked
by Themistius, the learned interpreter of Aristotle, that to
collect many notions into one, and to consider them as
one, is the work of intellect and not of sense or fancy.

356. Aristotle himself, in his third book *Of the Soul*, saith
it is the mind that maketh each thing to be one.   How
this is done, Themistius is more particular, observing that,
as being conferreth essence, the mind, by virtue of her

[1] [See *Princ.*, Sect. 12.—ED.]

276

simplicity, conferreth simplicity upon compounded beings. And, indeed, it seemeth that the mind, so far forth as person, is individual (Sects. 346, 347), therein resembling the divine One by participation, and imparting to other things what itself participates from above. This is agreeable to the doctrine of the ancients, however the contrary opinion of supposing number to be an original primary quality in things, independent of the mind, may obtain among the moderns.

357. The Peripatetics taught that in all divisible things there was somewhat indivisible, and in all compound things somewhat simple. This they derived from an act of the mind. And neither this simple indivisible unit, nor any sum of repeated units, consequently no number, can be separated from the things themselves, and from the operation of the mind. Themistius goeth so far as to affirm that it cannot be separated from the words or signs ; and, as it cannot be uttered without them, so, saith he, neither can it be conceived without them. Thus much upon the whole may be concluded, that, distinct from the mind and her operations, there is in created beings neither unit nor number.

367. As for the perfect intuition of divine things, that he [Plato] supposeth to be the lot of pure souls, beholding by a pure light, initiated, happy, free and unstained from those bodies wherein we are now imprisoned like oysters. But, in this mortal state, we must be satisfied to make the best of those glimpses within our reach. It is Plato's remark, in his *Theaetetus*, that while we sit still we are never the wiser, but going into the river and moving up and down is the way to discover its depths and shallows. If we exercise and bestir ourselves, we may even here discover something.

368. The eye by long use comes to see even in the

darkest cavern : and there is no subject so obscure but we may discern some glimpse of truth by long poring on it. Truth is the cry of all, but the game of a few. Certainly where it is the chief passion, it doth not give way to vulgar cares and views ; nor is it contented with a little ardour in the early time of life, active, perhaps, to pursue, but not so fit to weigh and revise. He that would make a real progress in knowledge must dedicate his age as well as youth, the later growth as well as first fruits, at the altar of Truth.

[FINIS]

PRINTED IN GREAT BRITAIN AT
THE PRESS OF THE PUBLISHERS